OXFORD TELEVISION STUDIES

General Editors **Charlotte Brunsdon**
John Caughie

The Intimate Screen

The Intimate Screen

Early British Television Drama

Jason Jacobs

Clarendon Press · Oxford

OXFORD
UNIVERSITY PRESS

Great Clarendon Street, Oxford OX2 6DP
Oxford University Press is a department of the University of Oxford.
It furthers the University's objective of excellence in research, scholarship,
and education by publishing worldwide in

Oxford New York

Athens Auckland Bangkok Bogotá Buenos Aires Calcutta
Cape Town Chennai Dar es Salaam Delhi Florence Hong Kong Istanbul
Karachi Kuala Lumpur Madrid Melbourne Mexico City Mumbai
Nairobi Paris São Paulo Singapore Taipei Tokyo Toronto Warsaw
and associated companies in Berlin Ibadan

Oxford is a registered trade mark of Oxford University Press
in the UK and certain other countries

Published in the United States
by Oxford University Press Inc., New York

© Jason Jacobs 2000

The moral rights of the author have been asserted
Database right Oxford University Press (maker)

First published 2000

British Library Cataloguing in Publication Data
Data available

Library of Congress Cataloging in Publication Data
Data available

ISBN 0–19–874234–7
ISBN 0–19–874233–9 (Pbk.)

1 3 5 7 9 10 8 6 4 2

Typeset by Graphicraft Ltd, Hong Kong
Printed in Great Britain
on acid-free paper by
Biddles Ltd,
Guildford and King's Lynn

Oxford Television Studies

General Editors
Charlotte Brunsdon and **John Caughie**

OXFORD TELEVISION STUDIES offers international authors—both established and emerging—an opportunity to reflect on particular problems of history, theory, and criticism which are specific to television and which are central to its critical understanding. The perspective of the series will be international, while respecting the peculiarities of the national; it will be historical, without proposing simple histories; and it will be grounded in the analysis of programmes and genres. The series is intended to be foundational without being introductory or routine, facilitating clearly focused critical reflection and engaging a range of debates, topics, and approaches which will offer a basis for the development of television studies.

For **Valerie Spall**

Acknowledgements

SINCERE THANKS to Charles Barr and John Caughie for their excellent comments on earlier versions of this book. Thanks also to Charlotte Brunsdon for originally suggesting the topic to me, many years ago.

The staff at the glorious BBC Written Archives Centre deserve more thanks than I can muster here: thanks in particular to Jeff Walden and Neil Somerville. Thanks to Philip Purser, John Jacobs, and Mike Savage for allowing me to interview them, and for the benefit of their experience. Thanks also to Paul Long.

Finally a sincere thank you to all my family for their generous support especially Henry, whose arrival provided a pleasant environment for the completion of the book.

Contents

List of Figures   xiii

1. The Intimate Screen   1

2. The End of the Photographed Stage Play: Television
   Drama, 1936–39   25

3. The Illustrated Broadcast? Defining Television
   Drama, 1946–50   77

4. 'Lost not cosy': Expanding the Screen of Television
   Drama, 1951–55   109

5. Conclusion   156

Bibliography   161

Index   173

List of Figures

1. Studio plan, *Clive of India* (1938)   54

2. Page two of George More O'Ferrall's continuity script for   58
   The Constant Nymph (1938)

3. Studio plan showing camera positions for *Juno and the*
   Paycock (1938)   62

4. Studio plan and camera positions for *The Ascent of F6* (1938)   65

5. Camera script synopsis for *The Ascent of F6* (1938)   70

6. Studio plan and camera positions for *Rope* (1947)   105

7. *Rope* (1950): script for camera 2 showing revisions   106

1

The Intimate Screen

AT WHAT POINT does television drama become self-conscious? In 1938 BBC drama producer George More O'Ferrall complained to his superior that television drama was too slow, and that he was going to speed it up. In 1952 another drama producer, Rudolph Cartier, informed his superior that BBC drama needed 'updating' that it was too 'stagey'; a few years later Sydney Newman, working for ITV's 'Armchair Theatre' signalled his desire to liven-up television drama by 'moving the cameras' on air; in the 1960s Troy Kennedy Martin said television drama was too dependent on dialogue and needed to be faster and 'more visual'.[1]

This recurrent pattern of modernization is a testament to the up-to-the-minute sensitivity of television drama, and to the appetite for innovation and change that characterized the practices and thinking of drama producers, directors, and writers.[2] Innovation and modernization in television drama is not located somewhere in the mid-1960s, but is also a characteristic of early drama production.

This book examines the aesthetics and style of early television drama from 1936 to 1955, a period for which virtually no retrievable examples of drama productions exist. Television drama is the form that is typically foregrounded, rightly or wrongly, as emblematic of the aesthetic state of the medium as a whole. After 1955, the history of early television drama has been understood as a development from a static, theatrical, visual style to a mobile, cinematic one. The evaluation of the subsequent development of television drama after 1955—from the innovations of Sydney Newman and 'Armchair Theatre', to the 'Golden Age' of 'The Wednesday Play', and Dennis Potter—depends on this idea of 'liberation' from the early static theatre of television drama, and on the assertion that early television drama (emblematic of television in general) did not develop its own aesthetic.

---

1 Newman: 'I insisted that the cameras definitely do move on the air'; in the documentary about 'Armchair Theatre', *And Now For Your Sunday Night Dramatic Entertainment* (Microcraze Productions/Channel Four, 8 February 1987). Troy Kennedy Martin, 'Nats Go Home: First Statement of a New Drama For Television', *Encore*, 48 (March–April 1964).

2 There was no distinction between drama producer and director before 1955. Early drama producers 'directed' their productions.

The essay that establishes this critical map of TV drama history is Carl Gardner and John Wyver's 'The Single Play: From Reithian Reverence to Cost Accounting and Censorship', which investigates the development of television drama in Britain, and examines the reasons for its decline. Early drama production is described as part of the 'Reithian phase' which lasted until the late 1950s, and succeeded by:

> the transitional phase dominated by Sydney Newman, from the late '50s until the beginning of the '70s; and the present phase currently dribbling to a conclusion, which one could dub the era of cost-effectiveness.[3]

In this reading, the influence of the first Director-General of the BBC, John Reith, was to set the moral and ideological parameters of early broadcasting, and this affected everything from organizational structure to the visual style of television drama (even though Reith did not like television). Reith is seen as the (controlling, restrictive) father of British broadcasting, and Sydney Newman as the (nurturing, permissive) father of British television drama. Newman had worked in Canada and the US during the late 1940s and 1950s, before his appointment as Head of Drama for one of the new ITV companies, ATV, in 1958. Newman's policy as Drama Head at the Canadian Broadcasting Company was to commission original plays by contemporary dramatists. It was the newness and innovation which Newman encouraged in his drama output that Gardner and Wyver find attractive, his concentration on 'television as television', for a mass popular audience, not one patronized by the middlebrow interests of the BBC elite.

It is true that the contrast between Reith and Newman is striking. Reith's photographs depict him as a sombre, austere minister, whereas Newman's show him as a white-suited blazing showbiz evangelist. In Gardner and Wyver's reading of history it is almost as if by some fantastic process of osmosis these personalities infect the stylistic dynamic of their drama productions: the early dramas of Reith's BBC become 'photographed stage plays', respectfully static and distant, whilst Newman's drama productions have an ingenious exhibitionistic mobility, with multiple cameras prodding their lenses into the action, and spiralling in and between the sets and actors, until their movement itself becomes the significant performance.[4]

3 This first appeared in *Programme of the Edinburgh International Television Festival* in 1980, 47–52. The version referred to here is Carl Gardner and John Wyver, 'The Single Play from Reithian Reverence to Cost-Accounting and Censorship' and 'The Single Play: An Afterword.' *Screen*, 24/4–5 (1983), 115.

4 Of course, Newman himself was only indirectly responsible for the style of his dramas: it was his directors who planned camera set-ups and movements. However, Newman has claimed that he always encouraged his directors to make the cameras mobile on air, as a contrast to what he claimed was the static nature of BBC drama production (*And Now For Your Sunday Night Dramatic Entertainment*).

For Gardner and Wyver, Newman refreshed the production of television drama by re-situating its mode of address and subject matter towards the majority working class, eschewing the West End middle-brow stage plays of the BBC for drama written for the medium. The Reithian era was a sterile 'last gasp':

> The first phase, primarily under the aegis of the BBC, was one of the last sustained gasps of a paternalistic Reithian project to bring 'the best of British culture' to a grateful and eager audience—a mission of middle-class enlightenment. Thus in its early days TV drama picked up the predominant patterns, concerns and style of both repertory theatre and radio drama (as well as many of their personnel, and their distinct training and working practices) and consisted of televized stage plays, 'faithfully' and tediously broadcast from the theatre, or reconstructed in the studio, even down to intervals, prosceniums and curtains. Such an approach, which takes the television process itself as transparent, almost by definition, precluded any innovation of TV style or any attempt to develop a specifically televisual form for small-screen drama.[5]

In their conclusion Wyver and Gardner refer to Channel 4's commitment (circa 1983) to a number of relay transmissions of dramas from the theatre (such as *Nicholas Nickleby* and *Kean*):

> How ironic then that, in a sense, it represents a return to the theatre on television which dominated the small screen in the 1950s. And how sad that a service committed to 'innovation and experiment' has to rely on one of television drama's oldest and least interesting forms.[6]

It is with these 'least interesting forms' that this book is concerned. It aims to revise significantly, rather than refute completely, the model of drama development asserted by Gardner and Wyver. Given the existence of considerable scholarship on early cinema, it seems no longer sufficient to offer a nebulous prehistory of television drama in terms of theatricality as a prerequisite to moving to the more exciting discussions of 'Armchair Theatre' and 'The Wednesday Play'. If early drama forms were static, boring, theatrical then surely this is interesting in itself, particularly given its existence at a time when cinema was fluid, mobile, and layered. If early television drama was static and theatrical, then how and why was it static and theatrical? If it was produced in terms of a Reithian ethic, then how did this translate into shots, composition, and mode of address? If it was parasitic on British West End theatre, why? And how was this theatre presented as television? In other words what did early television drama *look like*? As Charles Barr argues:

---

5 Gardner and Wyver, 'The Single Play', 115.
6 Ibid. 129.

> We need at least some tentative equivalents, in terms of
> TV history, for the authoritative analyses of the developing
> formal systems of early cinema that have been provided by
> writers like Barry Salt and the team of David Bordwell/Kristin
> Thompson/Janet Staiger . . . Between the blocks of 'dated' raw
> material and the institutional and technological histories, bridges
> need to be built.[7]

I planned and researched this book precisely as a 'tentative' and exploratory 'bridge', in order to outline possible ways of thinking and
writing about early television which would genuinely 'open the (historical) box' for further work. Barr also identifies what would become almost a defining problematic for my research, the absence
of audiovisual material from the earliest years of television. It is a
somewhat awkward historical legacy for those scholars wanting to *see*
precisely how television drama worked. John Caughie summarizes
the problem:

> While cinema historians have a continuous, though incomplete,
> history of films from the 1890s, television has a pre-history in
> which programmes themselves do not exist in recorded form.
> Transcription, or recording television on film, was not developed
> till 1947, and recording on tape was technologically possible first
> in the US in 1953, and was probably not readily available in
> Britain till around 1958. Neither was in routine use till the 1960s,
> and even when recording was possible there is a long chain of
> missing links which have been wiped from the record either to
> reuse the tapes or to save storage space . . . This makes the
> recovery of the early history of television form and style an
> archaeological, rather than a strictly historical procedure.[8]

These interrelated issues—the necessity to begin an analysis of the
style and forms of early television drama, and the corresponding
absence of audiovisual material—have shaped my subsequent research methodology and the structure of this book.

The bulk of the research presented here was conducted at the BBC
Written Archives Centre, Caversham Park. This *written* archive provided programme and policy information—studio plans, camera
scripts, memos, etc.—which was invaluable in the process of recon-
structing the *visual* sense of early television drama. Other primary
written sources included schedules, reviews, and criticism published

---

7 Charles Barr, 'Television on Television', *Sight and Sound*, 55/3 (1986), 159. He is
   referring to Barry Salt, *Film Style and Technology: History and Analysis* (London:
   Starword, 1983), and David Bordwell, Janet Staiger, Kristin Thompson, *The Classical
   Hollywood Cinema: Film Style and Mode of Production to 1960* (London: Routledge and
   Kegan Paul, 1985).

8 John Caughie, 'Before the Golden Age: Early Television Drama', in John Corner (ed.),
   Popular Television in Britain (London: British Film Institute, 1991), 24–5.

in the *Radio Times*, *The Listener*, *New Statesman*, *BBC Quarterly*, and *Sight and Sound* from the 1930s, 1940s, and 1950s. The use of still photographs of early television production was not satisfactory as a basis for analysis: the vast majority of them are production stills, presumably taken during camera rehearsals (one can often see the television cameras on the periphery of the photograph).[9]

I also draw on three other kinds of subsequently generated material. First, published anecdotal and interview-based writing provided some invaluable insights into the working practices of early television drama. Second, the 'gap' in academic scholarship in this area has been addressed more recently in some journals and books of collected essays, and this work provided me with some useful maps of hitherto unknown territory. Lastly, I conducted a number of interviews with production and engineering personnel who worked during the early period.

I consider 'early television' to mean programmes made up to 1955. It is important to separate the period of single-channel television broadcasting, within the public service epoch, as a discrete time in television history. As I note in Chapter 4, the introduction of a competing television service had a transformative effect on drama production and, whilst there was also some continuity with pre-1955 forms of drama, this is such an important moment in the history of British television that it is sensible to restrict my analysis to drama output before this date. The post-1955 period is also a transitional one, between a near total reliance on live studio drama productions, and the increasing use of pre-recorded material, on tape and film. This is reflected in the steep increase in the availability of visual archive material from 1955 onwards, a rich source for future research. The pre–1955 era also represents the most unexplored period of television drama production (and of television in general).

The aim of this analysis is not to pretend that early television drama was always mobile, never theatrical, and never dependent on some forms of radio drama. But restricting our understanding of early television drama to 'photographed stage plays' elides a great deal of stylistic and aesthetic development and debate, particularly as it is taken as the starting point for the transition of the medium as a whole from a literary to a cinematic mode. Robin Nelson has recently argued that:

> The shift from the studio-based, literary/theatrical to the
> visual/cinematic product is most marked in the historically
> cherished, authored, single play slot. In a gradual process,
> one-off, authored TV drama has loosened its tap-root in theatre
> and gravitated towards the visuality of cinema.[10]

---

9 See the stills in Tise Vahimagi (ed.), *British Television: An Illustrated Guide* (Oxford: Oxford University Press, 1994).

10 Robin Nelson, *TV Drama in Transition* (London: Macmillan, 1997), 19.

What is the 'cinematic' here—long shots? little dialogue? European art cinema? Hollywood high-concept? What counts as 'visuality' given that television is *always visual*, even when it transmits literary and theatrical subject matter? Is this a sensuous distinction between film and television images? I think that the distinction between visual styles is not reducible to a literary cinematic trope: sometimes the self-effacing television drama that relays performance and dialogue without drawing attention to its visual style might seem more 'cinematic' than the visually exhibitionistic television drama. As we shall see, even early television drama sometimes wanted to show off its visuals before its verbal.

Television was also more than radio that gained an eye and lost a voice: it had a visual imagination too. Stylistic change in television drama was often signalled by the claim not that it was 'more realistic' (as in film) but that it was 'more visual'. In the 1960s Troy Kennedy Martin's essay about alternative television drama, 'Nats Go Home' was written as a manifesto against the gravitational pull of dialogue on the style of television drama, arguing for the more visual appeal of collage and montage.[11] To assume that early television drama had limited visual imagination, and that a dependence on theatrical material entailed a 'theatrical visual style' of depiction, whereas writing for 'television as television' in the late 1950s and 1960s meant the liberation of cameras from their static theatrical chains, is to avoid confronting the reality of television history in preference for a neat metaphor.

The ability to choreograph multiple cameras through space in real-time is certainly indicative of a level of technological ability and also of the ambitions of drama producers: but it says little about the aesthetic value of the television drama (one could, for example, interpret a busy camera style as distracting). Where camera movement is a significant factor in the development of television drama is as part of a continuity of stylistic ambition whereby drama producers want to 'get in closer' to the dramatic action, to become intimate with it.

The desire to get in close to the dramatic action is not confined to drama production (it is clearly relevant to news and sports coverage —both in short supply during the early years of British television), but it is an appetite that provides a continuity between the early, pre-1955, television drama and later drama. Achieving 'nearness' to actors and moving a viewpoint with them through the diegetic spaces of the studio was a feature of early and later television drama. But where did this appetite for 'getting closer' originate?

11 Troy Kennedy Martin, 'Nats Go Home'. Kennedy Martin repeated his point thirty years later, 'Television is all dialogue, or a lot of it is, and cinema is all images', quoted in Sean Day-Lewis, *Talk of Drama: Views of the Television Dramatist Now and Then* (Luton: University of Luton Press/John Libbey Media, 1998), 210.

For Gardner and Wyver the development of indigenous television drama was blocked by a respect for theatre, and the push for dramatic freedom was personified by Sydney Newman. The arrival of Newman from North America to Britain in the mid-1950s, onto a psycho-social terrain apparently ripe for liberation has symbolic potential as Ted Willis demonstrates:

> Along came this man with this dream of putting the story of ordinary people and of our times, the contemporary times, on the screen, and doing this with quality, and giving writers freedom to write . . . this natural force blew through the corridors of television and blew a lot of the cobwebs out. That man probably had a greater influence on the development of television than anyone else.[12]

Newman's arrival more or less coincides with the arrival of commercial television in Britain in 1955 which has also been seen as a liberating force for change in television. However, it is possible to see this development toward a newly socialized popular 'closeness'—in terms of its popular address and a stylistic freedom—as part of a longstanding broadcasting tradition whose ambition from the beginning was to establish more intimate forms of communication.

Broadcasting provided the regular delivery to the home of developing structures of 'dailiness' that Paddy Scannell has shown characterized early broadcast programming. For Scannell, the address of broadcast programmes was developed toward the 'more direct, intimate personal style of speech', so that broadcast talk was aligned with conversational forms.[13]

'Intimacy' for early television drama was understood by critics and producers in terms of the reception of television in the private 'intimate' sphere of the home, something shared by all television programmes. Some critics believed that the delivery of drama to the domestic sphere required a softer vocal register, and restrained performance style—the conversational, rather than the declarative. For other critics, television plays should tackle psychological and emotional issues, using the 'intimate' interior setting of one or two sets, rendered through a close-up style. For them, intimacy as a quality of television drama meant close familiarity between characters in interior settings, and this was clearly distinguished from the more macho observational knowledge of the public sphere that television's Outside Broadcast abilities could provide. Television critics argued that the proper métier for television drama's intimacy meant the limitation of ambition away from film's space-expanding possibilities,

---

12 *And Now For Your Sunday Night Dramatic Entertainment.*
13 Paddy Scannell, *Radio, Television and Modern Life* (Oxford: Blackwell, 1996), 12–13.

and toward the enclosure of 'electronic theatre'. Intimacy meant the revelation and display of the character's inner feelings and emotions, effected by a close-up style of multi-camera studio production, rather than the exhibitionistic display of technological virtuosity that the 'come and see inside a submarine live' rhetoric of programmes like *Saturday Night Live!* offered the viewer. Early television drama's intimacy is then a very elastic idea that contains a variety of historical and aesthetic assumptions about early television.

The virtual absence of pre-1955 audio-visual material in the archives probably accounts for the bias of critical attention towards the post-1955 period, where viewing copies are available.[14] Although television studies scholarship still has not developed a well-defined and historically constituted sense of the medium and its apparatus, there is a growing body of work that considers television history in Britain and North America.[15] Previously, Asa Briggs's five-volume *History of Broadcasting in the UK* and Eric Barnouw's *Tube of Plenty* represented the most thorough social and institutional histories of broadcasting in Britain and the United States respectively.[16] One criticism of this kind of history was that it privileged the broadcasting institution's own self-definition at a management level, obscuring more local decisions and developments. The limitations of Briggs's monumental study is raised by Edward Buscombe in his review of Briggs's fourth volume:

> there remains the question of whether the book is indeed what it claims to be, a history of broadcasting in the UK. There are reasons why I think it cannot quite be that. One has to do with what Briggs takes broadcasting to be. Broadcasting is what the BBC does, and what the BBC does is largely to be discovered through an examination of internal records. By far the greater part of Briggs's story is told through the evidence of BBC memoranda, published policy statements, letters, speeches and so on. His book is therefore the history of the BBC's internal workings at the level of policy formation.[17]

14 See Steve Bryant, *The Television Heritage* (London: British Film Institute, 1989) for a history of television programme archiving.

15 For example, two seminal essays on early television drama are, John Caughie, 'Before the Golden Age: Early Television Drama', in John Corner (ed.), *Popular Television in Britain* (London: British Film Institute, 1991), and Charles Barr, ' "They Think It's All Over": The Dramatic Legacy of Live Television', in John Hill and Martin McLoone (eds.), *Big Picture, Small Screen: The Relations Between Film and Television* (Luton: University of Luton Press/John Libbey, 1997).

16 Asa Briggs, *History of Broadcasting in the UK*, i. *The Birth of Broadcasting* (1961), ii. *The Golden Age of Wireless* (1965), iii. *The War of Words* (1970; vols. i–iii, London: Oxford University Press); iv. *Sound and Vision* (1979), v. *Competition* (1995; vols. iv and v, Oxford: Oxford University Press). Eric Barnouw, *A Tower in Babel* (1966), *The Golden Web* (1968), *Tube of Plenty* (1975; all pub. New York: Oxford University Press).

17 Ed Buscombe, 'Broadcasting From Above', *Screen Education*, 37 (1980–1), 75.

Buscombe notes that the dependence on internal memos for evidence tends to present the BBC as a purely self-generating organization, and this approach necessarily elides attention to the actual content of the programmes themselves:

> it is obvious enough that a history of *broadcasting*, as opposed merely to a history of the internal workings of the BBC, ought surely to offer some analysis of the end product. What Briggs provides is for the most part merely a listing of the major shows the BBC put out between 1945 and 1955. One cannot understand the reasons why these programmes took the form they did simply by reference to the minutes of the BBC's Board of Governors.[18]

In recognition of the fact that official records are produced by 'those in charge', a more balanced history would reflect the thinking and practice of technicians, producers, and writers:

> Such research among those lower down in the hierarchy, involved in programme production, might also complicate and therefore improve our understanding of the BBC's ideological function . . . There must always have been more or less of a struggle. Indeed the stream of memos and policy papers is at least a priori evidence of this. For if there was never any resistance to the line pursued by those at the top, never any questioning of the proper way of doing things, why would the BBC's position need to be spelt out in such detail?[19]

For Buscombe, writing in 1980, the 'complete' history of broadcasting remains to be written, and it would be one where the programmes and the programme-makers are privileged. Clearly, broadcasting history needs both the monumental ambition and coverage of Briggs's excellent history and the more local specific analysis of particular genres and their production practices. As the Head of BBC television drama during the 1950s, Michael Barry says of Briggs:

> [His] History of Broadcasting in the United Kingdom gives the overall view of the development of drama during the period [1936–55]; but, as one sub-division in a massive work, the view is limited, and one that, in the main, is seen from distant and senior corridors. [My] essentially personal account seeks to convey the impressions, listen to the sounds and feel the pulse of another corridor, the studio corridor at Alexandra Palace; along which for a number of years the life blood of television seemed to flow. It attempts to describe what it was like to work in that first corridor of television . . .[20]

---

18 Ibid. 77.

19 Ibid.

20 Michael Barry, *From the Palace to the Grove* (London: Royal Television Society, 1992), p. xi.

The historical turn in television studies of the early 1990s combined both the macro-overview with more local analyses.[21] This history demonstrated that the absence of the programmes as 'raw material' was not necessarily a problem. The history of theatre has similar absences, many of which have been addressed using precisely the kind of written secondary material I intend to draw upon. Of course, what is written down is not necessarily the same thing as what happened on screen. There are many ways in which the live broadcast may differ from that which was planned in writing: actors and technicians may make mistakes, or a particular performance may differ in its emphasis, or quality, in ways that would be impossible to discern from the script alone. The absence of the epistemological guarantee of the audio-visual record *is* a limitation for any historical analysis that seeks to understand visual aesthetics and style. This absence is explained by a number of factors.

In the UK, by 1947 it was technically possible to record television on film so, theoretically, there should be a complete record of programmes from here onwards. Instead, for the pre-1955 period, we have two episodes of *The Quatermass Experiment*, the 1953 televising of the Coronation, an adaptation of *Nineteen Eighty-Four*, a selection of children's programmes from the early 1950s, and some sporting events (Test Match cricket, some football). Michael Barry noted that the fiftieth anniversary celebration of television that the BBC embarked on in November 1986 'revealed the lamentable poverty of a pictorial record of what is essentially a visual means of communication.'[22] There are three primary reasons for this, the limit of aesthetic horizons; copyright controls on recording material; talent unions' agreements with the BBC.[23]

A year after telerecording (recording television images on 16mm or 35mm film) was introduced in the BBC, an article in *BBC Quarterly* explored its potential.[24] It noted that the recording of 'important outside broadcasts of historic or sporting interest' (the Olympic games, the Cenotaph Ceremony, the Royal Wedding, etc.) was valuable in itself both for the BBC archives and for sale abroad. Recording was also seen to address the needs of an expanding national audience:

21 See e.g. William Boddy, *Fifties Television* (Urbana and Chicago: University of Illinois Press, 1990); William Urrichio (guest editor), *Historical Journal of Film Radio and Television*: special issue, *The History of German Television, 1935–1944*, 10/2 (1990), which includes Knut Hickethier's essay 'The Television Play in the Third Reich'; Paddy Scannell and David Cardiff, *A Social History of Broadcasting*, i. *1922–1939* (Oxford: Blackwell, 1991); John Corner (ed.), *Popular Television in Britain: Studies in Cultural History* (London: British Film Institute, 1991).

22 Barry, *From the Palace to the Grove*, p. xii. For details of the anniversary programming, see *Radio Times* 1 Nov. 1986.

23 See also Steve Bryant, *The Television Heritage* (London: British Film Institute, 1989).

24 H. W. Baker and W. D. Kemp, 'The Recording of Television Programmes', *BBC Quarterly*, 4/4 (1949–50), 236–50.

It is inevitable that the majority of important outside broadcasts take place during the day, with the result that the direct television broadcast is often missed by members of the family who are at work or at school. It is therefore very desirable to make a record of the event as televised . . . Little or no editing of the recording is required, since this has in effect been done at the time of the broadcast by the television producer.[25]

The existing Television Newsreel reports of such events were seen to be wasteful, taking on average twelve hours to add commentary and sound, compared to some four or five hours of processing of telerecorded film where editing and sound was already recorded. Telerecording would also allow technicians and producers for the first time to see the result of their electronic processing of the event, and it could be used for training purposes. The authors note that telerecording would be invaluable for drama productions, particularly when studio space and rehearsal time was very limited:

Two studios are available at Alexandra Palace, which allows one day only for the camera rehearsal and transmission of each production, assuming that there are only two programmes a day. Any easement of the studio load that could be obtained by making a television recording of the original production, and would result in more camera rehearsal time being available for following productions, would be most welcome.[26]

Television programmes were not perceived as valuable in themselves, though some were thought to be worth preserving as historical records of national events (which had a resale value abroad). A television play was not recorded because it was seen as worthy of recall or archival storage, but because the process would free up studio space and time, or facilitate repeats without the costs of a live re-presentation, and this practice did not become widespread until the start of ITV in 1955. Even when the recording of programmes was seen as a positive necessity this did not invalidate the conceptual and aesthetic horizons within which television was perceived: as strictly ephemeral. The dominance of such a standpoint can be seen (or, rather, it cannot) in the way videotaped material from the 1960s was routinely wiped by the BBC and ITV television companies, partly in order to re-use tapes and to save space, but crucially because tapes and space were more *valuable* than the preservation of *television* programmes. As a result, if television plays were telerecorded before 1955, very few were archived.

Copyright restrictions meant there was always a problem even when recording television on film was not a possibility: the BBC had

25 Ibid. 236.
26 Ibid. 237.

to get permission to produce its own live production of the theatre play *Clive of India* in 1938, because it had been filmed by 20th Century Fox four years earlier. When a large studio production of *The Scarlet Pimpernel* was filmed with non-synchronized 'lines and all' in 1939 (the only attempt to do this) Alexander Korda who owned the rights ordered the recording to be burned, with the bonfire itself filmed as evidence. The BBC could get the stage rights for a television transmission—a one-off performance (this is television—transient —see it now or never)—but not the mechanical (recorded, stable, retrievable) rights.

For example, Royston Morley produced a studio version of *The Petrified Forest* in 1951, but Warner Brothers Picture Company had acquired the film and television rights to Robert E. Sherwood's stage play in 1935 for fifteen years, with first refusal on the television rights at the end of that period (the film was released in 1936). Morley assumed that the production could be telerecorded (he was Head of Staff Training at this point and an example of a studio play would have been valuable training material for new drama producers), but Warner were insistent that no recording should be made.[27]

One solution to the copyright problem was to commission original plays for television. The setting up of a script unit in early 1950, and the hiring of Nigel Kneale and Philip Mackie as staff scriptwriters, can be seen as an attempt to generate fresh drama, and drama which could be recorded and owned by the BBC. This would not have been an issue before telerecording when television programmes simply could not be thought of as *material* commodities. As John Caughie notes,

> What recording did was to lift television out of ephemerality and give it a commodity form. The shift from direct transmission to recording turned television from use value to exchange value, re-forming even public service television as not only a cultural good but also a tradable good. Previously there had been some exchange of films of important events, but now what was conceived as cultural production entered the market place as commodity.[28]

In December 1952 the Television Transcription Unit was formed, its aim to 'distribute abroad films made by the BBC TV Service and telerecordings of BBC TV plays.'[29] Around the same time, Hugh Carleton Greene, later Director-General of the BBC (1960–9), wrote an article for the *BBC Quarterly* called, 'Television Transcriptions: The Economic Possibilities'. He defines 'transcription' as 'either a recording on film of a live television programme or a film specially

27 See memo R. G. Walford to Royston Morley, 15 May 1951, BBC Written Archives
    Centre (WAC) Programme File T5/391.
28 Caughie, 'Before the Golden Age', 39.
29 *BBC Handbook* (1958).

produced, whether with ordinary film cameras or by electronic methods, for showing on television.'[30] He makes the further distinction between telerecordings (recording a live television programme on film—called 'kinescopes' in the US) and television films (films specially made for television). It is a prophetic article, which notes that the expansion of television services internationally meant that there was a growing market for ready-made television packages. For the year ending 31 March 1956 the BBC had exported over 200 telerecordings and films to the Canadian Broadcasting Company and the Australian Film Commission. A year later this had risen to 550 (300 films, 200 telerecordings). By the next year (end March 1958) the proportions had changed somewhat with the sale of 200 films and 500 telerecordings, the vast majority of them drama serials. Despite the Transcription Unit's formation in 1952, there is little evidence to suggest that much was transcribed before 1955. The significance of increased telerecording was that it undermined one of the central planks of the television's 'immediacy' aesthetic: the simultaneous address of the actor to audience, the live relationship between drama production and reception in the home. With the use of 'canned' material, what was there to separate television from film?

The question of actors' and musicians' fees meant that there was also a certain resistance to using filmed material to replace live repeat performances. Although an actor's repeat fees for the second live performance was slightly lower than for the first, the prospect of the BBC being able to produce only one performance of a show or play and film it for repeat showing, clearly meant a dire loss of revenue, unless an agreement could be reached over filmed repeat fees.

Equity later agreed with the BBC that telerecordings could be made of programmes, but only of the repeat performance. Actors and musicians' repeat fees were guaranteed. Furthermore, the pre-1955 agreement stipulated that any telerecording made could only be viewed privately. The BBC's production of Marcelle Maurette's play *Anastasia* in 1953 provides a good example of the way the rules operated in this period. The play lasted nearly two hours, and won the Daily Mail 'Best TV Play of the Year' award for 1953–4. A telerecording of the programme was made, and sold to the Canadian Broadcasting Company. Eric von Stroheim wanted to view it but under the Equity agreement he could only do so in private, in a BBC building. In 1955 20th Century Fox acquired the mechanical rights (and subsequently made the 1956 film version) and the BBC's *Anastasia* had to be destroyed.[31]

30 Hugh Carleton Greene, 'Television Transcription: The Economic Possibilities', *BBC Quarterly*, 7/4, (1952–3), 216.

31 *Anastasia*, BBC WAC T5/15.

Given this absence of primary material, the study of this period, particularly a study which endeavours to explore aesthetic and stylistic qualities of drama production, needs to reformulate traditional notions of textual analysis. These are texts that do not exist in their original audio-visual form but exist instead as shadows, dispersed and refracted amongst buried files, bad memories, a flotsam of fragments. For the BBC, the resting-place for such remains is the BBC Written Archives Centre, where the historian can find scripts, studio plans, policy memos, committee minutes, and so on. My intention is the reconstitution or reconstruction, using this written material, of 'ghost texts' (or ghost-television dramas), in order to approximate the visual constitution of early television drama.

I see the period 1936–55 as 'early television'. There are compelling reasons to isolate this period, with due regard for the continuities of programming and form and institution that followed. First, in Britain, the pre-1955 fact of a *single* television channel. This means that a non-competitive (or non-complementary) schedule was designed, and that 'keeping the audience's interest' had a slightly different inflection from post-1955 considerations. Secondly, the pre-1955 technological basis of television production and transmission was the *live broadcast*. True, this continued well into the 1970s, but I am thinking here of the manner in which television was *conceived* aesthetically and technologically, and the way that television after 1955 was no longer—technologically and in practice—necessarily or essentially 'live-only'. The possibility of scheduling based on pre-recorded 'canned' programmes was considered in Britain as far back as 1949, but as a practice and a competing conceptual standpoint this had no significant currency before 1955. Furthermore, as I have already indicated, the recoverable period of television history in terms of audio-visual archive material dates, with a handful of notable exceptions, from 1955.[32] The National Film and Television Archive's catalogue, shows that the majority of pre-1955 surviving television is US television (usually serials filmed for television).[33]

---

32 These are telerecordings of the 1953 television coverage of the Coronation, some children's programmes, the first two episodes of *The Quatermass Experiment* (BBC, 1953), some sporting events, and the only example of the single television play before 1955, *Nineteen Eighty-Four* (Dec. 1954).

33 For a list of copies held at the National Film and Television Archive (these are not necessarily available for viewing), see Simon Baker and Olwen Terris (eds.), *A For Andromeda to Zoo Time: The TV Holdings of the National Film and Television Archive* (London: British Film Institute, 1994). See also, Dan Einstein *et al.*, 'Source Guide to Family Comedy, Drama, and Serial Drama, 1946–1970', in Lynn Spigel and Denise Mann (eds.), *Private Screenings: Television and the Female Consumer* (Minneapolis: University of Minneapolis Press, 1992)—this listing, and the Museum of Radio and Television (New York) catalogue of holdings, suggests that a continuous audio-visual record for US television begins around 1948–9, coinciding with the development of kinescope recording of television on film.

There is also a continuity between pre- and post-war television, as John Caughie explains:

> television in the immediate post-war years was still driven
> by the enthusiasm of the amateur inherited from the pre-war
> pioneers. The whole discourse of production, the celebration
> of disaster, the informal working relations, the try-outs, carried
> something of the 'wizard prang' about it, an extension of
> church-hall dramatics. In many ways, this period parallels the
> experimentalism and lack of standardization characteristic of
> 'primitive cinema' as described by Bordwell and Burch. The
> significance of the 50s with the arrival of competition and the
> technology of recording, was to install professionalism in the
> place of the enthusiastic amateur . . .[34]

What is also apparent from producer's memos, studio plans and later retrospectives is the extent of *aesthetic appetite* within a culture of *professional excellence* during the pre-war and immediate post-war years. The reliance on anecdotal material, such as that found in Denis Norden's *Coming to You Live!* which stresses the accidents, the fluffs, the unusual and entertaining, should not be confused with the actual, if less dramatic, history of regular drama production within strictly managed parameters.

The pre-1955 period also has a unity in terms of the development of television drama's *aesthetics*, *technology*, and *style*.

Aesthetics refers to the historical characterization of television's essential qualities, by those chiefly involved in the production process. The aesthetics of early drama production are inseparable from its technology. As John Caughie argues,

> the adaptation of theatre was not simply a question of reworking
> scripts, but rather of capturing on television something of the
> nature of theatrical performance. The absence of expressive *mise
> en scene* and editing—the absence, in other words, of 'style'—
> which comes to be confused with 'boring naturalism', was not
> simply a limitation borne out of technological constraint or
> imaginative failure; it was rather the logical aesthetic of a
> technology whose essence was conceived in term of immediacy,
> relay and the 'live'.[35]

In my discussion of technology I want to signal the importance of the technical developments which have influenced, in various ways, the nature and production of aesthetic discourses, and the stylistic features of television drama. Central to this aspect of the book is the

34 Caughie, 'Before the Golden Age', 40.

35 Ibid. 32.

status of a media service characterized by *live* production and the tension between this dominant characteristic and the availability of various recording technologies.

Bordwell and Thompson situate style within an overall context of form:

> Every film develops specific techniques in patterned ways. This unified, developed, and significant use of particular technical choices we shall call *style*.[36]

Considering aesthetics, technology and style is a first step in identifying and exploring the development of specific textual patterns of television drama production. For example it is possible to extrapolate from early cinema history aspects of technical and stylistic change that have been seen to be indicative of its modernization. Noel Burch's definition of the 'primitive mode of representation' (PMR) is partly based on shot scale and the absence of an editing process:

> The formal characteristics of Burch's 'primitive mode of representation' in their most abstract manifestations can . . . be briefly summarised: single shot scene, tableau composition, frontal staging; no scene dissection . . .[37]

Scene dissection is Barry Salt's useful term for cutting within a given space, rather than between different spaces.[38] Early television's 'photographed stage play' might at first seem to share certain characteristics with Burch's PMR, particularly in terms of the expected 'reverence' for the unity of the theatrical scene. Was the respect for theatre and the continuity of performance expressed by a refusal to change shots during the acting out of a theatrical 'scene'? How far did the 'dissection' of each scene in fact occur? This would be one way of estimating stylistic change during the early period. This is not to argue that a faster, more 'cinematic' cutting rate is necessarily equivalent to maturity or development. Thomas Elsaesser is cogent on this point as it applies to early cinema:

> 'Simultaneous playing areas' and 'editing within the frame' are features of early cinema that have increasingly become the object of attention. First, because they refer to and reformulate the

36 David Bordwell and Kristin Thompson, *Film Art: An Introduction*, 4th edn. (New York: McGraw-Hill Inc.: 1993), 144.

37 Thomas Elsaesser, 'Introduction' in Elsaesser (ed.), *Early Cinema: space, frame, narrative* (London: BFI, 1990), 24.

38 Barry Salt, *Film Style and Technology: History and Analysis* (London: Starword, 1983), 49–51.

oldest (and usually pejorative) distinction made between primitive and classical cinema: the charge that early films were 'theatrical'. . . . But . . . the formal features of early cinema cannot be equated with its presumed debts to the theatre. Second, tableau scenes and other forms of elaborate staging are not necessarily the sign of 'primitive' or 'retarded' practice. Rather, they are specific choices or strategies, available as alternatives to editing.[39]

As we shall see, one alternative to editing for live television drama was to use a continuous take with reframing to follow each actor's movements and to emphasize aspects of the performance. After all, it is the *static* nature of the photographed stage play which is attacked by Gardner and Wyver, and the mobility of the cameras for Newman's productions is one of the stylistic ways in which early drama is assumed to be separated from the more 'mature' styles of the late 1950s and the 'golden age' of the 1960s. As I will demonstrate, this kind of spatial mobility—achieved either by switching between studio cameras ('editing'), or by camera movement—was a characteristic of the earliest drama productions as well.

One concrete piece of evidence for this—like a mosquito preserved in fossilized amber—is an audio-visual fragment of television drama from the 1930s, a US television adaptation of Dion Boucicault's Victorian melodrama, *The Streets of New York* broadcast from a small studio on 31 August 1939. It was filmed off an early television tube using an experimental camera and is available for viewing at the Museum of Radio and Television in New York. Sadly, only six minutes of fragments remain, and there is no soundtrack. Initially, the fragments ooze precisely the kind of theatricality that Gardner and Wyver criticize: curtains, captions, an intermission, the respectful relay of a three-walled stage and some overblown acting. Yet a cursory glance shows that this is also a highly segmented presentation of that performance: three cameras cover the play, and there is often some very rapid cutting between close-up and medium shots, dialogue and reaction shots. There is also camera mobility—pans to follow characters across the stage, a track-in during a speech. Yes, this is a theatrical performance, but one mediated by a new means: live multi-camera studio television. We are given a *selection* of viewpoints, few of which could be equivalent to the position of a theatrical spectator.

In order to understand how the BBC television developed its own range of approaches to solving the problem of how to 'do' television drama it is necessary to situate the service within its institutional and technological context.

---

39 Elsaesser, *Early Cinema*, 13.

A Guide to the Institutional and Technological History of British Television[40]

On 2 November 1936 the first[41] BBC Television Service began regular, scheduled programme transmissions from Alexandra Palace, a dilapidated Victorian dance hall: by 1955 it had acquired seven more studios and was facing competition from two commercial television companies.[42] The history of television is therefore one of expansion and conflict.

The early and formative history of television is bound up with the history of radio. The process by which radio manufacturers developed national broadcasting networks and monopolies that replaced local and amateur broadcasting communities is well documented.[43] The transition from fragmented, local, home-made programming and equipment to national regulated systems of broadcasting allowed a rationalization of both product and audience. Television, as a broadcasting technology perceived by many as 'radio with pictures' was eventually developed and integrated within existing broadcasting institutions and industries (although it is important to note that television's developmental possibilities were not yet restricted to broadcasting to the domestic sphere).[44]

The formation of the British Broadcasting Company in 1922 marks the beginning of institutional broadcasting in Britain. From this point the development of radio schedules, programmes, ideology, and address had a direct bearing on the first television service. To a certain extent, the logic of programme length, selection, theme, genre, and address are 'pre-loaded' for television by the BBC's sound broadcasting rationale and tradition, one forged within particular circumstances of the 1920s.

If the institutional history of television begins with radio, the history of television in Britain begins with BBC radio, and the ideology of public service broadcasting first espoused by its first Director-General, John Reith:

40 This section is intended to be a very selective guide to broad aspects of British television history as it pertains to the development of early television drama. For more detail and coverage see Andrew Crisell, *An Introductory History of British Broadcasting* (London: Routledge, 1997).

41 In fact the BBC had regular, if experimental, television broadcasts from Broadcasting House between 1932 and 1935, using Baird's 30-line system.

42 The Television Act, legislating for a commercial television channel, was passed on 30 July 1954. The first two commercial television companies awarded franchises to broadcast by the Independent Television Authority were Associated-Rediffusion and ATV who began transmission in September 1955.

43 See William Boddy, 'Archaeologies of Electronic Vision and the Gendered Spectator', *Screen* 35/2 (1994), Eric Barnouw, *Tube of Plenty* (New York: Oxford University Press, 1975), chapters 1–2; Briggs, *The Birth of Broadcasting*.

44 See Ed Buscombe, 'Thinking it Differently: Television and the Film Industry', *Quarterly Review of Film Studies* 9/3 (Summer 1984), 196–203. For the history of the Scophony company which attempted to develop large screen public television in Britain during the 1930s, see, T. Singleton, *The Story of Scophony* (London: Royal Television Society, 1988).

His message for the infant medium of sound broadcasting was that it had to be as morally sound as a church bell. He wanted it to take the high cultural road and educate popular taste rather than merely pander to the lowest common denominator. There was thus a heavy stress on the best that had been thought, written, known and heard. Reith's book of prophecies, *Broadcast Over Britain* (1924), was a mixture of the theocratic ramblings of a Carlyle with the cultural poise of an Arnold.[45]

This squares somewhat uneasily with the BBC television's transmission of John Snuggs, the troubadour, 'demonstrating paper tearing with his partner accordionist' in December 1936: the 'vulgar visuality' of television was to trouble the moral unity of the BBC's self-definition.[46]

The Selsdon Committee was appointed by the Government in 1934 to consider the development of television and advise the Postmaster-General on the relative merit of competing systems of television transmission. Despite his reservations about television, Reith himself agreed when giving evidence to the Committee that, 'The relationship between sight and sound broadcasting is absolutely indissoluble.'[47]

The Committee reported in 1935, and gave the BBC responsibility for the production of television programmes using two television systems which would alternate weekly (Baird's mechanical system, and EMI-Marconi's electronic cathode-ray tube system). By 11 November 1936 the BBC Television Service began regular broadcasts across London (they had been broadcasting to the manufacturer's exhibition, RadiOlympia, during the summer), albeit only two hour's worth of programmes a day, between 3.00 and 4.00 p.m. and between 9.00 and 10.00 p.m.

The recommendation that rival television systems be used alternately until one or other proved compatible with the requirements of the new service at Alexandra Palace immediately prevented any standardization in terms of production practices. Baird's obsolete and cumbersome mechanical system was axed in February 1937, and the television service continued to broadcast until the beginning of the Second World War using the EMI-Marconi system.

The BBC Television Service at Alexandra Palace was both physically isolated from Broadcasting House, and organizationally isolated. Like the radio Empire Service, it was treated as a parallel service rather than an integrated one, and executive control was located with the

45 Roger Sales, 'An Introduction to Broadcasting History', in David Punter (ed.), *Introduction to Contemporary Cultural Studies* (London: Longmans, 1986), 48.

46 Part of an early series of 10-minute skits called 'London Characters', *Radio Times* 11 Dec. 1936 (Television Edition).

47 Quoted in Briggs, *The Golden Age of Wireless*, 585.

sound broadcasters. Hence the first Director of Television was responsible to the Controller of (all) Programmes, Cecil Graves, and throughout the late 1930s there was increasing frustration that BBC management refused to recognize the 'special needs' of television, and instead regarded it as a luxury or novelty service.[48] The service also proved to be far more expensive than was foreseen, so much so that, in March 1939, sponsored programmes were seriously considered as the only solution to the financial crisis. The Treasury was unwilling to release more cash, and both the Postmaster-General and the Television Advisory Committee wanted sponsored television so that the service could develop. As Asa Briggs argues, 'Had there been no war in 1939, it is conceivable that commercial television would have come to Britain fifteen years before it did.'[49]

What might have been a significant restructuring of the BBC's ideology was averted by the closedown of the Television Service in September 1939 on the eve of the war. The Hankey Report, published in March 1945, suggested the restoration of the pre-war television model rather than a revision of it. The example of the failure, in America, of sponsored commercial networks to develop television successfully, convinced the committee that the BBC should be entrusted with providing a public service television system at least for the immediate future.[50]

The Service was restored in 1946 as part of a changed BBC, one that had won considerable public and political kudos for its wartime broadcasting. One element of continuity remained: the isolation and implicit denigration of the restored Television Service by the rest of the Sound broadcasters. The BBC may have won the 'war of words', but it had yet to recognize the potential of sound *and* vision. During the late 1930s and the immediate post-war years, television was perceived by the BBC as something of a 'Cinderella' service, lacking the aesthetic kudos that German television producers had fostered before the war, or the publicity engendered by the competition between NBC and CBS systems in the US.[51] In a survey of BBC Sound personnel conducted in 1947, the majority of respondents considered the Television Service too similar to the Light Programme.[52] Television was also seen, correctly, as a luxury toy, which *ipso facto* prevented the

---

48 See Briggs, *The Golden Age of Wireless*, 570 and 602–3.

49 Briggs, *Sound and Vision*, 181.

50 Although the Hankey Report did not question the logic of the Postmaster-General's suggestion that television frequencies could, in principle, be leased to any organization including cinema. Briggs, *Sound and Vision*, 180.

51 See Knut Hickethier, 'The Television Play in the Third Reich', *Historical Journal of Film, Television and Radio*, 10/3 (1990).

52 Briggs, *Sound and Vision*, 214.

wide democratic coverage that the principles of public service broadcasting demanded.

The continuing denial of organizational parity with Sound broadcasting can be seen as a consequence of this attitude, which lasted until well into the 1950s. As John Caughie notes:

> Director-General Haley's cultural mission to use broadcasting as an institution of national improvement seems always to have had a slightly edgy relationship with television, preferring the known territory of radio to the *terra incognita* of television with its slightly heady entertainment potential. Asa Briggs points out that 'key figures in the BBC itself were more interested in 1946 in the starting of the Third Programme than in the resumption of television'[53]

Maurice Gorham was appointed Head of the Television Service in 1946 and he pressed for the expansion of the Service for the next 18 months. He resigned in 1947 in response to Haley's reorganization of the BBC which left the Television Service integrated as only one of six divisions within 'Home Output'. This meant that television still had no representation on the BBC Board of Management. He was replaced by Norman Collins who was also a television enthusiast. Financial conditions began to improve, and in June 1947, two years after Hankey's recommendations, plans for a new transmitter serving the Midlands area were announced. With his Programme Director, Cecil McGivern, Collins was able to carry out a rational restructuring of the television output into four 'Programme Groups': drama; light entertainment; talks and talk features; outside broadcasts and films. Using the threat that US television expansion was already ahead of British developments, Collins was further able to convince BBC management that the Service required new studios and equipment to maintain its prestige, so that by August 1948 BBC Governors approved an expansion programme for television. In March 1949 the BBC acquired a 13.5-acre site at the White City Exhibition where Television Centre was planned to open by 1960. In the meantime, the Rank Film Studios at Lime Grove were bought in November 1949 and the process of converting its five studios began.

This expansion needs to be contrasted with the relative political insignificance of television in the late 1940s. The Beveridge Committee, set up in 1949 to investigate the BBC monopoly, devoted only eighteen out of 325 pages of its 1951 Report to television, perceiving it as still in the experimental stage.[54] The publication of the Beveridge Report is significant chiefly for the Minority Report that it engendered, Selwyn Lloyd dissenting from the rest of the Committee by

---

53 Caughie, 'Before the Golden Age', 26.

54 For a discussion of the Beveridge Report (1951) see Sales, 'An Introduction to Broadcasting History', 54–6.

arguing for the establishment of a commercial television network. Undoubtedly this threat to the BBC broadcasting monopoly via television raised the profile of television within the BBC.[55]

The rapidly increasing television audience also had an impact on the expansion of television in the early 1950s. The BBC consistently underestimated the growth of combined sound and television licences: its estimate for 1955 was 2 million, and the actual figure 4.5 million.[56] The televising of the 1953 Coronation is the best-known measure of television's increased visibility as a *national broadcasting* medium.

The debates leading up to the Television Act, legislating for commercial television and passed in July 1954, mark the point where political and institutional discussion of broadcasting refocuses on television over radio as the key medium.

The technological history of television has been dealt with exhaustively elsewhere, and the following is a brief sketch necessary for an understanding of the rest of the book.[57]

During the 1920s and 1930s television's status as a viable apparatus and the nature of its application were in continual debate. Here television, rather than what was broadcast, is the novelty, an attraction in itself. Television in the 1930s was necessarily live and ephemeral. It had a distinctive ability as a medium that could relay pictures over space but maintain a co-temporality between event and spectator. Hence the recording of programmes themselves was not seen as a priority. Given this conceptual and aesthetic orientation, recording a television programme would have seemed as pointless as recording a telephone conversation. Filmed material could be transmitted electronically through television, using a telecine machine. This process could be used to provide inserts, usually stock scenes (battle, landscapes, rain, fog, etc.) which were used within the live studio transmission. Feature films could also be transmitted on television,

---

55 For a thorough description of the genesis of commercial television in Britain see, H. H. Wilson, *Pressure Group* (London: Weidenfeld and Nicolson, 1961), Peter Black, *The Mirror in the Corner* (London: Hutchinson and Co. Ltd, 1972), Bernard Sendall, *Independent Television in Britain*, i. *Origin and Foundation, 1946–62*, (London: Macmillan, 1982).

56 Quoted in Briggs, *Sound and Vision*, 241.

57 See: Albert Abramson, *The History of Television, 1880 to 1941* (Jefferson, NC: McFarland, 1987); Briggs, *The Golden Age of Wireless*, 520–4; R. W. Burns, *British Television: The Formative Years* (London: Peregrinus Press, 1986); Raymond Fielding (ed.), *A Technological History of Motion Pictures and Television* (Los Angeles and Berkeley: University of California, 1967); N. Goldstein, *The History of Television* (New York: Portland House, 1990); D. W. Kreuter, *British Radio and Television Pioneers: A Patent Bibliography* (London: Scarecrow Press, 1993); George Shiers (ed.), *Technical Development of Television* (New York: Arno Press, 1977); Brian Winston, *Misunderstanding Media* (Cambridge: Harvard University Press, 1986).

although film companies were reluctant to supply them.[58] During the pre-war and immediate post-war years the Television Service had little money to produce its own filmed material, let alone its own filmed dramas. In January 1948 the BBC begins to produce its own films regularly, in the form of the *BBC Television Newsreel* (BBC, 1948–54). Filming inserts for live drama and light entertainment (rather than using stock library film) was rare until the early 1950s.

The BBC *did* produce several 'Demonstration films' advertising its television service: *Television Comes to London* (1936)[59] and the *TV Demonstration Film* (1937) were broadcast in the morning during the pre-war years so that retailers would have something to show prospective buyers during the day (this was also a factor in the afternoon schedule where large drama productions would take place between 3 and 4 p.m.). Both films contain illustrative material, which attempted to re-create for the film camera something of the flavour of television for prospective buyers of sets.

Given the scarcity of studio space and rehearsal time at Alexandra Palace during the 1930s, the filming of programmes, had it been technically possible, would seem to offer an immediate solution: canned programmes would free-up both studio time and space, and allow producers to assess their own work. This did not happen until after the war. Instead, the impetus to record the television signal on film came from the US Navy and Air Force.[60] Not until 1947 was a means devised to record television pictures on film which minimized synchronization problems.[61] The result was called a *kinescope* or, in the UK, a telerecording.

Recording on film had huge advantages. Television programmes no longer had to be live one-off transmissions disappearing into the ether. Theoretically, the day's viewing could be recorded weeks before it was transmitted. Recording on film in the US was particularly useful as the differing state time zones meant that television programmes produced in New York and Hollywood could be filmed and sent (or 'bicycled') to distant syndicated stations. As Brian Winston notes:

> Without a national system of coaxial cables, programmes had to be . . . 'bicycled' to stations outside the . . . network. As the net was built, another problem arose—time differences between the two coasts. This led to the era of 'hot' or 'quick' *kines*, requiring

58 For more detail see, Edward Buscombe, 'All Bark and No Bite: The Film Industry's Response to Television', in Corner, *Popular Television*, 197–207.

59 Its post-war successor was *Television is Here Again* (1946).

60 Albert Abramson, 'A Short History of Television Recording', in Fielding, *A Technological History of Motion Pictures and Television*, 251. Abramson provides an excellent technical history of the development of television recording technologies in the US and Britain.

61 See Abramson, 'Short History of Television Recording', 252.

that the telerecording be produced in under three hours to enable the other coast to see it, via coaxial cable, at the same point in the evening schedule. The growing industry insisted on a national audience; it promised the delivery of no less to its sponsors and advertisers.[62]

One of the reasons a far greater proportion of American television from the late 1940s and 1950s has survived when compared to Britain is precisely the institutional and commercial necessity of networking a national schedule over different time zones.

The ability to record a television signal *electronically* rather than photographically was demonstrated in 1951 in the US, when the Electronic Division of Bing Crosby Enterprises developed a black and white video recorder. Recording electronically had huge advantages over recording on film. The optical and photographic developing losses of film recording were eliminated; as videotape recorded electronic signals rather than visible images, there were no optical distortions at all. It could be replayed instantly; and it could also be recorded over and used again.

The BBC did not use videotape until 1958.[63] At first, the recordings were of complete programmes, without edits: the recordings were, like the telerecordings, of entire live performances, film inserts and all. Methods of editing videotape were at first unavailable and then cost too much to implement (cutting a tape made it unusable; an uncut tape could be wiped and used again).[64] Videotape was a cheaper alternative to telerecording programmes, a way of taking television out of the control of the schedule, allowing programmes to be made and stockpiled, before transmission. The 'videotape age' reformulates the aesthetics of drama and the organization of production in various ways, but even so, segments of drama lasting up to thirty minutes continued to be recorded on videotape in continuous time 'as if live' until the introduction of time-coded signals on the tape in the mid-1970s, which allowed faster and more accurate postproduction editing.[65] In this way some of the style and aesthetics of early pre-1955 television had considerable longevity in the modern period of television.

62   Brian Winston, *Misunderstanding Media* (London: Routledge and Kegan Paul, 1986), 88.

63   They initially used an experimental prototype, VERA (Vision Electronic Recording Apparatus) where the tape itself was very quickly passed over a static pickup head. The Ampex Corporation in the US had already set an industry standard (using a spinning head) by 1956, and the BBC subsequently adopted this. See Winston, *Misunderstanding Media*, 90.

64   The post-1955 history of videotape editing offers a fascinating insight into gradual decline of the 'live and continuous' aesthetic which had so far dominated television production. Future research in this area is essential for an understanding of television drama's alternation between 'live' and pre-recorded styles.

65   Barry Salt describes this development, *Film Style and Technology*, 282–3.

2

The End of the Photographed Stage Play: Television Drama, 1936–39

I will require three live rats on Thursday, Nov. 11th for rehearsal at 4.30 and transmission at 9 o'clock . . . I would like them to be as photogenic as possible, so in choosing your rats you might bear this in mind. I believe rats are obtainable in almost any colour. They should be as large as possible and as hungry as possible, as I shall expect them to eat a candle.

George More O'Ferrall, BBC television drama producer, 1937[1]

GEORGE MORE O'FERRALL'S 1937 live production of *Journey's End* vanished into the ether with the rest of pre-war television, so it is difficult to estimate how the rats fared with the candle, either during rehearsal or at the crucial moment of transmission. The endeavour of this chapter is to rescue the pre-war period from the accusation of amateur dramatics and argue that O'Ferrall's request was indicative of the aesthetic appetite for innovation and experiment among drama producers who were faced with organizational, financial, and technological limitations.

The form and aesthetic of early television has its origins as part of a wider cultural and technological change. During television's prehistory, the proposals, patents, and outlines for early television devices frequently refer to other nascent telecommunication technology, amenities, or forms of transport as reference points for the new possibilities of television. Early television itself was also promoted in terms of mobility—from the 'transport' of images *to* the home, to the invitation to journey *from* the living room with the broadcasters to distant events and locations:

---

1 Memo George More O'Ferrall to Peter Bax, Head of Design, 3 Nov. 1937, BBC Written Archives Centre (WAC), Programme File T5/271. Bax replies, 'Three cream-coloured rats will be here at 10.30 tomorrow'.

> Television is concerned *at present* with the *transport* of
> Entertainment and Information, i.e. the recipient of these entities
> has them projected to him, rather than he having to go to their
> source.[2]

The novelty of television's modernity was expressed in terms of this
relationship between movement and stillness, and many of the critical tropes about early television can be linked to the collapsing of
distance between viewer and object, enabled by technology and
broadcasting institution. Raymond Williams captures this dialectic
in his idea of 'mobile privatization':

> [There are] two apparently paradoxical yet deeply connected
> tendencies of modern urban industrial living: on the one hand
> mobility, on the other hand the more apparently self-sufficient
> family home. The earlier period of public technology, best
> exemplified by the railways and city lighting, was being replaced a
> kind of technology for which no satisfactory name has yet been
> found: that which served an at once mobile and home-centred
> way of living: a form of *mobile privatization*. Broadcasting in its
> applied form was a social product of this distinctive tendency.[3]

The potential of the new broadcast technology was compared to
the old. The BBC Television Service was modelled on its parent organization, BBC Sound broadcasting, a convenient model of an already
professional broadcasting service on which to base television's management and administrative structure. However, this modelling provided the Television Service with little further indication of how to
produce *visual* programming. As far as BBC Sound were concerned,
images were way below words in the moral and aesthetic hierarchy, as
Grace Wyndham Goldie noted:

> their speciality was the use of words; they had no knowledge of
> how to present either entertainment or information in vision, nor
> any experience of handling visual material. Moreover, most of
> them distrusted the visual; they associated vision with the movies
> and the music hall and were afraid that the high purposes of the
> Corporation would be trivialised by the influence of those
> concerned with what could be transmitted in visual terms.[4]

The relationship between words and pictures was initially understood in terms of family relations: parent (sound radio) and child
(television), and the dominant model for television's development

---

2 Dallas Bower, 24 Oct. 1938, Public Records Office: GPO/INF 5:56.

3 Raymond Williams, *Television: Technology and Cultural Form* (London: Fontana, 1974), 26.

4 Grace Wyndham Goldie, *Facing the Nation: Television and Politics, 1936–1976*
(London: Bodley Head, 1977), 18–19.

was an *evolutionary* one: television is born of radio. William Haley, the post-war Director General of the BBC, expressed this commonly held view when he argued that television is the 'natural extension of sound'; other descriptions included 'illustrated broadcasting', 'radio-vision', a kind of enhanced radio, sound with picture-plug-ins.[5] The theme for the BBC's pre-Service television programme, *Here's Looking At You* (26 August to 9 September 1936, twice daily) contained the chorus, 'Here's looking at you | It seems hardly true | That radio can let you sit and watch the show.'

In the post-war years the relationship between television and other media was expressed explicitly in terms of the 'family of media':

Television studio production has grown up like the child thrust into the middle of the party and told to perform to its elders and betters. Criticism of the prodigy will reflect the knowledge possessed by each elder and better of the more familiar kinds of entertainment:
'The little blighter takes after Auntie Film, eh?'
'Tch!' sniffs Grandmother Theatre. 'A young monster!'
'Of course, there's promise, but it's not—well, really it ought to grow up', Elder Brother Radio morosely bites his nails.
One misconception follows another—and how are they to be avoided? Discipline is required to think of television in terms of television and not in the idiom of theatre, or film, or radio. How is the onlooker to distinguish between the awkward faults of youth and the manifestation of original character?[6]

The 'original character' of the 'lusty young infant' was something that continued to elude precise description. Cecil Madden, Television Programmes Organizer, in a press release in 1939 noted the difficulties with choosing material for television drama were a result of the bastard nature of the medium itself:

'Material': This presents difficulties, as television is a mixture of stage, film and something else which we will call television technique. Plays have to be very carefully adapted by our producers, for it is not possible to bring anything direct from the theatre without much careful thought and re-rehearsal.[7]

'Television technique' suggests a *processing* of preformed material, in the same way that 'annealing' is a technique of burning colours onto metal, enamel or glass. This non-invasive description misses the

5 Haley is quoted in Asa Briggs, *History of Broadcasting in the UK*, iv. *Sound and Vision* (Oxford: Oxford University Press, 1979), 4.

6 Michael Barry, 'Problems of a Producer', *BBC Quarterly*, 3/3 (Autumn 1951), 167.

7 Cecil Madden, Press release 1939, BBC WAC special collection: Cecil Madden.

point that a pattern of 'television technique' might reasonably be called television style. For television historians the problem with talking about television style, given the absence of surviving audio-visual material, is that the technique of showing becomes less important than what was shown (for which there is a record). But formal, technical and stylistic choices still had to be made by programme makers. In the late 1940s Madden continues to signal the unresolved hybridity of television:

> Some people ask where television drama is going, whether it aims to be a photographed stage play, a competitor to the film, or an illustrated broadcast. The truth probably belongs somewhere between them all.[8]

'Somewhere between them all' is obviously something of a cop-out, but it is also indicative of the uncertainty and lack of confidence in thinking about television's agency as a medium. The sense of television as a *process* rather than as a text, de-activates its potential for aesthetic substance. It is as if television's natural state is aesthetically and stylistically passive, that to become valuable it requires 'activation' by, for example, its audience. In terms of television drama, the prejudice still exists that the true qualities of the medium can only be activated by writers writing for 'television as television' (whatever that means). Directors, set-designers, producers, and other technical staff—television professionals that new writers often have to consult in order to find out what 'television as television' actually means—are frequently downplayed or ignored.[9]

Nonetheless, as Madden's comment indicates, issues about television's aesthetic and stylistic qualities were being discussed. The ideas were not systematic and often emerged in a piecemeal and under-developed form, but they were a recognition of the hybridity and fascination with new techniques of mediation that television technology offered. Three key discourses constructed around television were in circulation during the pre-war period:

1. The live immediacy of television is its defining characteristic: television is a means of instant transportation of material. The co-temporality of viewing and event signifies authenticity and realism.
2. Television is a medium of 'intimacy'; it is the delivery of images to the private domestic sphere (as with radio broadcasting), and the visual 'closeness' described by the television close-up, that are the characteristic features of television. This intimate form of direct visual address to the viewer in the domestic (familial) home is

---

8 Cecil Madden, 'Television: Problems and Possibilities,' *BBC Quarterly*, 2/4 (1948), 225.

9 An exception to this is the collection of essays in George Brandt (ed.), *British Television Drama in the 1980s* (Cambridge: Cambridge University Press, 1993).

sometimes seen to set up a new social/communal relationship (although, of course, television is also later blamed for creating atomized and fragmented communities).[10]

3. Television is a hybrid medium (see above), a combination of theatre, newsprint, radio and film: it can do all the things these other media can do, but with the advantages of 1 and 2.[11]

Hence, a programme might be evaluated in terms of its immediacy, according to the access to reality television could give directly and instantly (like radio, unlike film), and also in terms of the ability to provide visual accounts of this reality (like film, unlike radio). These ideas about television were in circulation even before the Television Service began regular transmission on 2 November 1936. Ten days before, *The Times* anticipates:

> The healthiest curiosity, we may hazard, is that which will demand to see as much as possible of the real world, not of artificially composed entertainment. How delightful, again, to see, as well as hear, the Derby and the Boat race; to watch Hammond bat and Larwood bowl, Perry play tennis and Padgham play golf; to follow the expressions and gestures as well as the words of an orator, and to get the look of some event or ceremony at which it was impossible to be present. Thus will all the doings of the great world take on a new life and interest. There seems to be no doubt now of the power of television to improve rapidly in the exhibition of scenes that it can light to its own needs. Improvement in the harder task of representing things as they happen in the ordinary world and our indifferent climate will make it, perhaps, an ever greater power than the broadcasting of sounds.[12]

The first level of interest here is in the instant relay of public, national events and ceremonies (immediacy); then to contemporary celebrities (topicality); then to the *detail* afforded by vision ('expressions and gestures') that the optical and technical advantage of the television camera offers. There is also the convenience of television and its function as a substitute, in a busy modern world, for being there at the event.

The personal, direct nature of television's visual address to its viewers, in their homes, was also part of its uniqueness, a fact recognized by

10 In fact it is possible to consider the 'presence' of immediacy to be part of early television's intimacy, but in critical literature at the time immediacy was discussed as a separate factor.

11 What is missing in these early ideas about television is a notion of television's *seriality*: although early serials did exist, seriality was not a major characteristic of television before 1955.

12 'Television', *The Times*, 1 Nov. 1936.

John Grierson, Alberto Cavalcanti, and others in their 'Television Manifesto', again published before the Television Service began:

> Television represents showmanship to the same people who go to the theatres, but to the same people in a different mood. The atmosphere of the home and the smallness of the screen emphasise the privacy of television.[13]

A later Editorial in *World Film News* noted that a fundamental quality of television was its 'radio self' with its possibilities of direct, personal, address:

> Television takes over from radio the intimacy and the excitement of direct observation and, in this respect, cuts right away from an identity with film. Television is a process not of looking-at but of looking-in. Where, as in the example of the television film, *Television Comes to London*, comparison is sought with the cinema, television is poor thin-blooded stuff and does not compare. But where, as in the example of the direct television of a lesson in golf, television is its own radio self, no brilliant film by Bobby Jones and M.G.M. combined can match the atmosphere of personal tuition.[14]

By this rationale, the intimacy of personal address was best exemplified by the 'talks' and 'demonstrations' which are abundant throughout the pre-war and immediate post-war television schedules, a type of programming that did not demand the exhibition of visual style. The direct address to camera, largely avoided in cinema, was a novelty in itself, and also one which reinforced an entirely *new* sense of a *personal* address, something even closer than physical presence:

> This little screen provides a degree of intimacy which makes television only a remote relation to the cinema. The teacher of gardening with his blackboard illustrates, for example, a directness of appeal which is altogether extraordinary. He is a new phenomenon. He works in a new plane of communication: closer than the commentator of the films, closer even than the commentator of the lecture room. The focus of the screen and the darkness of television bring him, we are even willing to believe, closer than a neighbour. We can at least answer our neighbour

13 Alberto Cavalcanti, Cedric Belfrage, Thorold Dickinson, John Grierson, and Graham Greene, 'Broadcasting and Television Manifesto', *World Film News and Television Progress*, 1/1 (April 1936), 5.

14 Editorial, 'Television—Already a Medium', *World Film News and Television Progress*, 1/9 (Dec. 1936), 5. A similar aesthetic of intimacy had developed around radio during the early 1920s: see John Drakakis (ed.), *British Radio Drama* (Cambridge: Cambridge University Press, 1980), 1–3.

back, but here the speaker can fix us with glittering eye of the ancient mariner and control us completely. The possibilities in this direction are enormous. Those disembodied and never quite satisfactory voices of the Talks Department must soon become real, and lecturing, against every expectation in the world, will have a new lease of life.[15]

Again, there is the sense of television overcoming distance—getting closer—by means of the smaller, intimate, scale of the television screen. This nearness has the advantage of a benign controlling presence, and the visual embodiment of the broadcast radio voice.

The most sustained and elegant elaboration of pre-war television aesthetics was written in the late 1930s by Grace Wyndham Goldie, who was broadcast drama critic for *The Listener* and occasionally wrote about television in her column before becoming full-time television critic in March 1939. She would have seen most of the drama productions for this period:[16]

the surprising and interesting thing is that television is already showing that it has a whole field of entertainment in which it is master because it has a vividness which we cannot get from sightless broadcasting and a combination of reality and intimacy which we cannot get from the films. Look! There is Ivy St. Helier at the piano doing imitations of Gladys Cooper and Yvonne Arnaud and Elisabeth Bergner. And, amazingly, although we are seeing her in black and white and in two dimensions, just as we should in a film, the effect is quite different from that made by a turn of this kind in a cinema. Partly, I suppose, because the sound is reproduced so much better (I am told, incidentally, that it is even better than in ordinary broadcasting), partly because we are in a room of the usual size and seeing her at a small distance instead of being in a huge assembly and seeing her enormously magnified.[17]

Again, there is the positive contrast against the film and radio antecedents, articulated via 'vividness'—the advantage of vision—and 'intimacy'—the advantage of delivery to the private home with its different scale. For television it is the fundamental ability to address the viewer as contemporaneous with the events it is showing which sets up an authentic relationship akin to 'being there':

15 'The Glittering Eye of Television', *World Film News and Television Progress*, 2/1 (April 1937), 5.

16 See Goldie, *Facing the Nation*, 13.

17 Grace Wyndham Goldie, 'Viewing Television', *The Listener*, 16 June 1937. This was Goldie's first television column, and she remained 'broadcast drama' critic, intermittently writing about television drama, until March 1939 when she swaps with Peter Purbeck, who until then had supplied a regular 'Television' column.

in plays it is the soliloquy, the actor speaking direct to the audience, which comes over best. . . . So far, in fact, the secret of successful television appears to be intimacy. And I do not believe that anything, even a larger receiving screen and more experience of handling productions, can ever alter this.[18]

This is more than the private intimacy of a telephone call: it is an intimacy that addresses the individual viewer who is also part of a wider audience. Goldie describes television's intimate address and its wide coverage: many people can 'join in' without risking the vulgarity of the public spectacle. As *The Times* noted in 1938:

Meanwhile great strides are being made each month in producing for the little screen. The plays which succeed on television are the thriller, the intimate play, the conversation piece, and poetic drama or fantasy, which is not always easy to put across the footlights because the theatre is so big. If on Christmas afternoon Father Christmas, Pierrot, and a policeman are seen clambering over the roofs and popping down the chimneys in Mr. Housman's *Moonshine*, the fantasy may be followed by 40,000 or 50,000 people, but it will be an intimate fireside entertainment, not a spectacle.[19]

The implication for drama production and drama style was that it should be appropriate to the reception context of the 'intimate fireside': the limits to aesthetic and stylistic thinking were therefore dependent on how the BBC Television Service and drama producers, perceived the audience. One of the ways this was expressed was through the drama schedule.

The programming policy of the Television Service was developed by its first Director, Gerald Cock, whose policy of 'variety and balance' was co-ordinated through Cecil Madden, Programme Organizer and chief liaison with the producers.[20] Airtime was limited (initially just 2 hours per day), and Cock wanted the early programmes to be topical and demonstrational in nature—not a good recipe for drama.[21]

In late 1936 and until the BBC rejected the Baird system in February 1937, the weekly alternation between Baird and EMI television systems had a significant impact on the length and type of programmes. During the weeks that used the Baird system no one programme would last longer that 15 minutes. If the BBC had adopted the Baird system, then the description of early television

---

18 Goldie, 'Viewing Television'.

19 *The Times*, 23 Dec. 1938.

20 See 'Television Today—All Over the World', *World Film News and Television Progress*, 1/1 (April 1936), 10.

21 Average airtime increased from around 20 hours per week in 1939 to around 25.5 hours in 1949.

drama as 'photographed stage plays' would be accurate. For drama productions Baird's team used the Intermediate Film (IF) technique, whereby the studio scene was filmed using non-standard 17.5 mm film, the film developed in under a minute and then scanned electronically to convert it into a television signal.[22] Its single camera was fixed in concrete, there was no camera mobility, no tracking, and only twenty minutes' worth of film capacity; to change to a close-up view the turret with four lenses had to be swung over, and this could not be done during recording without stopping the camera, halting transmission. As Cecil Madden recalled:

> You had absolutely no camera mobility at all. You were tied down to a specific set-up and all you could do was swing the turret on the camera. It meant you simply had to stay in one fixed long-shot position and come into the action by swinging the turret head— and swinging in full view of the audience who, on the home screen, saw a blur.[23]

The EMI-Marconi system was both more mobile and more flexible, and it could deploy multiple cameras. Once the Baird system was shut down we can begin to see some standardization in the schedules. The television day was divided into three blocks, morning–afternoon –evening. The 60-minute *Television Demonstration Film* was shown between 11.00 and noon, and live studio transmission would begin at 3.00 p.m. with either a repeat performance of a play or sports coverage (or sometimes a short film, such as a Disney cartoon). This block would last for 60 to 90 minutes. Programmes recommenced at 9.00 p.m. (pre-war) or 8.30 p.m. (post-war) for a further 90 minutes. The schedules varied during outside broadcast events (e.g. until the match/ fight/ play finished), but three to four hours a day in total was the norm.

The evening schedule was organized around a single 'main event' programme, either a play or a variety show, occasionally sports coverage or opera. Weekend evening viewing was devoted to plays, a 'classic' on Sunday night (repeated on Thursday night), a popular play for Saturday, and a comedy or thriller for Tuesday night. (The repeat of a play meant just that: the entire cast and technical staff performed the play again in the studio.) Drama played a central role in the schedules and was consistently popular, although the repeats were not, as consistent viewers effectively lost a night's viewing.

There were three main forms of drama output that developed in the pre-war years: extracts from current theatre productions, Outside Broadcasts (OBs) of theatre productions; and full-length adaptations.

---

22 See Bruce Norman, *Here's Looking At You* (London: British Broadcasting Corporation and Royal Television Society, 1984), 14–15.

23 Quoted in Norman, *Here's Looking At You*, 130.

For the first months of the service (November 1936–June 1937), extracts or 'scenes' from plays were the dominant form of drama presentation. They were short, typically lasting from 10 to 20 minutes, and tailored for the limitations of the Baird system: after March 1937, the EMI-Marconi system allowed the standard length of extracts to increase to around 30 minutes. The material used took two forms, extracts from current West End productions under the rubric 'Theatre Parade',[24] and adapted scenes from well-known—but not currently running—theatre classics, often showcasing the talents of celebrity actors; both forms were far less common after June 1937.[25]

It is this form of drama presentation, perhaps more than any other, that exemplifies the idea of the 'photographed stage play': static, 'boring', and relayed, with due reverence to the performance, to the television audience. However, the dependence on theatrical material was not so much an effect of the limited imagination of the drama producers as a result of pragmatic assumptions about the advantages of using current West End material. First, the idea that fewer rehearsals were needed, as the actors would be familiar with their lines: this could save time and space. In fact, as I discuss below, it turned out that *more* rehearsals were needed with actors who were generally unfamiliar with the demands of performing for multiple television cameras. The second assumption was that, as the plays were already running in the West End, television would gain publicity, as would the West End plays. Televised 'scenes' could act as 'trailers', helping future theatre bookings, and promoting the demonstrational function of television. As I discuss below, these assumptions proved faulty.

The second type of drama production involved OBs of live stage performances transmitted by television cameras from the theatre. This format came under the control of Outside Broadcast personnel rather than drama producers. In his television column for *The Listener*, Peter Purbeck remarked that the televising of *When We Are Married* encouraged him to go to the theatre to see it, and he goes on to contrast this OB drama with drama originated in the studio:

> How then did last Wednesday's performance compare as television with a play produced in the ordinary way in the studio? . . . coming from the theatre it had the immense advantage of an assembled audience as well as a dispersed and invisible one. Obviously it is easier to act before a public whose reactions you can feel and watch than it is in front of a camera which does not appear to care a pin; so the stage performance helps the actor . . .

24 Various titles were suggested before this: 'Play Parade', 'From the London Theatre', 'Stage Parade', 'The Living Theatre'. Memo, 9 Nov. 1936, BBC WAC T5/517.

25 'Theatre Parade' makes two brief reappearances in 1938, and a final one in 1939 as 'Play Parade'.

Where the studio production scores over last Wednesday's performance is in the movement of the actors . . . the television screen, owing to its size, cannot show more than two of three players in detail at one time. In the studio this trouble is overcome by grouping the actors accordingly. On the stage they could not be so neatly grouped; and so the camera had to chase from one speaker to another with rather bewildering effect.[26]

The relay of a performance from the theatre was therefore rather like covering a football match, a form of drama coverage rather than drama production, and one which deliberately set out to capture the 'feel' of a theatrical event with voyeuristic back-stage interviews with the stars, and shots of the audience arriving (a form very similar to present-day television coverage of concerts and opera performances).[27]

But organizationally and formally OBs were distinct from drama production proper:

Television plays shown from the theatre are in the same class as Royal Processions and Test Matches and outside events generally. These are things we could see better if we were actually there ourselves but which it is marvellous to see like this if there is no other way of seeing them. Television studio plays on the other hand, are adventures in a new medium. They are bound to go on getting better and better as they leave film on the one side and theatre on the other and become more purely television.[28]

Developing the 'art' of television drama was seen as a distinct project, separate from the relay and extraction of theatrical forms, and found in the third drama format: the adaptations. During the summer and autumn of 1937, 'Theatre Parade' extracts and one-act dramas and sketches were gradually superseded by half-hour adaptations, no longer described as 'scenes'.[29] The increase in running time indicated

26 Peter Purbeck, 'We Go to the Theatre', *The Listener* 24 Nov. 1938. '8.30–10.40 p.m. *When We Are Married*. For the first time in the history of the theatre a play with its West End cast, and given before an audience, will be televised direct from a theatre stage. By permission of Basil Dean, J. B. Priestley, and the theatre lessees, viewers will see the entire performance direct from St. Martins Theatre, London.' *Radio Times*, 11 Nov. 1938.

27 Peter Reynolds notes a similar voyeuristic impulse, the 'camera's ability to penetrate beyond the policed stage door' in his description of 1990s *Omnibus* documentaries about the theatre, 'Actors and Television', in Jeremy Ridgman (ed.), *Boxed Sets: Television Representations of Theatre* (Luton: Arts Council of England/John Libbey Media/University of Luton, 1998), 164–5.

28 Grace Wyndham Goldie, *The Listener*, 19 Jan. 1939.

29 Occasionally, plays originally presented in the 'Theatre Parade' extract form were re-presented in full versions later. In May 1937 the *Radio Times* announced 'Scenes from Rupert Doone's Little Theatre Production of *The Ascent of F6* by W. H. Auden and Christopher Isherwood. Presented by Royston Morley'; a year later, Morley produces a longer version of the play with the entire plot intact.

an increase in ambition and technical proficiency: George More O'Ferrall's production of *Journey's End* in November 1937 ran at 60 minutes, and in December Eric Crozier presented the first 90-minute adaptation, *Once in A Lifetime*. These were the exceptions until May 1938 onwards when there was at least one play per week running at around an hour, with the occasional production of 90 minutes such as *The Constant Nymph* (3.00–4.30 p.m., 31 May 1938). Shorter 30-minute one-act plays were also part of the schedule, but they clearly do not have the same status of a drama 'event'.

For example, a typical week in August 1938 (Sunday 21st to Saturday 27th) offered the following drama: a 90-minute play as the main event on Sunday evening, *Libel*; a 75-minute version of *The Importance of Being Earnest* shown on Tuesday evening; a repeat of *The Rivals* on Thursday evening (also 75 minutes), and a Friday afternoon repeat of *The End of the Beginning* (30 minutes). The rhythm of the 'first night' presentation and later repeats is not a consistent one yet (sometimes a Sunday night play will be repeated Tuesday afternoon, or the next Saturday evening), but there is an emergent standard of running time at 90 minutes, which indicates increased standardization in drama planning.

There is also some repetition, as producers perfect their technique, or try out something new with the same material: Michael Barry produced *Libel* twice, in August 1938 and March 1939, Eric Crozier produced *Once in A Lifetime* in January and December 1938. Some successful plays, such as these and *Rope*, became part of the television drama repertoire and were repeated in the immediate post-war years. In this period revisions marked on studio plans, and camera set-ups indicate that the purpose in repetition is modification and improvement in technique; in the late 1940s the repertoire served more of a stand-by function.

Executive decisions for the selection of plays were taken during the meetings of the Programme Board, but it was left to the producers to come up with specific suggestions for programme material. As far as early television drama is concerned the source of material was current or recent West End plays. As John Caughie argues:

> It was an additional attraction if the drama came with critical of popular guarantees. The vast majority of the single plays and serials produced by the BBC until the 1960s were adaptations, coming to the viewer with a prior seal of approval from the West End theatre, the classics, or the best-seller lists.[30]

Producers were the driving force behind the selection, planning and realization of programmes. In November 1936 there were just

---

30 John Caughie, 'Before the Golden Age: Early Television Drama', in John Corner, (ed.), *Popular Television in Britain* (London: British Film Institute, 1991), 27.

five producers for the entire television output. Cecil Madden was the Programme Organizer and also produced Variety programmes, such as *Picture Page*. George More O'Ferrall was responsible for drama, Stephen Thomas for music, ballet, and opera, Mary Adams for talks, and Dallas Bower for opera and film. In practice these were only nominal responsibilities, and producers would work on variety, talks, or opera as production contingencies required. By 1939 there were fifteen drama producers, and just nine others to take care of the rest of television output.

Few drama producers had transferred to television from a career in BBC radio (Royston Morley, who had worked in radio drama and features, is a notable exception), and almost all of them had a background in visual arts, mainly theatre or cinema. Stephen Harrison worked for Paramount as an editor; Stephen Thomas had a theatre background; Dallas Bower directed *The Path of Glory* (GB, 1934); George More O'Ferrall had been an assistant film director; Lanham Titchener also had a background in film, Michael Barry had been a stage director at the Garrick and Playhouse theatres; Fred O'Donovan had an extensive theatre background. Denis Johnston, hired by the Service in 1938, was already established as a playwright and theatre director.[31]

For the 'Theatre Parade' format drama producers were sent to the London West End theatres to find plays that were suitable and practicable for television. Their selection of plays was governed by rules of 'suitability', which meant compliance with Reithian norms of taste and decency as well as more practical considerations, such as the length of the play, whether the theatre manager was willing to allow a television performance, the co-operation of actors, the size of the cast, and whether the Service could borrow scenery and props. Adultery, violence, and swearing and sexual references were definitely taboo.[32] For example, one of Madden's 'London Theatre Play Reports' on *Yes, My Darling* at the St James: 'Theme entirely unsuitable: based on the emancipation of the modern girl.'[33] Or this, from Madden to drama producer Reginald Smith, about the play *Quiet Wedding*, a Rattigan play in which two characters sleep together before they are married. Smith was insistent that the scene that suggests this should be retained, as it was essential for an understanding of the play.

---

31 See John Swift, *Adventure in Vision: The First Twenty-Five Years of Television* (London: John Lehman, 1950), 74 and 99. The full list of drama producers working by 1939: Michael Barry, Dallas Bower, Jan Bussell, Eric Crozier, Desmond Davis, Stephen Harrison, Moultrie Kelsall, George More O'Ferrall, Royston Morley, Fred O'Donovan, Harry Pringle, Reginald Smith, Denis Johnston, Lanham Tichener, Stephen Thomas. Many of them were to later work in British cinema during the 1950s: Kelsall as an actor; Barry, O'Ferrall, Bower, Davis as directors.

32 Memo, Cecil Madden to Drama Producers, 3 May 1937, BBC WAC T5/517.

33 Memo, 4 June 1937, BBC WAC, T5/517.

Madden replies, 'I do not agree. The scene is against BBC policy. I think that blood, strong language and violence are unsuitable on Sundays for actors and audience.'[34] When Sunday broadcasts began in March 1938 the type of material selected had to be sensitive to the Christian associations of that day. Political themes were also treated with caution. The *Radio Times* gave some space to the announcement of a forthcoming 'controversial' production:

> Clifford Odets's *Waiting for Lefty*, a propagandist play, is to be televised on February 17th . . . make a point of watching it on television, for it will probably be your only chance of seeing it; official permission has been withheld for performing *Waiting for Lefty* on the English stage.
>
> You may disagree violently with the heavy 'Left' bias of the play; but producer Eric Crozier hopes you will forget politics and consider *Waiting for Lefty* purely as an experiment in drama.[35]

The advantage of television in this case is the privileged view it can offer of officially censored material, although in this case the definition of the 'English stage' was eventually extended by the BBC to include the 'television stage' and Odets' play was not televised.[36]

In early 1937 when the 'Theatre Parade' form was the primary mode of drama presentation, the vetting process meant selecting suitable scenes or extractable material rather than entire plays:

> *Housemaster* (Shaftesbury)
> Light farce comedy. Might be possible to find an extract, but would not be strong material.
> *Mile away Murder* (Duchess)
> Very complicated drama of small clues. Could only be made effective if the opening only is done—as a trailer.[37]

While there was no evidence that the impact of television had any detrimental effect on attendance at the theatres, by 1938 there were reports of a rivalry between television and the theatre.[38] The assumption that selecting scenes from current West End productions had advantages—a rehearsed cast, publicity for the West End, some cultural and topical kudos for the Television Service had become

---

34 Cecil Madden, Memo, 24 Nov. 1938, BBC WAC T5/499.

35 *Radio Times*, 29 Jan. 1939.

36 Press release, BBC WAC, T5/569. No explanation for the withdrawal of the play was given in subsequent editions of the *Radio Times*: instead, on 17 Feb., the drama presentation was billed as a Crozier production of Hubert Griffith's *Youth at the Helm*, a comedy.

37 Memo, Cecil Madden to Drama Producers, 3 May 1937, BBC WAC T5/517.

38 See 'Television and Theatre—A Coming Rivalry', *The Times*, 27 Oct. 1938.

untenable. The exigencies of the small studio, the unfamiliar nature of television production for the actors, meant that actors had to have several rehearsals for the cameras. The extra rehearsals and consequent demand upon actors' time were not reflected in the fees paid to them and to the theatre management. Fifty pounds for a single performance was same amount paid for radio productions of theatre extracts. Madden stressed the urgency of revising this position, to include what he called 'special demands of vision' in the estimation of fees paid to a theatre cast:

> It is absolutely essential that we should review the position
> of fees in connection with stage plays. . . . The fact that Sound
> Broadcasting pay fifty-pounds (which involves little rehearsal and
> a wide public) is in my opinion no reason why it should apply to
> us, as we need special advance rehearsals and all the added
> complications of vision.[39]

William Streeton, the television booking manager, further outlines the problem:

> Sound broadcasting requires no rehearsal other than the brief
> run-through on the day of transmission, when the artists are
> provided with a specially marked script from which they are able
> to read their parts without the necessity of memorising the
> necessary cuts etc.—and of course, without movement gesture
> or costume . . .
> [For television] All cuts in the script require to be memorised
> and there is a good deal of revision in the movements and
> gestures, etc. for each artist, necessitated by television technique.
> While this is common to all television programmes, the
> essential point is that this memorising has to be kept quite distinct
> in the artists' minds from the stage requirements to which they
> have to revert the same evening on returning to the theatre.[40]

The key phrases in this exchange are 'complications of vision' and 'television technique': they indicate that the aesthetic ambitions of drama producers were placing extra demands on rehearsal time. If the aesthetic horizons of those producers were limited to the simple, efficient relay of performance, this would not be an issue: rehearsal time for West End transfers was at least three to four times that of rehearsal time needed for radio.

The bottom line was that West End productions were becoming expensive at a time when the Television Service as a whole was

39 Cecil Madden to D. H. Munro, 4 Oct. 1937, BBC WAC, T5/517.

40 William Streeton, Memo, 25 Oct. 1937, BBC WAC, T5/517.

overrunning its budget allocations, and the Treasury was unwilling to release more finance.[41] A year later, Madden notes that it is too expensive and time-consuming to rely primarily on material from the West End, and that plays originated within the Service 'pay more', in other words they were more economical for the BBC to produce, bypassing the need to negotiate with theatre managers, and allowing the BBC to hire actors individually.[42] Along with the desire by producers to expand drama production full-length, this was a determining factor in the move away from a parasitic reliance on current West End material and towards material which the producers had more overall control.

The limitations of studio size and technical equipment had an impact on the development on the television technique. Before the Television Service started regular transmissions, the BBC chief engineer Douglas Birkenshaw sent frequent letters to the Director of Television, Gerald Cock, warning that more studio space and staff to maintain it would be needed.[43] Cock considered television's function as a relay, with its benefits and attractions supplied by the Outside Broadcast.[44] There was no need for large studios to house spectacular drama productions, as the world itself was the stage. Cock misjudged the popularity of studio drama production with producers and the small television audience.[45] A BBC survey in 1939 discovered that:

> The popularity of studio drama is a remarkable feature of television today and the preference is for full length rather than for short plays. Asked whether an hour and a half was too long for a television play, over 80 percent replied 'No'; but most people like the practice which has lately been introduced of including occasional intervals in such plays.[46]

It is interesting to speculate about the function of these intervals. Clearly they provide a welcome breathing space for the production team, allowing costume and set changes, and they also strengthened the connection with theatre. It is possible that some producers

41 Briggs, *Sound and Vision*, 181.

42 '. . . original Alexandra Palace plays pay more than theatre transfers', Cecil Madden to D. H. Munro, 18 Oct. 1938, BBC WAC, T5/517.

43 In an essay 'Planning a Television Studio', H. W. Baker says of the Alexandra Palace studios: 'Their size, each $70 \times 30 \times 27$ feet high, is completely inadequate for large-scale productions, a fact which was realised even before the war.' *BBC Yearbook 1951*.

44 Before his appointment as Director of Television, Cock had been Director of Outside Broadcasts for BBC radio since 1925. See Asa Briggs, *History of Broadcasting in the UK, ii. The Golden Age of Wireless* (London: Oxford University Press, 1965), 80.

45 The standard figure for this audience is 20,000 by the close of the Service in 1939. Briggs, *The Golden Age of Wireless*, 620.

46 *The Times*, 3 May 1939.

assumed that sustained viewing in the home required the occasional break. That audiences expressed a preference for them suggest that they recognized—and welcomed—television's ability to offer rest-periods—interruptions—as commercial television continues to do today.

The 'Theatre Parade' extraction of scenes from the West End theatre was less popular that complete narrative adaptation. This implied a growing demand on studio time and space, a demand that was exacerbated by the ambition of drama producers indicated by the increase in the running time of drama productions.

The two studios, A and B, had been used to house the rival television systems of EMI-Marconi and Baird. The rejection of the Baird system in early 1937, did not immediately free up its studio B which was used for storage and rehearsals until its refit was complete in autumn 1938. As Bruce Norman notes, 'As productions became increasingly ambitious, space—even utilising both studios, one for production and one for rehearsals—was still not enough.'[47] In June 1938 a Central Control Room was built which separated engineering staff from production staff, and provided the means for multi-channel mixing, from up to seven camera channels and two telecine machines, allowing the rapid selection between the image sources, which might originate from cameras in studio A or B, or telecine, or outside broadcast. The significance of this should not be underestimated. It meant, for example, that a reverse shot between two actors could be achieved using two cameras in separate studios, between a film source on telecine and a studio-generated source. The possibilities for spatial manipulation were vastly augmented.

By the autumn of 1938 all the elements of a new production standard were in place; the consequences of the Selsdon Report recommendation of competing television systems had lasted nearly two years after the service began, retarding the development and routinization of television production. The length and variety of the schedules had been curtailed up to this point. It is important to understand the increase in the length and ambition of drama productions in the light of these technical limitations. Once the single standard was consolidated the amateur, stuttering, nature of drama production began to diminish:

> The adoption of a single standard enormously simplified the
> task of programme production at Alexandra Palace whereas,
> formerly, the entire routine of the station had to be changed each
> week to allow alternate transmissions by the two systems. . . . the

---

47 Norman, *Here's Looking At You*, 165. Plans were drawn up for a larger 'studio C' to be completed in the early 1940s, and dedicated to drama productions. The closedown of the Service meant this was not implemented.

programmes improved; they became more 'professional', the rough edges were trimmed off, more careful study was given to the development of studio lighting, multicamera work, and general presentation; and, imperceptibly at first, there developed a new technique which owed more to TV than theatre or cinema.[48]

Technological standardization was an integral part of the distinctive aesthetic and stylistic development of television production. The link between technical and stylistic development continued in the post-war years. A technical paper written in 1945 by Campbell and Birkenshaw, the Television Service's Chief Engineers, 'Studio Technique in Television', consolidated all that was learned about the technical aspects of television production during the pre-war service.[49] It is the first outline of the 'television technique' from a technical point of view, and contains the definitive guide to studio lighting, make-up, scenery, and design.

Studio A was the largest studio and was used mainly for drama production. Measuring 70 by 30 feet, it was separated into two distinct areas; the top section of the rectangle finishing in a curved cyclorama where the main sets were located, and the opposite section situated just below the Central Control Room. The main performances were staged at the cyclorama end, and opposite section was used to place caption-machines or as seating for an orchestra, if live accompaniment was required. By 1938 the main set was kept at the larger end, but many other sets were spread around the walls of the studio.

Evidence from surviving studio plans indicates that a standard format for drama production was in place by 1939.[50] Campbell and Birkenshaw refer to a production of *The Fame of Grace Darling* (July 1939) as an example of standard studio practice.[51] The *Radio Times* billing for the play states:

> The action of the play takes place from September 1838 to 1842, in the Langstone Lighthouse, Farne Islands, Northumbria; at cousin McFarlane's shop at Alnwick; and in Grandfather Hersley's cottage at Bamburgh.[52]

At least main three sets were therefore required. The main lighthouse set at the cyclorama end was covered by the two main cameras, both mobile, and a third camera, static, behind the main set to cover the

---

48 'Television Today', *BBC Handbook 1938* (London: Norman Jarrold and Sons Ltd, 1938), 41.

49 D. C. Birkenshaw and D. R. Campbell, 'Studio Technique in Television', *Journal of Institute of Electrical Engineers*, 92/19 (Sept. 1945), 165.

50 The studio plans used for examples in this chapter and later ones often were the two-dimensional templates upon which three-dimensional models were built. See Swift, *Adventure in Vision*, pl. 26.

51 9.05–11.05 p.m., Sunday 9 July, written by Yvette Pienne, produced by Fred O'Donovan.

52 *Radio Times*, 7th July 1939.

'exterior' scenes. The remaining sets, the shop and the cottage are confined to the opposite end of the studio, towards which both main cameras will eventually turn.[53] This studio set-up represents the standard means of organizing studio space for television drama until the move to new television studios at Lime Grove in 1950: one studio divided into three sets, with a main set at one end of the studio where the majority of the dramatic action would take place, and two others dispersed either at the other end or along the sides (perhaps with some auxiliary sets and a caption-board area). These areas were covered by four cameras, two of which were mobile and covered action on the main sets. One other camera was used for 'special' shots (possibly close-ups, or brief scenes away from the main sets), and a fourth camera was reserved for captions.

The standard studio set up after autumn 1938 therefore had a *centrifugal* organization with sets pushed up around the walls of the studio, whilst the cameras were free to move and select angles from the centre hub. This model parallels early television drama production in Germany, in particular the 'bright round studio' that Knut Hickethier describes:

> The studio was five metres high with a circular floor plan, and situated at its outer edges were five single stages passing into one another, all illuminated by a fixed lighting system. The middle was left free for the cameras. The stages were 13 centimetres higher than the centre, so that the cameras could only record the action on stage from the front. This construction reflected the stage-bound conception of the tele-play (and therefore the term 'television stage'). A contemporary television cameraman, Herbert Kutschbach, looking back on the period wrote in 1956, that 'one wanted to make the viewer of the television image believe he saw the picture from the point of view of a theatre spectator sitting in the parquet.'[54]

There was never a suggestion that BBC television producers wanted to make the same equivalence in their studio drama productions; the relay of scenes during 'Theatre Parade' was seen as a relayed showcase of actor and performance rather than an attempt to situate the viewer as theatre spectator. Similarly, in outside broadcasts from the theatre, the cameras were placed to get a better view of the performance and the theatre experience as a whole, rather than mimicking the fixed viewpoint of a member of the audience.

Theatrical tropes did survive in early television drama production for good practical reasons. Television plays were sometimes divided

---

53 Birkenshaw and Campbell, 'Studio Technique', 174.

54 Knut Hickethier, 'The Television Play in the Third Reich', *Historical Journal of Film Radio and Television*, 10/2 (1990), 172–3.

into 'Acts', using the interval time (during which a camera might be trained on some props from the play or a caption) to reposition cameras towards another set, and to allow actors to change costume. This was a *convenient* adherence to the norms of theatre rather than aesthetic allegiance to it. During a lengthy live performance, and within a non-commercial television output, intervals provided much-needed breathing space for the production team and performers, as well as a familiar resting point for the audience.

One way of solving the puzzle of co-ordinating live studio performance for cameras was to break up the action with the interval. But this necessarily meant an interruption. Another method would be the use of film inserts, using either stock film or specially filmed material that would be inserted via a telecine machine in between the live studio transmission. In 1950, John Swift outlined three functions of film within the Television Service:

(a) as a stop-gap between 'live' studio programmes, or as a substitute for programmes unexpectedly postponed or cancelled. Examples: Rain may stop play at the Oval or at Lords. The sudden illness of a leading artist may cause postponement of a play or other programme. In such cases the commercial cinema film is generally used.

(b) as a 'convenience', such as continuity shots to link action (if necessary) between studio scenes. Also to establish scenes other than those in the studio. Examples: A character may be telling of his experiences earlier in his life, and realism is added by the film 'flashback' technique. A play may well be set in the village smithy, and as it might be as embarrassing as inconvenient to have a horse in the studio the scene is pre-shot elsewhere by the film unit, as in the first example. Exterior shots are also taken for intercutting with studio programmes.

(c) to bring to the screen something that can only be shown by film, including news—news of events, that is, taking place outside the range of the O.B. units, or where it is inconvenient for O.B. cameras to operate.[55]

The theatrical interval and the film insert could be used to free up live studio time and space, and to provide continuity. Captions were also used to provide continuity within the dramas, as well as for their opening title sequences, sometimes to provide narrative information, sometimes simply to indicate the end of an Act. Another continuity device was the use of *narrators* to set scenes and guide the viewer. This would usually take the form of a voice-over provided either by an off-screen BBC announcer (Leslie Mitchell, Jasmine Bligh, or Elizabeth

55 John Swift, *Adventure in Vision*, 185.

Cowell), 'The action takes place in . . .', or even by their direct address to camera.

Maintaining continuity, and structuring the on-screen performance and narrative space into a meaningful order was also a live process, rather than one completed in 'post-production'. Directing live drama from the Central Control Room meant the live mediation of an already rehearsed performance.[56] This mediation is exemplified in D. H. Munro's description of the drama producer at work in the Central Control Room:

> You were transmitting, say, camera 1; your next shot was on camera 2, then from the script which you'd worked out in advance, you could see that you wanted camera 3 set up at a certain angle. So you OKed 2 on the preview monitor and you called out to the vision mixer, 'I want to preview camera 3'. He'd set that up and you'd say, 'That's fine. 3, stand-by. I'll be coming over to you later.' There was no great bank of monitors, one for each camera as there is today so that you know everything that is happening. You only had the transmission monitor and the preview monitor, and in anything complicated the producer was doing a running commentary all the time through his microphone not only to the cameramen on the floor but to his stage manager on the floor and to the vision and sound mixers in the gallery.[57]

This continuous, live, nature of the segmentation of space and time demanded a different production aesthetic from film. Usually, the period of principle photography in making a film involves a short period of shooting a set-up, lit and miked for that particular shot before the camera is stopped, the actors, lights and mikes repositioned, and the process continued. Live television production is a *continuous* process of selection, choosing the appropriate shots from a planned performance in the studio: cameras, lighting, and sound have to be co-ordinated for the entire performance, in planned order, rather than for each particular shot. As Bower points out:

> by virtue of the fact that it was 'live' there were certain restrictions in what you could ask any given cameraman to do. Could he, for example, get into one position from the one he was in previously in time to give me that close-up? Particularly as we had only three cameras it meant a good deal of hard arithmetic on paper and the need for very careful timing.[58]

56 As I note in Ch. 1, the distinction between director and producer did not exist before the mid-1950s. Television 'producers' controlled technical decisions from the Central Control Room during transmission.

57 Norman, *Here's Looking At You*, 170.

58 Ibid.

In a similar way, Marie Seton describes this new form of image-making production:

> Usually four cameras are employed, differently angled. Since the producer must, during a second or two before the public receives the transmitted picture, select the best of two or possibly three of the different camera shots, he must, before rehearsals commence, work out carefully each shot of the four cameras employed and put them on paper. Since the playing area for a scene is often as small as six square feet, and a single movement or gesture outside that range will invalidate the transmission, he must see that every move made by the actor is kept within prescribed lines during rehearsal. During the actual transmission the producer can communicate from the 'bridge' to the cameramen and sound technicians on the studio floor, but not to the actors. He is, therefore, virtually in the position of a conductor who is invisible to the first violinist. For all these reasons he must be adept in making rapid decisions.[59]

The tension, anxiety, and danger of this live assemblage is captured by this account from *The Times*:

> Television is above all else a triumph of co-operation, and when the actual transmission is on there is great tension in the studio. The producer up in his control room, surrounded by his technicians, has everything noted in the script, the change from camera to camera, the interpolations of film, the captions, the change from studio to open air—rarely attempted but very effective—which are all unknown in a theatre production. He does not need to see the actors, as he has before him two television sets, one the pre-view, the other the actual person on the air. At the word 'Mix!' the mixer turns a knob, the pre-view picture is prepared. Rehearsals take place in a sort of frozen silence while detailed instructions, inaudible to everyone else, are given to the cameramen or the stage manager. A loudspeaker breaks in occasionally with general instructions, and the rehearsal goes on. It is all unlike anything else.[60]

Munro's account mentions changing 'shots', *The Times* of changing 'pictures', rather than 'editing'. For the pre-war BBC Television Service the cinematic instant 'cut' did not exist at all, and transitions from 'picture to picture' were achieved by *mixing* between available camera images, a process that took up to eight seconds. Birkenshaw's team gradually quickened the mixing rate down to (a still significant)

---

59 Marie Seton, 'Television Drama', *Theatre Arts Monthly* (Dec. 1938), 879–80.
60 *The Times*, 23 Dec. 1938.

two seconds.[61] Instant 'cutting' was made available in 1946, but there was still a sense of the virtue and artistry of the slower 'mix', as Maurice Gorham noted in 1949:

> before the war the BBC Television Service had no equipment for making instantaneous cuts from picture to picture, and the result was that producers and technicians acquired a high degree of skill in mixing and fading; scripts were even written with this requirement in mind. Since the Service reopened in 1946 it has been possible to cut as well as mix, but the cut has not yet driven out the mix as it has done in America, where cutting has a far longer history.[62]

The movement from picture to picture, however achieved, is reminiscent of the transition from slide to slide in nineteenth-century magic lantern shows. Indeed the hybridity of the nineteenth-century magic lantern shows have a great affinity with the 'screen practice' of pre-war television. Charles Musser argues that:

> During the second half of the nineteenth century, the lanternists' preoccupation with the faithful duplication of reality and the creation of a seamless spatial world remained limited as disparate representational techniques were routinely juxtaposed in the course of a program. As with many other forms of popular entertainment, the screen often relied on strategies inimical to the principles of 19th century naturalism. Lithographic and photographic slides were often integrated into the same program. In travel lectures like John Stoddard's exhibition on Japan, actuality material and studio photographed artifice were combined in the same sequence. In some cases the synthesis of different mimetic strategies occurred within the same slide. Slide producers often placed actors against sets which combined real objects and objects painted on the backdrop. Sometimes the actor was shot against a white background and the milieu subsequently drawn in.[63]

In a similar way early television's made an eclectic use of different source material in demonstrations, talks, dramas, variety shows, and outside broadcasts, and the different ways that were used to *show* these programmes, from live studio sources mixed with film, to the variety of camera angles, and the later use of puppets, models and superimposition effects. As the following examples show, early

61 Norman, *Here's Looking At You*, 136.

62 Maurice Gorham, *Television: Medium of the Future* (London: Percival Marshall, 1949), 24.

63 Charles Musser, 'Toward a History of Screen Practice', *Quarterly Review of Film Studies* (Winter 1984), 67.

television drama, far from being limited, could draw upon and combine a wide range of sound and image sources.

Case Studies As I discuss in Chapter 1, the textual analysis of early drama is made problematic by the absence of surviving television programmes. As a result the reconstructions below are tentative and provisional.[64] I have not paid detailed attention to the narrative aspects of the drama scripts themselves, mainly because the adaptation of theme and content in early television drama is less central to my investigation than the reconstruction of its visual style.

The planned organization of studio space in terms of sets and performers and the structured segmentation of that space by the cameras in real time was further inflected by the stylistic preferences of individual producers, some of them well-known—such as Fred O'Donovan's 'one camera technique' or 'George More O'Ferrall's close-up technique'. Different producers ascribed different levels of agency to the technology itself: some situated the performance as that which took place beyond the television cameras and was relayed by it; others conceived of television drama as an art form constructed live in the Control Room.

It seems to me that the latter view of television's agency is indicative of aesthetic ambition. At one end of the production scale we might posit the television camera-as-monitor: pointed in the general direction of a performance, but with minimal creative human intervention, and with minimal regard by the performers for the camera. At the other end of the scale, the combination of a range of images and sounds with creative ambition. This is not to say that the latter necessarily creates 'good television' whereas the other does not. (Indeed there is a critical tradition that would praise the minimal non-invasive aesthetic of the first mode, in television documentary for example.) For example, scene dissection—the cutting within a given space, rather than between different spaces—is indicative of the ability to divide dramatic spaces beyond the requirements of the dramatic act or pause, and also of an ambition to intervene and organize narrative space and time. Similarly, variation in shot-scale achieved by camera movement may also indicate (rather than necessarily fulfil) aesthetic ambition. The following categories, in no particular order, I take to be indicative of stylistic ambition in television drama production.

(The following list uses the word 'transition' instead of 'cutting' or 'editing' because the instant cut was not a technical choice in the

---

64 The reconstructions are primarily based on written material in the form of production memos and studio plans, available at the BBC Written Archives Centre.

pre-war period and, in any case, it signals a tradition of editing-centred film criticism that is distracting in this context.)

1. Transitions between sound and image sources and types. This would include mixing between live studio, and filmed inserts, or outside broadcast, or caption, or graphic. This category includes the simultaneous layering of image sources (to superimpose title captions over live studio image, for example). Requires multiple image/sound source and mixing ability.
2. Transitions between narrative spaces, for example, 'inside' and 'outside'. Requires multiple image sources, from cameras or telecine.
3. Scene dissection: transitions within the same narrative space. Requires multiple cameras or telecine.
4. Camera movement (when camera is off-air).
5. Camera movement (when camera is on-air).

Clearly, the evaluation of stylistic ambition in these terms is difficult to complete definitively where audio-visual texts are not available. What follows is an attempt to reconstruct the plays in as much detail as possible, rebuilding important examples in tabular form so that the planned structure of scene, segment, and camera changes can be approximated.

■ **Clive of India (1938)**   *Clive* was a West End hit in 1934 for authors W. P. Lipscomb and R. J. Minney, and ran for almost a year; BBC Television transmitted an adaptation of it in 1938—this was not a current West End play.[65] The play dramatizes the life of Robert Clive, the man credited with conquering India for the British Empire; its main action alternates between scenes showing Clive's skill as a cynical manipulator of the competing feudal interests of Indian regional rulers, and his unsatisfactory domestic life.

The stage play has three acts, each with three scenes. The time scale of the play is over twenty-five years, from 1748 to 1773, in various settings, with only a few central characters, and interior scenes without spectacular action. The play is *a character study*, an interrogation not only of what Clive did but his psychological motivation, namely, How do great men become great men? and What makes them tick? Whatever the spectacular historical background, it is also an 'intimate study'.

George More O'Ferrall decided to produce *Clive* for television and to adapt it in conjunction with its co-author W. P. Lipscomb.[66] It was

---

65 *Clive of India*, 9.00–10 p.m., Saturday 9 Feb.; repeated 3.20–4.20 p.m., Wednesday 23 Feb. It was first produced at Wyndham's Theatre, 25 Jan. 1934. For a production history of the stage version see, R. J. Minney, Foreword to *Clive of India*, in *Famous Plays of 1933–34* (London: Victor Gollancz Ltd., 1934).

66 Lipscomb worked as a screenwriter for Ealing and Gainsborough studios in the 1930s, and again at Ealing in the 1950s.

planned for transmission in February 1938, in a pioneering 60-minute slot.

It is worth contrasting the television adaptation of *Clive* with the career of the film version.[67] In 1934 Darryl Zanuck, studio chief at Twentieth Century-Fox, commissioned the other co-author Minney to write the screenplay for Hollywood production. Minney reports the script conference with Zanuck:

> Without further ado he [Zanuck] began talking about *Clive*.
> 'I have seen the play and I've read your book. Now for the picture. We'll have to put him over big . . . There will have to be titles. Lots of titles. The public must be told all this happened. There *was* a man Clive and he lived in—whenever it was. When they can accept that we can put over the rest of the stuff.
>
> I'll get sixty elephants. We'll have a hell of a charge for the Battle of Plassey . . . now, when we come to crossing that river. In the play you couldn't show it, but in the film—we'll cut from Clive's tent and show the Governor and the four other bozos, sitting by themselves their arms folded saying, 'We've fixed that bastard Clive.' And then the rain. All the hurrying and scurrying . . . and the bugles. The Governor and the—five—other bozos look out. They don't know what the hell's happening. Suddenly one of them says, 'Christ that son of a bitch Clive is crossing the river!' Cut. Save film footage—jump to the actual crossing.[68]

Zanuck's interpretation literally transforms and visualizes the play: look what film can show compared to theatre—elephants, cross-cutting between interior and exteriors, sound effects, the spectacle of a river crossing. Film is about the attractions of spectacle and action, and Zanuck's vision of *Clive* is a showcase of what film can do—such as using editing to move between spaces instantaneously.

A comparable moment takes place for the television version of the play where it was adapted, in some respects, in order to showcase television's visual abilities. Two months before *Clive* was transmitted, George More O'Ferrall met W. P. Lipscomb, to discuss the possibility of televising two of his plays, *Clive* and *Thank You, Mr. Pepys*. O'Ferrall reports the substance of the meeting back to the Programme Organizer, Madden:

> I suggest that Mr. Lipscomb (who, as you know, is a very successful scenario writer) should in collaboration with me make a television scenario similar to a film script, consisting of very short scenes following one another very rapidly, which I imagine will be our technique in the future.[69]

67 *Clive of India*, 20th Century-Fox, 1934, 90 minutes.

68 R. J. Minney, *Hollywood by Starlight* (London: Chapman Hall Ltd., 1935), 47.

69 Memo George More O'Ferrall to Cecil Madden, 6 Jan. 1938, BBC WAC T5/98.

This implies a significant shift in thinking, away from the theatrical and towards a more segmented style, 'very short scenes following one another very rapidly', indicating transitions between scenes rather than within them. Of course there is still the retention of the theatrical sense of 'scene' here, but the rigid subordination to the published theatrical script is rejected. It is also interesting that the slippage or uncertainty in the distinction between theatre and film is reflected in O'Ferrall's choice of format for the scripts: 'I like the names placed out in the margin as you usually do, and not in the centre of the page as in this [Lipscomb's] script. Please leave a fairly wide margin on the right-hand side of the page, and a space of about 20 lines between each scene.'[70] The extra space is for camera directions and yet O'Ferrall insists on the theatrical convention of using the left-hand margin for the character names.

In his memo to Madden, O'Ferrall continues to outline a new way of thinking about television drama production:

> I also propose that we make such a script of *Thank You, Mr. Pepys* compressing the whole action of the play into about 40 minutes, instead of producing a Theatre Parade which merely consists of photographing a scene of a play. . . . It would entail a good deal of script writing with Lipscomb . . .[71]

O'Ferrall's desire to transcend the passive, limited achievement of 'merely . . . photographing a scene of a stage play' existed in 1938, at the beginning of—even before—the phase of 'Reithian reverence' which Carl Gardner and John Wyver identify as *characterized by the photographed stage play* up to the late 1950s.[72] It demonstrates that television drama producers were actively engaged with the formal and stylistic possibilities of the new medium, rather than slavishly relaying West End theatre performances.

Lipscomb's response to O'Ferrall's enthusiasm is interesting in this respect: he aligns television with film and radio and the stage, but is clear that for him the medium is a distinct form:

> A television story will have to be devised and written in an entirely different way—halfway between sound broadcasting and films. In preparing *Clive of India* for television, we are televising a play which will be neither a stage play nor a screen play. It should be more mobile than a stage play, using the film technique, but not the whole technique. My ideal arrangement for future television plays would be to have perhaps twenty rooms under

70 Memo O'Ferrall to Miss Steeds (secretary), 7 Feb. 1938, BBC WAC T5/98.

71 Memo O'Ferrall to Madden, 6 Jan. 1938, BBC WAC T5/98.

72 Carl Gardner and John Wyver, 'The Single Play from Reithian Reverence to Cost-Accounting and Censorship' and 'The Single Play: An Afterword.', *Screen*, 24/4–5 (1983), 114–29.

one's control, with the scenario devised so that a player can get from one room to another—but that is simply a question of technique.[73]

Again, there is the suggestion of the liminal 'somewhere between them all', and the uncertainty with which producers and writers considered visualizing production practice. It is worth returning to the 'magic lantern' analogy and the *range* of techniques, not yet strictly formalized, which drama producers were willing to draw upon.

One way of exploring television's nature as a medium was to showcase its visual abilities: like the film, the televised *Clive* had its own 'spectacular' moment, recollected by Bill Ward:[74]

Lipscomb . . . had written a highly complicated 'montage' sequence. What this montage called for was a lot of fast and accurate cutting between four cameras in the studio and two film-outputs on telecine, one of them giving us various stock scenes of India—the Taj Mahal, Kashmir, all those places—while the other was a continuous loop of film showing just flames blazing and leaping. Down in the studio, we had one of four cameras on a caption that had the word 'war' written on it in very large letters, the camera starting a long way back from it so that the word 'war' looked very tiny, then gradually tracking forward till 'WAR' was screaming at you. That same camera then had to be switched to captions showing illustrations of various wars—Crecy, The Black Hole, all that lot—while another of the cameras stayed on a kettle-drum that just kept going brrm . . . brrm . . . terrap. And throughout that, the remaining two cameras took shots of the actors who played characters in the play . . . Clive, the Indians, so on, all standing against a plain grey background.

And assuming all that came together at the right moment, what the montage would show would be a full screen full of flames, then the word 'war' superimposed, gradually getting bigger as we tracked in; then, as that faded out, the face of Clive would come through, then Clive would fade out, in would come a shot of India, then—well, you can imagine the idea.

It was a long sequence, very long, went on for several minutes, which meant that everybody concerned—vision-mixer, sound-mixer, telecine operators, cameramen, Floor Manager—they were all depending on getting an enormous number of intricate split-second cues from the producer [. . .] It worked like a

---

73 Quoted in Memo from George More O'Ferrall, 28 Jan. 1938, BBC WAC T5/98.

74 This story, in various forms, is quoted in many other books and reminiscences. See e.g. Norman, *Here's Looking At You*, 169–70; Swift, *Adventure in Vision*, 99–100, and the report of an Alexandra Palace reunion, 'TV Pioneers Recall Days of Fun', *The Independent*, 24 April 1992.

dream. I mean it, it really did. Up came the flames, then 'war' came through, faded out, Clive's face came in, went out, India scenes, kettledrum, brrm . . . brrm . . . terrap. Everything! On and on it went. Beautiful! . . . And finally we came to the end of it, faded out, got onto the next scene—and George [More O'Ferrall] said, 'Oh that was wonderful. Can we do it again?'[75]

Of course, they *did* do it again, for the repeat a few days later. The full technical resources of the Television Service were in use for the montage sequence.[76] It is a description of a complex layering of performance, graphics, and sound that marks off early television as something distinct in itself, and not visually dependent on theatre or film. The example also illustrates the extent of the aesthetic appetite of those producers and writers.

By 7th February, a month after O'Ferrall's initial meeting with Lipscomb, the play was scheduled, budgeted and provisionally cast. It was given two 60-minute slots, Saturday night 9.00 to 10.00 p.m. (19th February 1938) and the following Wednesday afternoon 3.20–4.20 p.m. Three members of the original 1934 stage cast were hired for the leading parts. For the 17 character parts in the published play only 12 actors were hired, five of the actors playing two characters (minor parts).[77] Out of a budget of £180, most was spent on hiring actors, who would be paid for both performances. Costumes had to be designed, as the players could not use the costumes they would be wearing at the theatre (as was usual if plays were running at the time).[78]

The play was broadcast from Studio A (Figure 1). O'Ferrall further departed from the theatrical presentation by dispensing with 'Act 1, Sc.1' format captions. Instead, his caption list asks for 8 captions.[79] They signal time and place rather than offering theatrical dividers: 'Five Years later in London' replaces the interval between the first and second acts, whilst 'Do what you must' (in a woman's handwriting of the period) is an internarrative signal (Margaret to Clive). Similarly, with the caption 'My Lord Clive of Plassey Returns To His New Home At Walcot', O'Ferrall specifies that it should 'look like a heading in a newspaper of the period' rather than 'an ordinary caption'. Each

75 Quoted in Denis Norden (ed.), *Coming to You Live! Behind-the-Screen Memories of Forties and Fifties Television* (London: Methuen, 1985), 58–9.

76 'It will be necessary for me to have all four cameras in Studio 1 for this play. P. S. I want to use both Telecine projectors, with a film loop on the second projector.' Memo from O'Ferrall to Television Programme Manager, D. H. Munro, 12 Feb. 1938, BBC WAC T5/98.

77 This is modified on 18 Feb., when three extras are hired. Camera rehearsals had shown (presumably) it impractical for the actors to change costumes in time.

78 Memo O'Ferrall to Miss Allan (costumes), 9 Feb. 1938, BBC WAC T5/98.

79 Memo O'Ferrall to Peter Bax, 15 Feb. 1938, BBC WAC T5/98.

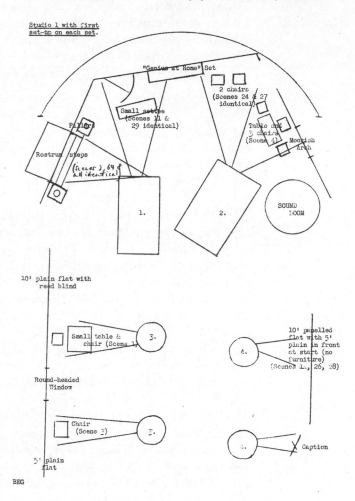

Fig. 1: Studio plan, *Clive of India* (1938). *Source*: BBC Written Archives Centre, T5/98

Studio A, Alexandra Palace. Without formal stencils, most studio plans were sketched by the producers longhand. This sketch indicates that the main stage contains three sets: the rostrum steps, the Moorish arch, and the 'Genius at Home' set. The latter was constructed for that play but, as a 'drawing-room' interior, it could be reused when suitable interior scenes were required. This repertoire of scenery was obviously cost-effective. These sets are covered by two cameras (1 and 2, on dollies), each with two angles drawn in. The lines representing the view of the cameras do not cross, suggesting that each scene was covered by one camera only. The typewritten notes near the sets ('used for scenes . . .') suggests that set, scene and camera were congruent: camera one would shoot the small settee in scene 11. Reverse main stage contains two cameras, 3 and 4, each with two positions, with camera 4—as was usual—used for caption requirements.

caption operates to mark out segments of the dramatic narrative. O'Ferrall then introduces a further innovation and departure from the play. He requests

a special outline map of India, with marks representing the relative positions of Port St. David, Trichinopoli and Arcot. I also want labels of these towns which can be stuck on the map or removed at will. Calcutta and Bombay ought to be marked permanently on the map. The map should be drawn on a caption card.[80]

---

80 Memo O'Ferrall, 15 Feb. 1938.

Unlike the stage play, O'Ferrall expects a visual representation of the geography of Clive's activity, and is therefore able to show Clive's movement across, and therefore conquest of, India, from Bombay to Calcutta. However simplistic this might seem, it was an attempt to distance the production from a pure relay of continuous performance, adopting instead a variety of visual graphic devices to maintain narrative continuity and novelty.

The play was transmitted at 9.00 p.m. on Saturday night, after the scheduled variety show finished at 8.30 (there was a half-hour interval, without vision, before the play began). *Clive* was introduced with a title caption, music, and a BBC spoken announcement. After the opening titles, the actors are introduced, in character, using dialogue from within the play, alternating between cameras, before the title caption is faded up once more and the announcer sets the scene verbally.[81]

Opening sequence of Clive of India *(BBC WAC T5/98)*

VISION: Caption   CLIVE OF INDIA
CAM 1

SOUND: Backed by record HMV.D.1945 (Symphony No.1 in
             A flat major   Elgar   No.1)

ANNOUNCER on cue:

          TONIGHT WE PRESENT THE PLAY 'CLIVE OF
          INDIA' BY W. J. LIPSCOMB AND R. J. MINNEY,
          ADAPTED FOR TELEVISION BY W. J. LIPSCOMB.
          THE PLAYERS ARE:—

CAM 3   COLIN KEITH JOHNSTON AS ROBERT CLIVE
(C.U.)   ('You think I am mad. Oh, yes, you do   they all do.
           Well, I am, thank God.')

On cue: DEERING WELLS AS EDMUND MASKELYNE
CAM 4   ('Bob, be careful. He is the most cunning and
           treacherous scoundrel in all India.')

On cue: W. E. HOLLOWAY AS MIR JAFFAR
CAM 3   ('My countrymen are unwise to call the English
(C.U.)   fools.')

On cue: GILLIAN LIND AS MARGARET MASKELYNE
CAM 4   ('Bob, they say you are in great danger—they hint
(C.U.)   terrible to me. Not withstanding all they say Bob, do
           what you must.')

81 A convention which frustrated Grace Wyndham Goldie: 'Couldn't television now abandon the childish business of letting us see the actors grimace in turn before the play begins?', *The Listener*, 15 Dec. 1938.

VISION: Caption   CLIVE OF INDIA
CAM 1

SOUND: ANNOUNCER, on cue:

THE ACTION BEGINS IN SOUTHERN INDIA
ABOUT 1748, WHEN THE WORKING
CONDITIONS OF CLERKS IN THE EAST INDIA
COMPANY WERE INCREDIBLY HARD. THE PAY
WAS ONLY FIVE POUNDS A YEAR AND
THERE WERE FEW OPPORTUNITIES OF
ADVANCEMENT. SUCH A MAN AS CLIVE
FOUND IT DIFFICULT TO STOMACH THE
OVERBEARING MANNER OF THE RICH
MERCHANTS AND THIS SO PREYED UPON HIS
MIND THAT WE FIND HIM FIRST AS A YOUNG
MAN OF NINETEEN IN A DESPERATE
SITUATION.

The studio plans indicate that was a highly segmented production. A 'faithful' rendering of the stage play would require dividing the action at the end of each theatrical scene, giving nine segments (three acts, each with three scenes). The studio plans indicate twenty-nine scenes, and each scene with a dedicated camera position, which points to the equivalence of scene with 'shot', but relocates the sense of a 'scene' away from the divisions in the published theatrical script. 'Scene' here retains the unity of continuous time, space and action, and its boundaries are clearly punctuated by camera transitions from one to another. The plans also indicate that the two cameras which cover the main sets at the cyclorama end of studio A—although they pivot to cover adjacent sets—do not cross their lines of coverage, which further indicates that O'Ferrall did not cut between them within scenes, meaning that scene dissection was not an aspect of this production.

Three main cameras are used to cover the action, with the fourth used for captions. In a 60-minute play there are at least twenty-nine camera changes (ignoring for a moment the 'montage' sequence and the opening credit sequence), which works out at an average shot length of just over two minutes. What is interesting is the way in which this television adaptation of the play attempts to recreate theatrical spaces whilst also trying to transcend them. The transition between cameras may be seen as a modification of the 'exit' and 'entrance' of actors on stage, but the motivation for camera changes is various: sometimes to change location, or show a caption, sometimes to reveal the entrance of new characters. But always the change is dependent on the sense of 'scene' which introduces a new locale, time or action, as in the theatre.

■ *The Constant*
Nymph and *St*
Simeon Stylites
(1938)

The Constant Nymph is a production that used space in both Studio A and Studio B.[82] The play begins in a similar way to *Clive*: a film insert of Big Ben (with chimes on record), a sound announcement, 'This is the BBC Television Service at Alexandra Palace', and then Big Ben fades out to be replaced by a caption, 'The Constant Nymph' (sound is Verdi's *Aida*—ballet suite). Then the announcer (on sound only): 'We now present an adaptation of *The Constant Nymph* by Margaret Kennedy. The players include . . .' As in *Clive*, the five main actors are presented to camera, in close-up, saying lines from the play; we move back to the title caption, then dissolve to 30 seconds of film of a Tyrolean landscape (these film inserts are taken from the 1933 cinema version), before a mix back to a plain set in Studio B.[83] The main scenes in each studio were covered by two cameras, whilst captions indicated setting or the passing of time: 'England. Strand on the Green' (backed by still of the Thames) and 'Some Weeks Later'. The film inserts are used to show spaces impossible to show in the studio and were mixed with live action from the studio. At one point a film source is used to show the point-of-view of a character in the studio: this is achieved by running a 2-minute film sequence of concert orchestra on telecine, and cutting back to the live image of the actor in the studio 'watching' the concert. (Figure 2)[84]

In this production the performance is segmented by the alternation between cameras, and by the use of continuity devices (either caption or telecine or both) which separate all but one of the scenes. The 'Theatre Parade' relay of extracts is here expanded to become a succession of 'scenes' organized by a narrative logic, and joined together by film and/or caption continuity devices. Taking the running time at 78 minutes (according to continuity notes rather than the schedule) the average length of each scene (excluding the opening credits and captions) would be around 11 minutes. However, it seems sensible to assume that O'Ferrall would employ a method of scene dissection, especially given his remarks made over a year before:

> Although the television producer's studio work is closely allied to that of the film director, it is essential that he should have a real knowledge of the theatre. To his sense of tempo and rhythm in acting he must add correct tempo and rhythm in the tracking and panning of his camera and a faculty for deciding in a split second

82 *The Constant Nymph*, 3.00–4.30 p.m., Tuesday 31 May, 1938; repeated 9.00–10.30 p.m., Saturday 4 June. Produced by George More O'Ferrall. The scheduling had certain advantages: as a fairly big production, Tuesday's afternoon performance was a useful rehearsal session before the more high-profile performance on Saturday evening.

83 *The Constant Nymph* (Basil Dean, GB 1933, adapted by Margaret Kennedy (from her novel) and Basil Dean). The *Radio Times* billing for the play notes that 'extracts from the film' will be used, and that main role of Tessa will be played by Victoria Hopper who played the part in the film.

84 *The Constant Nymph*, BBC WAC T5/108.

-2-

V	On cue dissolve to Caption (Austrian telegram) backed by record, faded out at opening of Scene 1A	CAM.3
S & V.	On cue dissolve to C.U. on Main Set Studio A for Scene 1A on Cam.4.	CAM.4
	(Scene ends on. "Florence Churchill" second time spoken)	
V S	On cue dissolve to Caption SOME WEEKS LATER backed by record faded out at opening of Scene 2.	CAM.3
S & V.	On cue dissolve to Side Set Studio B for Scene 2 on Cam.2	CAM.2
	(Scene ends on: "They always do when you've got a use for them.")	
S & V.	On cue dissolve to plain Set Studio B. for Scene 3 on Cams. 1 and 2 as directed.	CAM.1
	(Scene ends on: "We don't want you. Go away! Go away!)	
V S	(On cue dissolve to Caption ENGLAND (Still of Thames superimposed. Backed by record faded at opening of Scene 4	CAM.4 TELECINE
V	On cue dissolve to Caption STRAND-ON-THE-GREEN Still of Thames superimposed.	CAM.2 TELECINE
S & V .	On cue dissolve to Main Set Studio A for Scene 4 on Cams. 3 and 4 as directed	CAM.3
	(Scene ends on: "No Tessa. You'll go straight to bed.")	
V. S	On cue dissolve to Caption FOUR MONTHS LATER backed by record faded at opening of Scene 5	CAM.2
S & V.	On cue dissolve to Main Set Studio A for Scene 5 on Cams. 3 and 4 as directed	CAM.4
	(Scene ends on: "Roberto! Dear Roberto!")	
S & V.	On cue dissolve to film sequence (concert etc.) 200 ft. = 2 mins. 13 seconds (N.B. After 20 seconds of film C.U. of Lewis Main Set Studio A for 12 seconds.)	TELECINE CAM.4
S & V	On cue dissolve to Side Set Studio A for Scene 6 on Cam.3	CAM.3
	(Scene ends on: "The train! The train! Goodbye! Goodbye!")	
S & V	On cue dissolve to film sequence (journey) 20 seconds	TELECINE

Fig. 2: Page two of George More O'Ferrall's continuity script for *The Constant Nymph* (1938). *Source*: BBC Written Archives Centre, T5/108

A basic continuity script noting sound and vision cues between scenes. Telecine film inserts are used in three ways here. First, to provide a still background (the Thames) over which two captions are superimposed. Second, to expand the space of the studio interiors. O'Ferrall uses a clip from the film version of the play (the concert) and intercuts it with live studio action (a close up of Lewis: the concert insert would then represent a point-of-view shot, presumably.) Third, a film insert is used to represent space outside the studio (film of a train journey—bottom of page). Note that O'Ferrall calls transitions between cameras 'dissolves' the film term for what was in fact a television 'mix'.

the exact moment to mix to another camera in order to give greater dramatic value . . . If television is a new drama medium, then its strength is in the close-up and semi-close-up. A play may have its characters first introduced in close up . . . or the main action can be shown in long shot, tracking up into close-up in any important speech.[85]

This suggests that camera movement, and a 'rhythm' of mixing was already a standard technique for the shorter 'Theatre Parade' extracts. It does not necessarily mean that shot and scene were never equivalent, but it does point to a greater mobility and flexibility in terms of a mixing rate and even a sense of spontaneous mixing ('deciding in a split second to mix').

Camera transitions between and within narrative space are not the only indication of stylistic ambition. *St Simeon Stylites* was a one-act play transmitted in 1938 and produced by Denis Johnston, and

---

85 George More O'Ferrall, 'The Televising of Drama', *Radio Times*, 19 March 1937.

illustrates the way in which spatial mobility could be achieved through superimposition as an alternative to transitions between cameras.[86] In the published play, all of the action takes place atop a column in the desert, where a grumpy ascetic is visited (via a ladder) by a pilgrim, a king, a woman, and 'the Devil and his Friend'. The stage play requires no action, special effects, or substantial movement, although it is expressionistic: the author's Foreword warns that 'As any attempt to render this scene naturalistically is foredoomed to failure, the setting should be as decorative as possible.'[87]

In the television version, the set—a rostrum representing the top of the column—is placed against the cyclorama, and the dialogue covered by two cameras on dollies. To get the effect of height, a third camera is placed on a low tripod, shooting past plaster models of tree tops.[88] Shorter scenes set in a different locale were usually covered at the side of the studio with a flat backgrounds. Here, although all the action takes place on top of the column, the fourth camera is used both for captions and a close-up of the 'Devil and his Friend'. The intention was to superimpose the arrival of these characters over the main action that would take place on the column set.

As in *Clive of India* and *The Constant Nymph*, camera movement was confined to off-air repositioning whilst the live image source was chosen from another camera. For example, camera 1 offers first a distant shot of the column top: this covers virtually all of the dramatic space in long shot. This camera's second and third positions move it closer and angle it, narrowing the focus and bringing the actors into a close-up. Camera 2 also moves in closer; camera 4 remains fixed for the 'special' low angle shot over the tree-tops, whilst camera 3 is used for captions and a later effect where the 'Devil and his Friend' will be superimposed over a shot of the ascetic on his column. The superimposition was probably thought of as a visually innovative effect, as indeed it was. However, this layering of images, as with the 'montage' sequence in *Clive of India*, was probably not the fast rush of thick graphic intensity that contemporary television viewers are used to: it no doubt lasted several minutes.

■ *Juno and the Paycock* (1938) Fred O'Donovan produced *Juno and the Paycock* in October 1938.[89] It began in the usual manner for this time: introductory music, a white on black title caption faded up, the credit sequence for the

---

86 *St. Simeon Stylites*, 9.00–9.30 p.m. Friday 23 Sept. 1938; repeated 3.45–4.15 Saturday 1 Oct. It was redone in Aug. 1946, with Harold Clayton as producer.

87 F. Sladen Smith, 'St. Simeon Stylites', in *Four One-Act Plays* (Oxford: Basil Blackwell, 1923), 27.

88 *St. Simeon Stylites*, BBC WAC T5/447.

89 *Juno and the Paycock*, 3.00–4.30 p.m. Friday 21 Oct. 1938; repeated 9.10–10.40 Tuesday 25 Oct. Adapted and produced by Fred O'Donovan from Sean O'Casey's 1924 stage play.

introduction of actors, and a final introductory caption sets the scene, 'The Year 1922—Civil War in Ireland'. This was superimposed over stock film footage of street fighting supplied by the telecine machine. The short amount of footage would be faded out and a studio scene faded up.

O'Donovan also wrote and designed a scene referred to but not shown in the stage play: the execution of an Irish Republican, Robbie Tancred, and this scene forms a prologue to the rest of the television production. O'Donovan used one camera for this prologue scene, which lasted some 90 seconds. The 'Prologue Set' was situated at the rear of the studio, opposite the main set, and consisted of cardboard cut-outs of a stone wall with a gate, surrounded by a few trees. Beyond the gate was a 'woodland cloth' backdrop.

According to the existing programme files, this is how the scene should have looked:[90]

> Behind one of the trees we see a sentry; the sound of a car, and the sentry draws his gun—a .45 service revolver. An officer enters through the gate and asks the sentry, 'Is it all clear?' 'All clear.' The camera remains static, some eight feet from the actors. We see two gunmen enter with Robbie Tancred, who is pushed against a tree and shot dead.[91] The officer takes a card from the sentry and hangs it on the tree above Tancred's body, and the gunmen exit. The sound of a car driving away. We track in closer and see Tancred's body up close, crumpled near the tree with the card, 'Traitor. Executed by Order.' The music returns and we mix to another caption (and camera) as the first camera is moved around to its new position facing the main set: 'Act I: A Dublin Tenement House'. The play finishes 90 minutes later, with three intervals.

The above reconstruction demonstrates the slippage between the cinematic, the theatrical, and the live radio broadcast. It supports the hypothesis that early television drama was a hybrid, a unique but structured mixture similar to other forms of presentation and representation familiar in radio, theatre and the cinema.

For example, consider the opening sequence introducing the actors in character, speaking lines from the play. Its function is twofold: to introduce the performer as a familiar name (usually in close-up), and to identify his or her character using an illustrative piece of dialogue. It is not a theatrical form, but here introduces theatrical performers. From this point each 'segment' moves the narrative from the outside

90 Based on material in *Juno and the Paycock* Programme File, BBC WAC T5/273.

91 Originally O'Donovan wanted this character to die in a spectacular volley of fire from four revolvers, but the damage to the microphones from blank ammunition meant that the sound had to be dubbed. BBC WAC T5/273.

inwards. The title sets the time and the place, and some film footage of street fighting has a cinematic expository style, establishing the spectacle of public violence; the subsequent move 'inside' the studio for the prologue offers a particular example of the consequences of public disorder. Whilst the studio set suggests pure stage—a painted backdrop, sparse scenery—O'Donovan's notes specify that the sentry is '*discovered* behind a tree cautiously looking about him' [my italics], suggesting that it is the camera which interrogates this space, a camera which actively *reveals* it, rather than passively showing it. Seconds later the camera is static and we see a tableau scene with sound effects as the sentry and officer speak; O'Donovan's reluctance to move in or cut for reaction gives the scene an impassive quality, until the camera tracks in close to the body and the card. The legend on the card has a narrative function, the purported reason for Tancred's execution. With the return of the captions: 'Act I, A Dublin Tenement House . . . the home of the Boyle family.' the scene becomes familiar, the domestic space of a living room. The play continues live in three acts with three 30-second intervals.[92] This is partly radio, (live broadcast to the domestic receiver), partly theatre (the intervals allowing costume changes); but also cinema (tracking in to close-up to reveal narrative information). During the rest of the play, despite the apparent theatrical stasis of the living room set, O'Donovan 'cuts' to the 'outside' (using sets built behind the main set) and into a bedroom, revealing further spaces (Figure 3).

Commentators during the late 1940s and early 1950s made much of Fred O'Donovan's 'one-camera technique'. This refers to his practice of using one camera *per scene*. John Swift discusses this in his 1950 survey of the medium:

> So far I have dealt with production by means of multiple cameras. There is one other system, known as the one-camera technique. It is the speciality of one producer in particular, Fred O'Donovan, who is steeped in stage traditions and to my knowledge has adhered to this method throughout his time as a television producer. . . . Particular successes of O'Donovan's, each with the use of the one-camera technique—that is, one camera to each scene—were Priestley's *The Good Companions* and Patrick Hamilton's *The Duke in Darkness*.[93]

Swift notes the equation of theatrical tradition with a 'one scene, one camera' style, but it is likely that O'Donovan's technique might have been seen as relatively standard during the pre-war years; only when instant 'cutting' became available in 1946 does the technique become

92 Intervals after the first and second act, with one near the end of act three.

93 Swift, *Adventure in Vision*, 167–68.

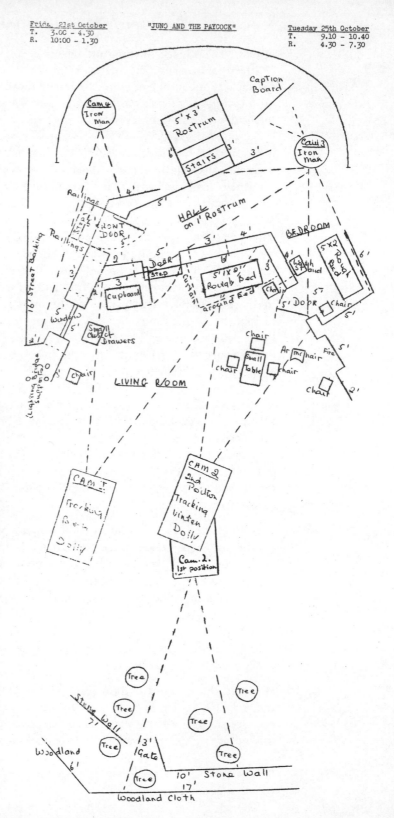

Fig. 3: Studio plan showing camera positions for *Juno and the Paycock* (1938). *Source*: BBC Written Archives, T5/273

Studio A. Two mobile cameras are used to cover the main stage set of the living room; camera 2 is also used for the prologue scene, reverse main stage. Behind the main set camera 4 covers a set of an exterior. Camera 3 has three functions: to cover a bedroom set, a hallway, and to provide captions. Camera 4 covers a set of a street, complete with railings and the outside of the house (again, like Tancred's execution this is not represented visually in the stage version) Building sets behind the main set (a hallway, some stairs and a bedroom), is a more complex method of organizing space *around* the camera angles, rather than moving the cameras within the sets. O'Donovan's 'one-camera-technique' encouraged this kind of complex set design, because using a variety of spaces was an alternative to camera movement.

visible as either an anachronism or as a consciously chosen alternative style.

But even with the most 'theatrical' of producers, it is clear that this is no static relay of performance, one-scene/one-camera or not. Where shot length is equivalent to scene length this should not deter us from noting the importance of the planned segmentation of the performance, by caption, telecine and intervals. And despite O'Donovan's much reported stylistic adherence to theatre, this production was criticized by Grace Wyndham Goldie for its debt to cinematic style:

> Television plays are doing marvellously. But there is increasing danger in this business of imitating the methods of film. The other night a producer nearly ruined a finely acted performance of *Juno and the Paycock* through trying to give it the continuity which is good in television by unnecessary bits of sight. Again and again he spoiled the effect the playwright intended by making us see unnecessary things, a man knocking instead of merely letting us hear the knock, a procession passing instead of merely letting us hear the singing.[94]

■ **The Ascent of F6 (1937 and 1938)** *The Ascent of F6*, written by W. H. Auden and Christopher Isherwood in the spring of 1936 concerns the attempt to conquer a mountain, F6, by Michael Ransom, a heroic figure (Isherwood would later say that the play was all about T. E. Lawrence) who is convinced by his brother James, a Colonial Office official, to climb the mountain because a legend claims that the first white man to conquer it will rule over the fictional Ostnian Sudolands for a thousand years. Ransom reluctantly agrees, and a newspaper sponsors the expedition. The play employs some esoteric symbolism (largely drawn from Jung) whereby Ransom's ascent becomes a quest for his mother's love. It is also politically critical: Edward Mendelson suggests that Auden's unhappy experience at the government-sponsored GPO film unit a few months before writing the play had taught him that state control vitiates artistic integrity, or any integrity.[95] The psychological nightmare of Ransom's ascent is therefore contrasted simultaneously on-stage with the presence of a suburban public, Mr and Mrs A, who listen to a BBC radio announcer on their wireless reporting the glory of Ransom's ascent.

Three of Ransom's climbing companions are killed and one other left behind; eventually Ransom collapses, and the remainder of the play is acted out as an expressionistic fantasy, with his 'Demon'

94 Grace Wyndham Goldie, *The Listener* 10 Nov. 1938.

95 Edward Mendelson, *Early Auden* (London: Faber, 1981), 285.

personified on the summit and its victims (Ransom's climbing companions Shawcross, Lamp, Gunn and the Doctor) returning to pass judgement. Ransom eventually unveils the Demon as his mother, and he dies.

Although different in style and address from *Clive of India*, this too is a psychological study of one 'great man'. The play's challenge for early television is the 'crosscutting' between Ransom's ascent and the BBC reports heard by Mr and Mrs A in their drawing room, requiring a rapid transition between spaces in order to emphasize a significant relationship. The directions in the published theatre script divide the stage into three spaces: 'stage boxes' on the left and right for the BBC Announcer and Mr and Mrs A and centre stage for the majority of the action. The division of the stage into these spaces allows a double interpretation of the events centre stage, first by the announcer, and then by Mr and Mrs A who are listening to the radio across stage. Part of the play's project is to dramatize visually the process of mediation whereby Ransom's heroic struggle with his psychology is distorted and trivialized through its state and media appropriation, and through its reception by the bourgeois listeners.

It was televised twice, in May 1937 and September 1938, with both versions produced by Royston Morley.[96] Unlike most of the other major television adaptations it did not run in the West End, but toured with Rupert Doone's Little Theatre Company (and was subject to many rewrites between 1936 and 1938).[97] The 1937 television version is of the 'Theatre Parade' variety (although not billed under this heading): 'Scenes from Rupert Doone's Little Theatre Production of *The Ascent of F6* by W. H. Auden and Christopher Isherwood.'

For this production, Morley uses the drama standard of four cameras: 'I should like to use Camera 1 (dolly), Camera 2 on the O.B. dolly, Camera 3 on a low tripod and Camera 4 for captions. The details of Camera positions, set up etc., will follow shortly.'[98] Morley has also developed a new form of shot notation for television drama (borrowed from film script notation): medium close-shot—M.C.S., close-shot—C.S., medium long shot—M.L.S. (Figure 4). This indicates the need to discriminate between different shot-scales at the planning stage, and that the distinction between them was important. This is evidence of a greater *precision* when planning and an ambition to visualize a narrative and spatial continuity that is not primarily segmented around the 'scene'.

96 *The Ascent of F6*, 3.00–3.20, Monday 31 May 1937. 9.35–10.50, Sunday 18 Sept. 1938; repeated 3.00–4.15, Monday 26 Sept.

97 For a history of changes to the text of this play, see Edward Mendelson (ed.), *Plays and Other Dramatic Writings by W. H. Auden, 1928–1938* (Princeton, NJ: Princeton University Press, 1988), 598–652.

98 Memo, Royston Morley to Programmes Manager, 28 May 1937, BBC WAC T5/29.

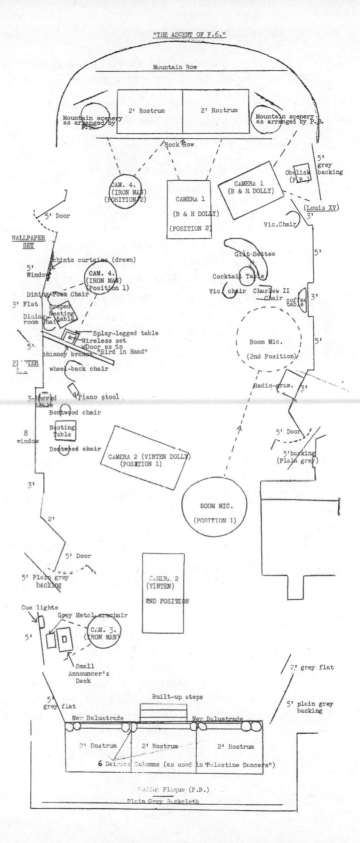

Fig. 4: Studio plan and camera positions for *The Ascent of F6* (1938). *Source*: BBC Written Archives, T5/29

Clearly this is a more sophisticated organization of studio A space than that used in *Clive of India* or *The Constant Nymph*. The main stage end houses one set intended to represent the mountain top; other sets are spread around the sides of the studio and at the reverse main stage end. Cameras 1, 2 and 4 have two positions each, with camera 3 covering the 'BBC Announcer's' desk. We can see that the main stage end of the studio contains five sets. They are (clockwise): the mountain top, the obelisk against a grey backing; the stock 'Louis XV' set with settee, cocktail table, chairs, and a radiogram; the 'plaster set' with a nesting table and two chairs; a wallpaper set with a wireless. Although it is not marked, clearly camera 1 or 4 would have to move to cover the 'Louis XV' set.

Studio plans are not infallible guides to what took place during transmission. The plan also shows that there were a further three sets at the reverse main stage end of the studio: the three rostrums with six columns, and the small Announcer's desk. The space of the studio is therefore filled with sets but, unlike O'Donovan's complex staging for *Juno and the Paycock*, this method of pushing the sets against the sides of the studio allows far greater camera movement.

The following labels appear within the studio plan figure:

"THE ASCENT OF F.6."

Mountain Row

2' Rostrum   2' Rostrum

Mountain scenery as arranged by F.B.   Mountain scenery as arranged by F.B.

Rock Row

CAM. 4. (IRON MAN) (POSITION 2)

CAMERA 1 (B & H DOLLY) (POSITION 2)

CAMERA 1 (B & H DOLLY)

5' grey backing

Obelisk (F.B.)

Louis XV   3'

Vic. Chair

5' Door

WALLPAPER SET

Chintz curtains (drawn)

5' Window

CAM. 4. (IRON MAN) (Position 1)

Grit Settee   5'

Cocktail Table

Dining-room Chair

Vic chair   Charles II Chair   coffee table   3'

3' Flat   Draped Nesting table

Dining room Chair

Splay-legged table

Wireless set

Door as in "Bird in Hand"

5'

Chimney breast

wheel-back chair

Boom Mic. (2nd Position)   5'

PLASTER SET

Radio-gram.   3'

3-legged Table

Piano stool

Bentwood chair

Nesting Table

8 window

Bentwood chair

CAMERA 2 (VINTEN DOLLY) (POSITION 1)

5' Door

5' backing (Plain grey)

BOOM MIC. (POSITION 1)

3'

2'

5' Door

5' Plain grey backing

CAMERA 2 (VINTEN) 2ND POSITION

Cue lights

Grey Metal armchair

5'

CAM. 3. (IRON MAN)

Small Announcer's Desk

2' grey flat

5' grey flat

5' plain grey backing

Built-up steps

New Balustrade   New Balustrade

2' Rostrum   2' Rostrum   2' Rostrum

6 Deirdre Columns (as used in "Palestine Dancers")

Welding Plaque (F.B.)

Plain Grey Backcloth

The studio plan available for this production indicates a sparse set, encircled by three cameras. A note from Morley states:

> All the action on main stage, against cyclorama. One change of set (boxes out, tent set) during telecine.
>
> Stand mike required with green cue-light. All props from theatre, except two stools draped with grey cloth to represent boulders (or bank used in Midsummer Night's Dream draped in grey, if practicable).[99]

Even when selecting only 'scenes' and with the bare minimum of scenery, the aim was to use multiple cameras to obtain variety of angles. The archival material available for this production demonstrates that both scene dissection and on-air camera movement *were* used as early as May 1937.

Table 1 is based on the continuity script for the play. The script details camera transitions, movements and shot scale. For a 20-minute production, it was highly segmented. Italics are used to indicate when a camera is directed to prepare for its next shot.

Scenes and extracts from plays, here using props from the current theatre production, might be described as the most 'primitive' form of television drama, and yet this is a sophisticated mediation of the performance space.

Morley divides the production into shots, noting the scale and movement of each; transitions between scenes are marked by telecine film inserts (4, 6, 22, 27, 35), but often these also provide continuity when accompanied by voice-overs (Ransom, BBC Announcer) narrating the progress of the ascent (one insert also allows a scenery change, 27).

Variation in shots is typically provided by reframing (6, 10, 17, 19, 25, 26, 29, 31, 33, 38), and in one shot (13) the camera moves to follow the exit of a character. This reframing or variation in shot-scale seems to go contrary to ideas of theatrical pictorialism in early television drama in preference for the mobile frame. Close-ups are used mostly for Ransom's soliloquies (shots 14, 26, 38), and sometimes track in or out of this position (26, 38), and camera transitions are motivated by character movement (7–8).

For this 20-minute production the average shot length is just under 30 seconds. This production must stand as the exemplary example of a 'photographed stage play' which is neither static nor dependent on the equivalence of shot with scene. Morley's production is exemplary to the extent to which it matches the later drama productions of the 1950s, in particular the organization of the cameras into a 'triangle'

99 BBC WAC T5/29.

TABLE 1: *The Ascent of F6* (May 1937) breakdown

Shot	Description	Sound	Shot Detail	Cameras and Telecine				
				T	1	2	3	4
1	Caption: 'The Ascent of F6.'	Record—classical						4
2	Telecine loop (of mountain)	Record (louder)		T				
3	Ransom's opening soliloquy.	Record slowly fades out	M.C.S.		1			
4	Telecine loop (of mountain)	Newsboys report that Ransom is to climb F6 (from stand mike)		T				
5	Ransom packing supplies for the expedition		M.C.S.		1			
6	Shawcross is packing with him		M.C.S. Cam. 1 track back			2		
7	Entrance of monk		M.L.S.		1			
8	As Ransom steps towards Camera 3						3	
9	Ransom steps back to table				1			
10	Doctor finds a flower and shows it to Lamp and Gunn		M.C.S. Cam. 3 pan on to Lamp and Gunn				3	
11	Gunn		M.C.S.		1			
12	Ransom		M.C.S.				3	
13	Gunn, Doctor and Lamp. They eventually exit.		M.C.S. Cam. 2 pans to follow exit. *Cam. 1 into C.U. of Ransom.*			2		
14	Ransom soliloquy	Record in background	C.U.		1			
15	Enter Shawcross, Gunn, Doctor and Lamp	Record out	M.C.S. *Cam. 1 track back*			2		
16	Telecine film of climbing	Ransom voice over and record.		T				

Table 1: (cont'd)

Shot	Description	Sound	Shot Detail	Cameras and Telecine				
				T	1	2	3	4
17	Ransom talking to Tom	Record out.	M.C.S. then track back to M.L.S.		1			
18	Ransom		M.C.S.				3	
19	Shawcross		M.C.S. Cam. 1 pan to Ransom and Doctor.		1			
20	Ransom		M.C.S.			2		
21	Ransom is handed a skull. Begins soliloquy	Fade up record	M.C.S. tracking up		1			
22	Telecine of avalanche	Cross-fade record to effects record of avalanche. Doctor voice over: 'Oh god he's done for!'		T				
23	Shawcross describes how Lamp dies	Fade out record.	M.L.S.		1			
24	Begins on close-up then Shawcross		C.U.				3	
25	Doctor then Shawcross and Gunn. All exit except Ransom.		M.C.S. panning onto rucksack, then track back to show Shawcross and Gunn			2		
26	Ransom soliloquy; eventually the others re-enter		Tracking into C.U. of Ransom; then track back to show group.		1			
27	Telecine loop	Announcer: announces death of Lamp	Make up tent set on stage during the film sequence.	T				
28	Doctor, Gunn and Shawcross enter		M.C.S. Gunn and Shawcross enter from behind cameraman			2		
29	Doctor and Gunn		M.L.S. track to Gunn and Doctor		1			

TABLE 1: (cont'd)

Shot	Description	Sound	Shot Detail	Cameras and Telecine				
				T	1	2	3	4
30	Shawcross		M.C.S. *Move Cam 1 to show Ransom and Shawcross*				3	
31	Ransom then Gunn then Gunn and Doctor		Tracking in to Gunn; then track back to show Gunn and Doctor		1			
32	Shawcross		M.C.S.				3	
33	Ransom then Shawcross		M.L.S. track into M.C.S then track out to M.L.S.		1			
34			M.L.S.			2		
35	Telecine loop	Announcer (anxiety about safety of expedition) Fade up wind effects record.		T				
36	Ransom climbing	Fade out record at end	M.C.S.		1			
37	Gunn dies	Fade up record of wind effects then fade out.	M.C.S.				3	
38	Ransom soliloquy, falls as if dying.		C.U. then track back to M.L.S.		1			
39	Telecine loop			T				
40	Ransom lying dead on stage	Fade up record	Mix to telecine loop and superimpose over Cam. 1; fade out Cam. 1	T	1			
41	Caption: 'The Ascent of F6'		Fade out telecine then caption as music ends.	T				4
42	Closing announcement						3	
43	Alexandra Palace Mast			T				

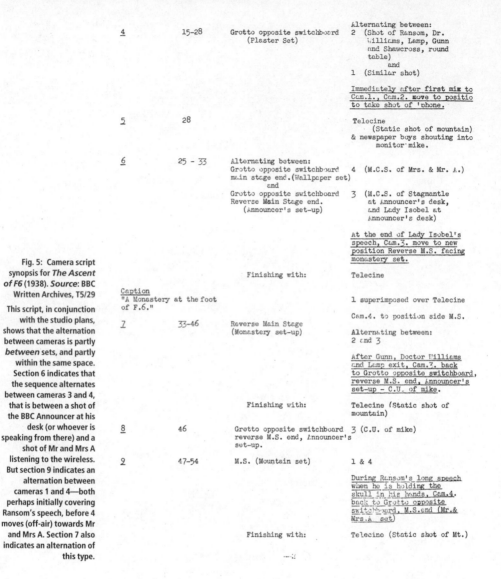

<u>4</u>	15–28	Grotto opposite switchboard (Plaster Set)	Alternating between: 2 (Shot of Ransom, Dr. Williams, Lamp, Gunn and Shawcross, round table) and 1 (Similar shot) <u>Immediately after first mix to Cam.1., Cam.2. move to positio to take shot of 'phone.</u>
<u>5</u>	28		Telecine (Static shot of mountain) & newspaper boys shouting into monitor mike.
<u>6</u>	25 – 33	Alternating between: Grotto opposite switchboard main stage end.(Wallpaper set) and Grotto opposite switchboard Reverse Main Stage end. (Announcer's set-up)	4 (M.C.S. of Mrs. & Mr. A.) 3 (M.C.S. of Stagmantle at Announcer's desk, and Lady Isobel at Announcer's desk) <u>At the end of Lady Isobel's speech, Cam.3. move to new position Reverse M.S. facing monastery set.</u>
		Finishing with:	Telecine

Caption
"A Monastery at the foot
of F.6."

			1 superimposed over Telecine Cam.4. to position side M.S.
<u>7</u>	33–46	Reverse Main Stage (Monastery set-up)	Alternating between: 2 and 3 <u>After Gunn, Doctor Williams and Lamp exit, Cam.3. back to Grotto opposite switchboard, reverse M.S. end, Announcer's set-up – C.U. of mike.</u>
		Finishing with:	Telecine (Static shot of mountain)
<u>8</u>	46	Grotto opposite switchboard reverse M.S. end, Announcer's set-up.	3 (C.U. of mike)
<u>9</u>	47–54	M.S. (Mountain set)	1 & 4 <u>During Ransom's long speech when he is holding the skull in his hands, Cam.4. back to Grotto opposite switchboard, M.S.end (Mr.& Mrs.A set)</u>
		Finishing with:	Telecine (Static shot of Mt.)

Fig. 5: Camera script synopsis for *The Ascent of F6* (1938). *Source*: BBC Written Archives, T5/29

This script, in conjunction with the studio plans, shows that the alternation between cameras is partly *between* sets, and partly within the same space. Section 6 indicates that the sequence alternates between cameras 3 and 4, that is between a shot of the BBC Announcer at his desk (or whoever is speaking from there) and a shot of Mr and Mrs A listening to the wireless. But section 9 indicates an alternation between cameras 1 and 4—both perhaps initially covering Ransom's speech, before 4 moves (off-air) towards Mr and Mrs A. Section 7 also indicates an alternation of this type.

position around the performance which matches exactly Ian Atkins's plan of the 'fundamentals' of television technique.[100]

The September 1938 version of the play is a full, seventy-five minute presentation. Again, Morley makes full use of the available technical sources: telecine; sound effects; captions; four cameras in various positions. The nine main sets are arranged centrifugally around the cameras (Figure 5). The shooting script indicates that Morley intended to mix between cameras *within* scenes, and that

100 Ian Atkins, 'Television Programme Production Problems in Relation to Engineering Technique', *Proceedings of the Institute of Electrical Engineers*, 99 (3a) no.17 (April–May 1952).

he planned camera movement (pan, track, tilt) whilst transmitting pictures. A month before, Morley had produced a new version of *The Importance of Being Earnest* which also had planning for alternation between cameras within scenes, and special directions for the camera-men (e.g., 'camera 1 pan for Lady Bracknell's entrance'; 'pan with movement').[101] Morley's continuity script for *Ascent* is similarly divided into columns that indicate greater precision in planning, with one column for 'cameras', one for the 'set', one for 'page no.' (of the script), and an organizing column—not shots—but 'Section No.'

Table 2 is derived from the camera synopsis for the 1938 version of the play. Italics are used when a camera is directed to move into pos-ition for subsequent shots. Where two cameras are directed to cover one scene, the first camera is highlighted in bold, the second in square brackets.

At first glance this breakdown seems more simplistic that the 1937 version: there are only fifteen sections (scenes) compared to more than forty shots in the earlier production. However, this is a *synopsis* of camera directions. Section 3 is a composite section, alternating between sets *and* cameras 3 and 4; the same is true of section 6, 10, 12. These sections all alternate between a shot of the Announcer (or a character making a broadcast) and Mr and Mrs A listening to the announcement. There is no way to gauge precisely how frequent these alternations took place, but this form of crosscutting between spaces, between announcement and reaction, is an example of the spatial mobility that early drama could achieve.

There is another form of shot alternation in the production, this time indicating scene dissection. Sections 4 and 7 use two cameras each to break down the performance space, giving a variation of views: 'shot of Ransom, Dr Williams' etc. and 'similar shot' on cam-eras 1 and 2. Judging by the studio plans, camera 1 is moved from the cyclorama end to the 'plaster set' to near camera 2 (first position), a movement already prepared for in section 3 ('During announcer's speech, Cam.1 move to new position, studio left'). Not only does the producer align shots when transmitted, he is also positioning cam-eras for future shots. This is also true for the earlier version, and is a kind of mobility that has traditionally been associated with television dramas of the late 1950s rather than the 'static' early period. And yet,

101 *The Importance of Being Earnest*, 9.00–10.15, Tuesday 23 Aug. 1938; repeated 3.00–4.15 Tuesday 6 Sept. The production was seen as a stylistic innovation at the time: Morley. '[It is] an entirely different and far more exciting set up of which it seems a pity to have no record.' Memo to D. H. Munro, 6 Sept. 1938, BBC WAC T5/248. One pre-war drama production, *The Scarlet Pimpernel*, was filmed (although this was of very poor quality due to the inability to synchronize television frame rate with that of the film camera), primarily because producers wanted a record of this big and expensive production. The film record was burned because it infringed copyright law. See Norman, *Here's Looking At You*, 188.

Table 2: *The Ascent of F6* (September 1938) breakdown

Section no.	Script page	Set	Shot Detail	T	1	2	3	4
				Cameras and Telecine				
Opening Sequence Captions	1		'The Ascent of F6.'			2		
—	1		'By Auden and Isherwood'				3	
—	1		'Produced by Royston Morley'			2		
—	1		Cast details				3	
—	1		Cast details			2		
—	1		Cast details				3	
—	1		'The Ascent of F6'					
—	1		Static mountain shot held in gate	T				
Prologue	2	Main stage, Studio Right (Side of Obelisk set-up)	C.U. of Ransom		1			
1	2–4	Grotto opposite switchboard, main stage end (wallpaper set)	M.C.S. Mr. and Mrs A *During this section Cam. 1 moves to position on studio right*					4
2	5–11	Grotto, switchboard side (Louis XV set)	Shot of Sir James, Lady Isobel, Lord Stagmantle and General Dellaby-Couch gathered round settee		1			
3	11–14	Alternating between: Announcer's set-up (Grotto opposite switchboard, reverse main stage end)	M.C.S. of Announcer *During the Announcer's speech, Cam. 1 move to new position studio left*				3	[4]
	11–14	and: Grotto opposite switchboard, main stage end (wallpaper set)	M.C.S. of Mrs A and Mr. A				[3]	4
4	15–28	Grotto opposite switchboard (Plaster set)	Alternating between: Shot of Ransom, Dr. Williams, Lamp, Gunn and Shawcross, round table		[1]	2		
			And: similar shot		1	[2]		

TABLE 2: (cont'd)

Section no.	Script page	Set	Shot Detail	Cameras and Telecine				
				T	1	2	3	4
5	28		Static shot of mountain	T				
6	25–33	Alternating between: Grotto opposite switchboard main stage end (wallpaper set)	M.C.S. of Mr. and Mrs A.				[3]	4
		and: Grotto opposite switchboard reverse main stage end (Announcer's set-up)	M.C.S. of Stagmantle at Announcer's desk and Lady Isobel at Announcer's desk; finishing with:				3	[4]
			Static shot of mountain	T				
Caption		'A monastery at the foot of F6'	Superimposed over telecine *Camera 4 to position side main stage*		1			
7	33–46	Reverse main stage (Monastery set-up)	Alternating between: *After Gunn, Dr. Williams and Lamp exit, Cam. 3 back to reverse main stage end, Announcer's set up, C.U. mike.*			2	3	
			Finishing with: Static shot of mountain	T				
8	46	Grotto opposite switchboard, reverse main stage end, Announcer's set-up.	C.U. mike				3	
9	47–54	Main stage (mountain set)	*During Ransom's long speech when he is holding the skull in his hands, Cam.4 back to Grotto opposite switchboard, main stage end (Mr. and Mrs A set)*		1			4
			Finishing with: Static shot of mountain	T				

TABLE 2: (cont'd)

Section no.	Script page	Set	Shot Detail	Cameras and Telecine				
				T	1	2	3	4
10	54–56	Alternating between: Grotto opposite switchboard main stage end	M.C.S. of Mr. and Mrs A					4
		And: Grotto opposite switchboard reverse main stage end	C.U. of Stagmantle at Announcer's desk				3	
			Finishing with: static shot of mountain	T				
11	57–62	Main stage (mountain set with tent and snow wings added)	Shot of 4 mountaineers		1			
			Finishing with: static shot of mountain	T				
12	62–64	Alternating between: Grotto opposite switchboard reverse main stage end (Announcer's set-up)					3	[4]
		And: Grotto opposite switchboard (the A's)					[3]	4
13	64–65	Main stage (mountain set without tent and snow wings)	Shot of Ransom and Gunn		1			
14	66		Static shot of mountain (with Mr. and Mrs A at Sound boom mike. Saying their piece in duet out of vision)	T				
15	67	Grotto switchboard side main stage end (obelisk set-up)	Shot of Mr. and Mrs A and obelisk		1			
			Finishing with: drifting cloud shot	T				
Caption			'The Ascent of F6. The End' Superimposed over telecine			2		

here there is evidence of a sophisticated planning and choreography of the cameras moving through sets in real-time that was to become the standard means of studio and camera organization even into the 1960s and after.[102]

The production history of this period contains few examples of plays encumbered by proscenium arches, curtains, or static and faithful rendering of theatrical performances. That the amateur 'photographed stage play' is a myth, is clearly shown in the television criticism of the time. Grace Wyndham Goldie and other critics confirm that television drama developed rapidly during the late 1930s:

> television plays are getting better and better every minute. Just consider the production of *Richard of Bordeaux* last week. There were dozens of scenes, scores of fourteenth-century costumes, an enormous cast . . . television plays in spite of their increasingly film-like handling, do succeed in remaining different in quality from film.[103]

As I indicated above, despite the segmentation of plays, the use of multiple spaces, and the new combination and layering of image-sound sources, the *pace* of pre-war television drama was certainly a lot slower than those of the 1950s and 1960s. Paradoxically, this was probably a result of television producers showing too much:

> It must be recognized that television slows up the action of the ordinary stage piece. Why? Because we see successively on television things that we see simultaneously on the stage. Take scenery. As the curtain goes up in the theatre we get the effect of the whole room. In television the camera pans round to show us first the door, then a window, then a piece of furniture. And similarly with the action. We have to have close-ups to give us the expression on the faces of the actors.[104]

Or consider the *Radio Times* description of a forthcoming drama production adapted by Denis Johnston from his radio play, *Death at Newtonstewart*:

> a reconstruction of an unparalleled murder of the 'seventies, extracted from the records of the Ulster Assizes, and produced by Denis Johnston. You will see witnesses giving evidence at the trial, and as they speak the picture will change to illustrate what they

---

102 See for example Philip Saville's studio plans and shooting script for the 1961 'Armchair Theatre' production, *Afternoon of a Nymph* published in John Russell Taylor (ed.), *Anatomy of a Television Play* (London: Weidenfeld & Nicolson, 1962), 138–9 and 175–203.

103 Grace Wyndham Goldie, *The Listener*, 29 Dec. 1938.

104 Grace Wyndham Goldie, *The Listener*, 15 Dec. 1938.

are saying. This is an old cinema trick, but two years ago the idea would have been much too complicated for television.[105]

For Goldie, this visual innovation also hinders the pace of the play:

> in television [compared to the radio version] the effect is quite different. For here everything is seen as well as described. Counsel says, 'The servant takes the sixpence and leaves the bank by the front door.' Do we then pass to the next point? Oh, no. We have to see the girl take the sixpence and walk down the corridor and into the street.[106]

Goldie's objection is that television shows too much, and therefore retards the flow of the action (a notion which is close to George More O'Ferrall's comment that live drama 'is rather like turning over the pages of a picture book for a child'[107]). One solution to this pedestrian style was to produce plays specially written for television. Goldie again:

> Most of the trouble is caused by adapting stage plays to a new medium and one day television plays will have to be written specially for television. But heaven forbid that they should imitate the films.[108]

> Television plays, unlike film, depend on words. So television drama is likely to be a new literary medium. Here, in fact, is a drama of the future for us to see and hear and for writers to write. And if being in at the birth of that isn't exciting I don't know what is.[109]

It was not until the late 1950s that plays written for the medium began to constitute the majority of television drama output. Until that point most of the material was adapted from stage plays; and yet, as we have seen, this dependence on theatrical material does not mean that the visual style was 'theatrical'. The adaptation of this material was not simply about compressing the narrative or cutting the number of sets and characters to fit studio space and the budget. There was a structured, and entirely new process of mediation: the multi-camera studio production which treated performance and narrative space in a manner both similar to other media (film, theatre, radio), and in a combination which was also very different: live, continuous, and 'intimate'.

105 *Radio Times*, 6 Jan. 1939.

106 Grace Wyndham Goldie, *The Listener*, 16 Feb. 1939.

107 George More O'Ferrall, Mary Adams, Michael Gough, R. K. Neilson Baxter, Roger Manvell, 'Television's Challenge to the Cinema', in *The Cinema, 1950* (Penguin Books, 1950), 178.

108 Grace Wyndham Goldie, *The Listener*, 15 Dec. 1938.

109 Grace Wyndham Goldie, *The Listener*, 29 Dec. 1938.

3

The Illustrated Broadcast?
Defining Television Drama,
1946–50

*apart from the practical difficulties of supply and demand economics,
and subject to indignant correction from Alexandra Palace, I am not
yet convinced that television drama is sure of its target. Does it aim
to be no more than a photographed stage play? Does it dream of
competition with the film? Or should its principal aim be that of
illustrating broadcasting?* For the practice and practitioners of
televised drama there can be nothing but undiluted admiration. But,
looking forward into the future, is it not perhaps out of place to suggest
that, as far as any genuine theory of television is concerned, a question
mark is still the most appropriate symbol.

Val Gielgud, 1947[1]

THE **QUESTION-MARK** remained throughout this period, and
even beyond.[2] Gielgud's comments reveal a continuing uncertainty about the themes, form and style appropriate for television drama. Despite the hiatus of the wartime closedown, BBC
Television in the late 1940s demonstrated continuity with the developments of the pre-war period. The Alexandra Palace studios continued to be the primary site of television production; the Television
Service was still underfunded; it was still geographically and institu-
tionally isolated from BBC radio broadcasting, and there was still the
relatively unstructured selection of drama material chosen by the 're-
calcitrant band of individualists' that were drama producers.[3]

---

1 Val Gielgud, 'Policy and Problems of Broadcast Drama', *BBC Quarterly*, 2/1 (1947), 23.
Gielgud was Head of Television Drama 1950–1.

2 For example, as late as 1954 in a drama producer's meeting Ian Atkins asks the Head of
Drama, Michael Barry, ' "What is our drama policy?" Mr. Atkins felt that there was little
sense of direction. Where were we going?' Minutes for 5 Nov. 1954 in BBC Written
Archives Centre (WAC) file TV Routine Meetings: Drama Producers Meetings, T26/11/2.

3 Michael Barry's description in *From the Palace to the Grove* (London: Royal Television
Society, 1992), 186.

There was also discontinuity and change. As the last German television transmitter at Witzleben was bombed in September 1943, a British government committee was formed, under the chairmanship of Lord Hankey, to consider the 'reinstatement and development of the television service'. The committee recommended that the television service be reinstated under the control of the BBC, and that it should be expanded. The drive for expansion was also initiated by new BBC television management, in particular Maurice Gorham, the post-war Head of the Television Service, 'one of the two BBC live wires', the other being Norman Collins who replaced Gorham as Controller of the Television Service in 1947.[4] Both pushed hard for the expansion of the Television Service and by 1950 the Service had acquired five more studios at Lime Grove, a new transmitter at Sutton Coldfield and a rapidly expanding audience.

The identity of television drama during this time was defined as much by policy and planning decisions as it was by the drama producers' decisions about such matters as camera mobility and shot-scale. This chapter will examine the way in which the Television Service, as it expanded, had to define and redefine itself and the medium of television. Television drama was central in this definitional process.

The restoration of the service within the BBC carried its own problems. BBC had gained considerable kudos for its broadcasting role during the war, and this popularity encouraged William Haley, Director-General since 1944, to initiate a reorganization of the Corporation. Haley's chief interest was the reorganization of radio especially the setting-up of the Third Programme (later criticized, like early television, as a privileged service, for a privileged minority). By 1948, the number of television licences was still only 45,564 out of a population of some 50 million, and television had little visibility as far as the rest of the BBC was concerned.

Continuity with the pre-war service was emphasized by the return of production staff. Cecil Madden took up his pre-war job as Programme Organizer; George More O'Ferrall returned to a higher rank as Senior Drama Producer and other former drama producers also returned: Royston Morley, Fred O'Donovan, Desmond Davis, Jan Bussell, Eric Fawcett, Stephen Harrison, Ian Atkins (formerly a pre-war studio manager), and Malcolm Baker-Smith (formerly a designer).

Denis Johnston, another pre-war drama producer, was appointed Programme Director and Deputy Head of Television, a position nominally senior to Madden's, but in practice parallel to it. Johnston made it clear that he would leave most of the Light Entertainment programming to Madden, whilst he concentrated on the development

---

4 See Val Gielgud, *Years in a Mirror* (London: The Bodley Head, 1965), 126.

of drama.[5] Johnston saw television as a 'shop window' for new plays of merit, and outlined the drama department's ambition to produce material written *for* television, saying 'open-minded producers' were 'awaiting adventurous authors'.[6] This was a pragmatic response to the refusal of London theatre managers to allow material to be televised, and also evidence of the ambitious desire of the television staff to expand creatively the range of the medium. The *ambition* to produce original material for television does not originate with 'Armchair Theatre', Sydney Newman or 'The Wednesday Play', even if the consistent *practice* of original play production does.

However, external limits were imposed on the overall development of television. The BBC Board of Governors fixed the operational costs of television for 1946/7 at a level below that of 1939 (when production costs were lower): the pressure on space, equipment and people increased, particularly as the length of programmes had expanded.[7] Gorham wrote to Haley in July 1947 pointing out that the inadequate studio accommodation and out-of-date equipment had seriously damaged the quality of programme production; by October of that year, programmes were beginning to be cancelled as a result of the strain on resources.[8] This was galling for Gorham who had recently returned from a visit to US television studios where he noted that 'Their studios were no better than ours, but they were building where we were not . . . if we had their equipment our staff could have produced a really excellent service.'[9]

In 1947 the Outside Broadcast and Film Supervisor, Philip Dorté, gave the first demonstration of the BBC's telerecording system, which enabled the recording of the television image on film. Gorham realized that this development could offer a possible solution to the problems of limited studio time and space:

> Recording programmes on film might relieve the strain on staff resources entailed by the current programme schedule, but it entails a revolution in thinking about programming as a whole.[10]

His ideas were not developed at the time but, writing two years later, Gorham lists the five main advantages that telerecording would have for the Television Service:

5 Barry, *From the Palace to the Grove*, 49.

6 *Radio Times*, 7 June 1946. This call was to be repeated again and again by critics and producers during this period. For example, Harold Hobson: 'Nevertheless, what one wants is not plays refurbished from the West End, but new plays, television plays, specially designed.' 'What We Want in Television Plays', *BBC Quarterly*, 5/2 (1950), 79.

7 Asa Briggs, *History of Broadcasting in the UK, iv. Sound and Vision* (Oxford: Oxford University Press, 1979), 207–8.

8 Ibid. 209–11.

9 Ibid. 219.

10 Gorham, Memo 18 July 1947, quoted in Briggs, *Sound and Vision*, 210.

1. It would save studio space and time (a repeat film makes no demands on the studio): 'At Alexandra Palace, for instance, it will be the equivalent of one new fully equipped studio, if not more.'[11]
2. Producers would be able to see and evaluate their own productions after transmission (during transmission the producer would see both preview and transmission monitors). Telerecordings could also be used as training material for new producers.
3. It would allow the repeat of important events that occur at bad viewing times: this is good for television newsreels.
4. Telerecording would facilitate the international exchange of programmes between TV companies: 'they can be sent all over the world and reproduced from the film.'
5. It could aid motion picture production by making the film-making process faster (using multi-camera studios).

The Television Service's chief engineers shared this view:

> I believe that in future developments of this very complex art very great dependence will remain on films. Chiefly, because few people can attend sporting events at inconvenient hours, so that these events will *have* to be filmed; otherwise large numbers will be disappointed. It is not possible for people to stop work in the afternoon to see the Derby. High-speed methods of developing and printing film, much faster than employed today, will be needed. . . . The taking of the film of, say, a play, too, will reduce costs enormously, and it can be televised frequently—it would be too costly to put on special 'live' shows continually.[12]

However, these potential benefits of telerecording were not explored until after 1955. In the post-war period the film industry refused to supply any films, whether long or short, for television.[13] Movietone even refused to sell the BBC a copy of the 1946 reopening service, which it had filmed for its own cinema newsreel and Disney cartoons were no longer available.[14] This meant that there was virtually no filmed material available in the late 1940s other than some scientific documentaries and some European films. Even film library stock-shots, previously used for superimposition effects and as inserts, were no longer available.

In response to these restrictions the Television Service created a Film Unit which produced the twice-weekly Newsreel (January

---

11 Maurice Gorham, *Television: Medium of the Future* (London: Percival Marshall, 1949), 39.

12 F. Watts quoted in D. C. Birkenshaw and D. R. Campbell, 'Studio Technique in Television', *Journal of Institute of Electrical Engineers*, 92/19 (Sept. 1945), 180.

13 See Edward Buscombe, 'All Bark and No Bite: The Film Industry's Response to Television', in John Corner (ed.), *Popular Television in Britain: Studies in Cultural History* (London: British Film Institute, 1991), 197–207.

14 The sale was banned by the American Federation of Musicians, see Gorham, *Television: Medium of the Future*, 36–9.

1948), as well as travelogues and documentary material.[15] The OB (Outside Broadcast) televising of West End plays was also eliminated as a result of the hostility of theatre management, and of actors' and musicians' unions. OBs from the theatre now came from Repertory theatres. In March 1948 the OB and Film Department was separated, with Ian Orr-Ewing the new Head of Outside Broadcasts and Philip Dorté Head of the new Film Department.[16]

Despite these problems, the Television Service was expanding: staff at Alexandra Palace increased from 456 in June 1946 to 677 in June 1948. But Gorham's position in the BBC organization overall meant that he had to clear even minor staff increases with Broadcasting House. Haley's reorganization of the BBC in 1948 had left the Television Service as one of six divisions of the Home Service.[17] Whereas before Gorham had dealt with Haley directly on policy matters, he now had to clear all matters through Basil Nicolls, the Senior Controller of Home Output. Exasperated, Gorham resigned on 24 November 1947.

An important theme in this chapter is the way that aesthetic debate about the 'nature of the medium' was conducted by BBC management. It is the period when television managers try to convince their seniors in BBC Sound that television is different from sound broadcasting. Gorham resigned because he believed television was significantly distinct from radio to demand a separate management and organizational structure, and he was willing to stake his career on it. As Val Gielgud notes, Gorham had consistently fought to 'destroy any vestige of Broadcasting House control over the Television Service'.[18] A measure of Gorham's disappointment after eighteen months of hardship can be seen in Michael Barry's recollection of the announcement of his resignation to television producers:

> He was very upset, and told us at once that the Director-General had accepted his resignation from the BBC. He made a few explanatory remarks following the silence that followed his announcement, describing the difficulties he had faced and the reorganisation that left the Head of Television still without a separate command within the BBC, and direct access to the Director-General . . . Gorham got up to leave and beckoned me to follow him . . . in the privacy of his office, it became clear that he found it increasingly difficult to control his distress.[19]

15 Memo, 'Development of Television Programmes Since the War', Cecil Madden to Norman Collins, 10 Oct. 1949. BBC WAC Special Collection: Cecil Madden.

16 In fact Haley's policy of sound and television 'integration' was first tested on this department when the Head of Radio OBs, S. T. Lotbinière, was given control of Television OBs. Orr-Ewing resigned.

17 For details of this reorganization see Briggs, *Sound and Vision*, 117–37.

18 Val Gielgud, *Years in a Mirror*, 130.

19 Barry, *From the Palace to the Grove*, 92.

The last phrase is the well known code for weeping, a testament, I think, to the passion and frustration that those committed to developing television in Britain felt during this time. Gorham was replaced by Norman Collins, who had worked as Head of the BBC General Forces and Light Programmes during which time he created *Radio Newsreel* and *Women's Hour*.[20] Like McGivern, Collins was a television enthusiast and was shrewd enough to bypass Haley altogether, meeting instead with the BBC Chairman of the Board of Governors, Lord Simon of Wythenshawe, and convincing him that the advanced state of US television development meant that it was essential that the BBC expand its television service in terms of studios and equipment, if it were not to be left behind. In June 1948 the Board of Governors agreed that the most urgent priority for the Television Service was the building of additional television studios.[21] Development proceeded rapidly: in March 1949 the BBC acquired a 13.5 acre site at the White City Exhibition where it planned to open a new purpose-built 'Television Centre' by 1960; the Rank Film Studios at Lime Grove were acquired in November 1949, providing 5 extra studios; in January 1950 a Television Studio Development Committee was set up.

As this development was planned, the drama schedule—its contents and organization—became the primary site where management and organizational conflicts were played out.

Denis Johnston resigned his post as Deputy Head of Television in 1947 and was replaced by Cecil McGivern, a former Newcastle school teacher, actor and stage manager, who had worked for the BBC Radio Features during the war, and subsequently at a Rank Organization script unit before his appointment as Television Programme Director. Peter Black has described McGivern as 'a true architect of television';[22] his enthusiasm for television was matched only by his organizational and planning skills. By December 1948 he had introduced a long-term programme planning system and had reorganized the Television Service into four 'programme groups': Drama, Light Entertainment, Talks, and Outside Broadcasts and Films. All television producers were ultimately responsible to him.

Denis Johnston's departure as Programmes Director left two vacancies: drama head and programme organizer. Johnston had concentrated on drama organization rather than programming output as a whole, so whilst McGivern restructured programming output, Robert MacDermot, a former announcer and programme planner for BBC radio, was appointed Head of Television Drama.

20 See John Swift, *Adventure in Vision: The First Twenty-Five Years of Television* (London: John Lehman, 1950), 127.

21 Briggs, *Sound and Vision*, 236.

22 Peter Black, *The Mirror in the Corner* (London: Hutchinson and Co. Ltd, 1972), 16.

MacDermot was conscious of the former dependence of television drama on stage successes and set out to change—or, at least, modify—the television drama landscape:

> I knew that it wouldn't be possible—nor, indeed, desirable—to concentrate exclusively on new material. I realised that the television audience would always need a staple ration of 'Shaftesbury Avenue Successes', but I was anxious that, in time, these would not constitute more than 50 per cent of our total output so that television would not appear to be borrowing only from established stage and screen successes. I wanted it to be realised that this was a medium which needed special study. Of the remaining 50 per cent of plays, it was my aim to make half of them specially written for the medium and the rest admittedly written originally for stage or screen but *not yet seen on either*. In making up the three-monthly drama schedule I contrived to approach as closely as possible these proportions of West End plays and classics, and plays untried or specially written, to obtain a balance that would please the largest number over any one month.[23]

This was an ambitious policy and it mirrored Johnston's earlier announcement that he wanted to recruit new writers for television. The ambition was curtailed by financial realities. Although the post-war period saw an increase in the amount of drama on screen (most productions lasting 90 minutes or over), there was an increased reliance on repeats: a typical week would include at least one new production and at least two further repeats of previous week's plays. The Sunday night performances were repeated on Tuesday afternoon, and a Thursday night play repeated on Friday afternoon, a rhythm that remained in place until February 1948. Repeat programming saved money, and the low visibility of afternoon repeats did not disgrace the Service and meant a varied evening schedule.

However, McGivern's planning acumen was applied to the drama schedules with a fiscal eye, and his solution to financial restrictions meant the repeat of major productions in the evenings. The bombshell was issued to the Head of Drama in February 1948:

> In order to keep down costs, it is going to be necessary to repeat plays in evening transmissions in the same week.
>
> The following procedure should be adopted whenever possible:
>
> 1. The Sunday night play to be the important drama offering in the week.

23 Quoted in Swift, *Adventure in Vision*, 154–5.

2. This play to be repeated on Thursday evening, not on Tuesday afternoon, as at present. This, unfortunately, will tend to weaken the casting, as the present system allows actors and actresses in the theatre shows to be booked. Producers should attempt to get over this to a certain extent by arranging to book star actors and leads well ahead, fitting in plays to suit their free periods.

3. Whenever the Sunday night play is repeated on Thursday night, the second play of the week will be produced on Tuesday night with a repeat on Friday afternoon.[24]

The original system allowed actors to work on Sunday evening (when theatres were closed) and Tuesday afternoons (before their evening performances); the 'saving' would come from replacing new evening programmes (such as variety and talks) with drama repeats.[25] However, the new schedule would cause congestion in terms of storage space.[26] Financial limitations caught the Service in a vicious circle: McGivern wanted to save money by using repeats as the main evening's television, but the lack of money meant no extra storage space for the sets was available. As the Studio Productions Manager, Imlay Newbiggin-Watts, argued:

It will be readily realised that the answer to most of the problems is space. The scheme [McGivern's] as outlined will have the following effects.

1. At the end of a Sunday night transmission the sets must be stored somewhere away from the Studios and Upper Scene Dock. They cannot remain, as at present, on the second floor.

2. The play on Tuesday night likewise.

3. Wardrobe will have to store two lots of costumes for productions in this very limited space. Costumes cannot be returned to Costumiers as under present planning.

Summing up, while appreciating the scheme from a financial point of view, from a studio operational point of view considerable congestion and confusion is foreseen.[27]

This argument was not about the desirability of repeats, but about the organization of work practices, and those in charge of storage argued that 'labour and costs' would go up because of McGivern's new plan, which was a veiled threat.[28]

---

24 Cecil McGivern to Robert MacDermot, Peter Bax (Head of Design), Imlay Newbiggin-Watts (Productions Manager), 17 Feb. 1948, BBC WAC T5/325.

25 Ibid. McGivern did not want to waste time: 'I will be glad if Mr MacDermot begins *now* to revise the drama schedule with reference to this new scheme.'

26 Peter Bax to Cecil McGivern, 17 Feb. 1948, BBC WAC T5/325.

27 Imlay Newbiggin-Watts to Cecil McGivern, 17 Feb. 1948, BBC WAC T5/325.

28 Peter Bax to Cecil McGivern, 20 Feb. 1948, BBC WAC T5/325.

Cecil Madden was still Programme Organizer but McGivern's organizational prowess had pushed him into an increasingly marginal role. Madden resented the shift away from 'speciality acts' to big Variety at the cost of drama output:

> Your memo . . . is surely a great comedown in programming. When we reopened . . . we could easily manage three plays a week, on Sundays, Tuesdays and Thursdays, on far lower general costs for the whole week. It was then reduced to two, and now by an upsurge of costs, mostly on Variety 'names', and abolition of small programmes, we can only afford one, knowing that by repeating it at night we shall cause irritation and get less good artists.[29]

MacDermot's response to McGivern's plan was equally negative; he argued that the proposal to compensate for evening repeats by hiring a 'big star' for the Sunday night performance was untenable:

> 1. It is hard enough as things are at present to book any star artist far ahead unless that star artist is unlikely to be in work on stage or film, and therefore probably not the star he or she once was.
>
> 2. With the new scheme the Thursday night repeat will mean that no star artist will be prepared to accept the loss of a theatre contract for the sake of two days on television. Should such a star agree verbally to appear for us it will be morally unsound . . . to insist on his playing the Thursday date should an attractive stage offer have come up in the meantime, which he would have to turn down if we held him to his contract.
>
> 3. I am naturally delighted at getting more peak times for drama productions, but have a strong suspicion that the audience will resent this new arrangement.[30]

Whatever the audience might think,—and what choice did they have anyway?—the fact remained that, 'With the exception of Copyright, the cost of a single performance of a play is about the same as a double.'[31] The result was a compromise between the old system and the new, with McGivern's system working intermittently against the trenchant demands of drama producers and of MacDermot.

Five months later, this compromise had effectively alienated the drama producers and management from McGivern: MacDermot was unwilling to divulge drama content before booking, and McGivern could see that his scheme was not being implemented. The abdication of programme selection and treatment to individual producers, as had been the case since the 1930s, was making planning for a balanced

29 Cecil Madden to Cecil McGivern, 17 Feb. 1948, BBC WAC T5/325.

30 Robert MacDermot to Cecil McGivern, 18 Feb. 1948, BBC WAC T5/325.

31 J. A. C. Knott to Cecil McGivern, 19 Feb. 1948, BBC WAC T5/325.

schedule very difficult. McGivern wanted to impose a centralized system of organization, and criticized MacDermot's lack of co-operation:

> I feel very much out of touch with the drama schedules and with the ideas which lie behind your lay-out for the quarter. . . . your layout of plays might be satisfactory from the point of view of your Section, but the order need not be satisfactory from the point of view of the week in which those plays are placed, when suggestions and demands of the other Sections are taken into account. It is . . . my business to make sure that the layout of every week's programmes is a considered and balanced one, with many factors taken into account.
>
> Will you in future please supply me each week with a few lines about the plays which are tentatively included in the schedule being considered that week, giving the type of play, the general atmosphere, whether there are any points which make it doubtful or unsuitable for Sunday night showing, etc.[32]

McGivern wanted integrated planning that provided, in the tradition of public service broadcasting, varied but balanced programming provision overall:

> I am very conscious at present that I am not managing to get the variation and diversity of interest into a week of television programmes that I should like to. We are becoming stereotyped and hidebound, and one week tends very much to resemble the previous week.[33]

McGivern also noted that MacDermot had effectively ignored his instruction to make the Sunday night play the linchpin of the drama schedule:

> The policy of repeats has gone wrong to some extent. When we started this scheme, I said that when we repeated a Sunday play on the following Thursday evening, there would inevitably be a strong reaction from viewers, and we should attempt to reduce the criticism as much as possible by making sure our Sunday night play was a very good one and, if possible, with a strong cast. I further said that if we had to put in an average play on Sunday night with an average cast, then we should repeat that on an afternoon. Perhaps I am wrong but it seems that we are automatically repeating the Sunday night play on Thursday evening and that some of them are really not worth the two evening performances. Here again, I sometimes sit helplessly in front of the schedules, lack of knowledge about a play making me

---

32 Cecil McGivern to Robert MacDermot, 8 July 1948, BBC WAC T5/325.

33 Ibid.

completely unable to decide whether it should be an evening or an afternoon repeat. A few lines from you about each play would be some help towards the following problem.[34]

Norman Collins supported McGivern's policy (also noting that, on investigation, MacDermot's claim that better artists could not booked for Sunday night plays was completely unfounded):[35]

FOR

1. The public is given a second chance of seeing *important* Television drama and does not work have to work out its own domestic timetable in terms of abject slavery to the BBC.

2. It is not 'fair' to the actors to ask them to spend *3 weeks rehearsing* and then give them less of a run than even amateur theatricals would provide.

3. Ditto the producer; also as regards the producer, it is woefully extravagant to put a man on a month's work for one production and there is a 50% saving automatically by giving it a second *evening* repeat.

4. *Thursday* repeats contribute substantially to easing Design congestion.

5. I do not think that it is any part of our job to encourage the public in the belief that they have an inalienable and prescriptive right to something new whenever they turn on the set.[36]

AGAINST

1. The public doesn't like 'em.

2. We must seek to give the public as fresh a programme as possible.

If the repeat of a play gave an automatic 50 per cent saving then an increase in repeats *and* a corresponding decrease in the rate of fresh drama productions was an obvious means of cost-cutting. Programming diversity could be provided by balancing drama against other output, rather than providing variety within the drama schedule, so the proposal meant no compromise of the public service ethic.

By 1949 MacDermot was even more disgruntled by the proposed reduction of drama output. In 1948 the average weekly drama output

---

34 Ibid.

35 Memo, 'Drama Repeats', Norman Collins to Cecil McGivern, 19 Aug. 1948, BBC WAC T5/325.

36 Ibid.

worked out at 2.5 plays per week; by 1949 the planned output was 1.5 per week. As MacDermot told McGivern, the decline in drama output meant that 'the repeat of the main one will stand out even more vividly to the public who, as we know, are already resentful of the repeat policy.'[37] MacDermot was also smarting from general criticism of his drama output offered at a recent Senior Staff Meeting, where it was attacked for lacking originality and variety.[38] In his defence, MacDermot blames McGivern's constant last minute readjustment to the schedules: 'I have realised from experience that making out the schedule for any length of time ahead and trying to balance the various types of plays is now of very little use since the first three weeks of the quarter have already been altered from my original suggestions.'

MacDermot suggested that planning should be organized around the 'fixed dates' that necessarily locked into the schedule, such as Outside Broadcast of events (the Coronation, Cenotaph ceremony) or the availability of stars. The major fixed points could be arranged in a skeleton plan and other material organized around it according to the current conventions of 'balance' and 'variety'.[39] Of course, such rigid planning restricted the advantage of the television's ability to be responsive and topical. McGivern's capriciousness continued under MacDermot's replacement, Val Gielgud:

> He [McGivern] was passionately addicted to off-the-cuff and last minute changes. He would hear of a new *diseuse* in Paris or a remarkable comedy duo just arrived from the States, and I would be told that a play, often already in rehearsal, must be changed for one costing less money because the budget was strained—it always was—and he needed the balance to pay for his new enthusiasm. The general programme may have been vitalised and brightened up: the drama schedule was knocked to pieces, its balance ruined.[40]

McGivern and his policy remained, MacDermot did not. Gielgud's appointment as Head of Drama was part of a wider reorganization of BBC Sound and Television output. In autumn 1949 Director-General Haley proposed the 'integration' of the Sound and Television output by seconding certain Heads of Radio Departments to oversee corresponding Departments in the Television Service: there would be a Head of Corporation Drama, Head of Corporation Children's Programmes, Head of Corporation Features and so on. Like Gorham before him, Collins was outraged by the apparent ignorance of BBC

37 Memo, 'Frequency of Drama Productions', Robert MacDermot to Cecil McGivern, 8 Feb. 1949, BBC WAC T5/325.

38 Ibid.

39 Memo, 'Suggested method for planning drama productions', Robert MacDermot to Cecil McGivern, 8 Feb. 1949, BBC WAC T5/325.

40 Val Gielgud, *Years in a Mirror*, 130.

management about the different demands of Sound and Television. In a memo to the Director of Home Broadcasting (his immediate superior), Collins cited television drama as a form that exemplified these differences.[41]

Collins agreed that co-ordination between the two outputs was organizationally attractive, but argued that the policy of integration necessarily ignored the 'essential differences between the two media'. Radio broadcasting had reached its technical limits:

> it is improbable that, in ten years' time, a Sound radio Saturday Night Theatre will be any different from the Saturday Night Theatre that was broadcast last Saturday . . . the *choice* of plays will be different. The *technique* will remain approximately the same.[42]

But television drama 'is still in its beginnings' and a drama from 1949 was unlikely to resemble one made a decade later:

> There is . . . every indication that the development of Television drama, if properly directed, will be more rapid than the development in the corresponding ten years of films, because the lessons of the film will be there for Television to have before it.[43]

Collins used film as the example because he saw television as a primarily visual medium, not a broadcasting medium with the 'added resources of vision' or amplified radio 'with pictures':

> Television production . . . is not the same as film production any more than it is the same as stage production and its relationship with Sound radio drama production is negligible and can be ignored. What is . . . essential for the most fruitful development of Television drama is the appointment of one man, the Val Gielgud of Television, working full time and without any other distractions whatsoever in this new, largely unknown, infinitely complicated and most exacting medium.[44]

Collins wanted a Television man for the job—probably Royston Morley, who had recently been promoted to Senior Drama Producer (replacing George More O'Ferrall who had left to work in cinema). Collins outlined the duties of the job:

> he must familiarise himself in the closest possible detail with studio production from the initial moment of discussion with designers to the handling of the controls at the time of the actual production. He must be so fully familiar with all the detail of caption design, scenic design, wardrobe design, make-up,

---

41 Memo, 'Integration of Sound and Television', Norman Collins, 14 Sept. 1949. BBC WAC T5/325.

42 Ibid.

43 Ibid.

44 Ibid.

lighting, telecine, television sound, studio lay-out, camera characteristics, studio characteristics and production gallery procedure, that he can alter them when he feels them to be wrong—all this in addition to the knowledge of the theatre, whether derived from stage or film, which originally qualified him for his post. Moreover, if the Head of Drama in Television is usefully and completely to fulfil his function he must work throughout in the closest association with the engineers in the design of new types of cameras and new types of lenses, the design of artificial scenic devices and the types of cranes and dollies, and the architecture of the studios that drama productions require, as well as giving his advice on the number of camera channels, the number of telecine channels, the number of caption channels, and so forth, that his productions require. Television is still so young that whoever takes over such a post must plan for the future as well as conduct operations in the present.[45]

Collins also raised the point that the new Drama Head would not be accountable to the Head of *Television* Programmes. How would the Head of Television Programmes control a Department Head who was accountable to the Corporation Management? For Collins, the plan seemed another way of absorbing television into the structure and thinking of Sound broadcasting.

The 'Val Gielgud of Television' turned out to be none other than Val Gielgud himself, who took up his post as Head of Drama (sound and vision) in January 1950. Gielgud had worked for BBC radio since the late 1920s, and became Productions Director in 1929, supervising drama and documentary output. He was perceived by BBC colleagues as responsible for the development of radio drama as a unique form in its own right, and had produced two plays for television in the pre-war years.[46] BBC management suggested in 1945 that Gielgud should join the Television Service, but this was vetoed by Maurice Gorham, who was against the appointment of 'people who had earned their positions in radio'.[47]

In his autobiography, Gielgud suggests that it was Collins himself who had wanted him as the new Drama Head, but given Collins's memo on integration it seems more likely that Haley imposed the appointment on the Television Service in a bid to offset Gielgud's

45 Ibid.

46 'Sir Cecil Graves had always considered that the growing isolation of Alexandra Palace from Broadcasting House was regrettable, and that it should not be established as permanent. I found him sympathetic to my suggestion that I should be seconded to Television, for the purpose of learning the elements of a new technique of dramatic production.' Val Gielgud, *British Radio Drama 1922–1956* (London: George Harrap, 1957), 76.

47 Gielgud, *Years in a Mirror*, 126.

threatened resignation from the BBC. Gielgud himself was initially optimistic:

> As I saw it, the case was one of starting again from scratch with two objectives in view. The first was to make a genuine Drama Department for the Television Service. The second was to produce a workable television drama policy. In my innocence I found myself running my head against a brick wall both above and below.[48]

Gielgud stayed for seventeen months before returning to Broadcasting House in June 1951, and it was an awkward period on all sides.[49] One problem was that Gielgud was now working under McGivern whom he had trained in the radio Features department; another was that McGivern had not wanted the insertion of a further level of management between him and drama producers. There was also the resentment felt by drama producers that Gielgud's twin objectives effectively invalidated the work they had already completed or, at least, implicitly suggested that it was not up to scratch. As Gielgud recollects 'I was asking them to admit that their present production standards were not as good as they ought to be. (They were not.)'[50]

His intention to form a better organized drama department had the implicit objective of removing what Gielgud would later describe as the 'rancid individualism' of drama producers:

> With no established script unit, and with no departmental control worth the name, it had been left almost entirely to each individual producer to choose the plays that he would handle according to his own tastes and whims. This obviously made balanced scheduling impossible.[51]

Gielgud also wanted to reduce the amount of drama, under the policy of 'fewer and better' plays, quality over quantity. In this respect, whatever the resentments 'from below', Gielgud might have assumed McGivern's support.

He did not get it. In a lengthy memo to McGivern, Gielgud's frustration with his immediate superior was clear. Gielgud complained that McGivern gave him little notice of scheduling changes, and that the 'embryonic state' of the Play Library and the absence of a 'reservoir of recorded plays on which to draw' meant that the rapid selection of replacement plays could not avoid the pulp 'gloom and brutality' genre (often short thrillers or murder-mysteries of the

48 Ibid. 129.

49 Barry gives a very full account of Gielgud's 17 months as drama head, from the point of view of a drama producer, *From the Palace to the Grove*, ch. 14, and 'A Head for Drama'.

50 Gielgud, *Years in a Mirror*, 132.

51 Ibid. 131.

Edgar Wallace type).[52] McGivern's capriciousness directly militated against Gielgud's desire for a planned and balanced schedule. As Gielgud told him in March 1950:

> In merely practical terms I must emphasise that alterations must not be made less than six weeks ahead if complete confusion and loss of money are to be avoided. Preliminary work has been done, designs have been discussed, casts have been booked, authors have been informed. A great deal of emphasis is laid on the importance of detailed advance planning up to almost three months ahead. If individual plays are to be put at the mercy of capricious alteration with no more than three or four weeks notice, much of this advance planning work becomes wasteful both of time and energy, and the effect on the general programme plans of the week is disastrous.[53]

Gielgud goes on to counter McGivern's accusation that the drama output has 'alienated quite substantial numbers of the public'. This is a reference to continuing complaints about 'horror plays', but Gielgud argues that the audience is typically 'unresponsive and apathetic' and that criticism and complaints arise from the few rather than the majority:

> You mention the 'extreme unsophistication' of a large proportion of our audience. This may be open to some question though it is difficult altogether to reconcile it with the present costs of television receivers. But once again, if we are to accept the lowest common denominator of viewing tastes as our yardstick of aim we may as well throw our hands in from the point of view of decent aesthetic standards.[54]

But Gielgud's aesthetic standards were really those of radio drama (although the receivers were cheaper than television). McGivern wanted more plays, at a cheaper cost, in order to keep standards high in terms of overall output across the schedules. Gielgud believed that higher quality meant fewer plays because higher quality could only be achieved through longer rehearsal times, especially longer camera rehearsals. The shortage of studio space had meant that the time available for camera rehearsals was often little more than the running time of the play itself and that was not enough:

> a play can be rehearsed *outside the studio* for three weeks or a month. *The camera rehearsals are the only ones that really count*, except for the learning of lines and the rough plotting of moves.[55]

52 Memo, Val Gielgud to Cecil McGivern, 29 March 1950, BBC WAC T5/325.

53 Ibid.

54 Ibid.

55 Gielgud, *Years in a Mirror*, 132–3.

Gielgud's desire for better quality drama production meant either waiting for more studio space, or reducing the number of drama productions. As we have seen, McGivern would no doubt have agreed with the reduction of fresh dramas, but not with the reduction of overall drama output. Gielgud also met with resistance from the drama producers themselves, and this was largely because of their perception of Gielgud's attitude to the type of 'trivial material' that television drama could produce:

> . . . Val Gielgud had agitated for longer time in the studio. He claimed that a maximum of two days was too few to prepare a play for transmission; and nobody disagreed in principle, but it was appreciated that additional time could be provided only by reducing studio productions, including the number of plays. Gielgud advocated the reduction, but it threatened a curtailment of opportunity that not everyone in his department welcomed. There was . . . an egotism in the energy that impelled us all. But the overriding factor was not as personal as this. The young service and McGivern, its programme head, needed the storytelling element of drama. The coverage of news, outside broadcasts, sport and film was far more restricted than it was to become. Val Gielgud did not conceal his dislike of the *Mrs Dale's Diary* kind of folk storytelling, and this probably made him suspect. He was alone, with little support as on other occasions, an idealist, possibly in the wrong place at the wrong time.[56]

As a result Gielgud felt he could exercise no authority. Frequently his memos to McGivern end on a personal note demanding that he is given 'a chance' to implement his restructuring:

> with diffidence for introducing a strictly personal note, I consider that I am entitled to be given a professional chance. I did not take over a 'going' concern and your drama department will not become, in the true sense of the word, a 'going' concern until it has been reorganised along the lines which I am proposing to put up to you in the next few weeks. Meanwhile it is, in my opinion, fair neither to me nor to the service not to give me a reasonably free hand in the choice of plays during the forthcoming months.[57]

Or, when told by McGivern to increase drama output:

> . . . It distresses me personally that this conflict on an aspect of what I hold to be a basic principle should arise between us, but I don't think it would be fair, either to you or to me, to conceal

56 Barry, *From the Palace to the Grove*, 167.
57 Memo, Val Gielgud to Cecil McGivern, 29 March 1950, BBC WAC T5/325.

my convictions. I think you know that I will without reserve
do my best to carry out any policy you may lay down, as long
as I am allowed to sit in this chair, but speaking strictly as your
professional drama advisor, I feel bound to say formally that in
my view, given our present circumstances and facilities, including
staff and money, you are asking for a quantitative output which
within a measurable time can only lead to a qualitative decline.[58]

Such a conflict was to be expected: Gielgud had set out his opinions of
television drama very clearly three years before. Writing in 1947, he
argued that a solid theory and aesthetics of television drama had to be
established before the form could develop in any significant way.[59] A
second article published in *BBC Quarterly* in 1951, and in many ways
a summation of his time as Head of Drama, is shot through with the
frustration about the rigidity of tradition which prevailed and complaints that drama production is not yet 'professional':

> In spite of all that has been written on the subject it has not yet
> been possible for television drama in this country to achieve what
> can be called genuine professional status. The space has not been
> available. The gear has not been available. More important than
> anything else, the *camera-rehearsal time* has not been available.
> There has been ferociously hard work; considerable ingenuity;
> great enthusiasm on the part of producers hard pressed by an
> inevitably merciless output routine. For experiment—so vital to
> the development of a new dramatic medium—there have been
> neither facilities nor time . . . what needs consideration is less the
> necessarily imperfect programme that will be seen next week,
> than the hypothetically first-rate programme that could be
> produced next year if the foundations of professional production
> were well and truly laid.[60]

Gielgud also makes it clear that he believes that the aesthetics of
television are skewed too far in favour of cinema. His central complaint is that the camera is privileged too often over the microphone.
For a 'radio man', indeed the man responsible for developing the form
and aesthetics of the radio play, it is unthinkable that the image could
have priority (contrast this with Collins's outline of the suitable can-
didate for Drama Head, above). For Gielgud the real answer to the
'question mark' about television drama can be found in the theory of
the 'illustrated broadcast':

58 Memo, Val Gielgud to Cecil McGivern, 21 July 1950, BBC WAC T5/325.
59 Val Gielgud, 'Policy and Problems of Broadcast Drama', *BBC Quarterly*, 2/1 (1947).
60 Val Gielgud, 'Drama in Television and Sound', *BBC Quarterly*, 5/4 (Winter 1950–1),
    200.

It is true that both the cinema product and the television product appear on a screen. It is true that both products are enabled to break away from the cramping conventions of the theatre. But there the truth ends—and a vast deal of rubbishy hot air begins . . . Once granted the use of cameras, the resultant ability to 'cut away' to 'dissolve' to 'superimpose' and so on, all of which certainly provides the television producer with a potential fluidity almost unimaginable in the theatre, the televised play—at the present moment—has far more in common with a mixture of stage and sound radio than with cinema . . . It is not for a professional specialist to make a case for or against such matters of policy. But I think he may be allowed to suggest that this 'isolationism' has tended to encourage one factor both disturbing and stupid. Where it has exalted the camera—drawing false analogies from the cinema—and despised or depreciated the microphone, it has thrown away valuable accumulated experience of sound in favour of thinking, largely wishful, in terms of vision.[61]

It is tempting to cite this last point as the fundamental reason why Gielgud could not succeed within the television service, and the reason why Michael Barry was appointed as Head of Drama a few weeks after Gielgud's return to radio drama. They have a radically different conception of the television image. For Gielgud, it depreciates the value of the sound element of broadcasting: '. . . Television's business is to give sight to the listener, *where sight is either essential or helpful*. It is not Television's business to radiate photographs. *Television should be an improved method of broadcasting*.'[62] For Barry the image offered all kinds of new aesthetic possibilities, not necessarily linked to cinema:

More exciting than the vitality in the shot itself was the discovery that moving pictures have a life of their own, an aesthetic unpredictability beyond the law of visual physics. I remember saying to the vision mixer, 'No, wait, wait. Don't mix. Let's see what will happen.' And we waited, watching the figures on the screen moulding and twisting until the images were rich with a character of their own.

And so my lessons in the grammar of visual storytelling continued. I studied the way to relate grouping and movement so that good picture composition would result. The prescience of editing in advance so that those compositions appeared on the screen as flowing sequences of pictures, or, when necessary, with a startling impact. But by what means and in whatever way the

61 Ibid. Gielgud makes some similar criticisms in 'Drama on the Television Screen', *Radio Times*, 12 Jan. 1951.

62 Val Gielgud, *British Radio Drama*, 82.

attention of the eye was arrested, it should be with the apparent effortlessness that distinguishes good style—in storytelling or in handwriting.[63]

This privileged the image over the sound transmission, and for Gielgud the demotion of sound reversed the proper hierarchy to something like 'pictures with the added resources of sound', and that was heresy, particularly as his own appointment had been part of a policy of integration of vision under sound.[64]

Gielgud's attempt to establish a script unit and a play library was successful, and the latter provided part of the solution to the planning and scheduling problems. Joanna Spicer, seconded from Broadcasting House as a 'trouble-shooter' rationalized the drama schedules, and designed a planning policy.[65] For the quarter January to March 1949 the number of new plays totals 19, in 1950 the drama output stood at 26 plays per quarter, with 600 scripts per quarter submitted to the Television Service by authors or adapters.[66] Spicer's solution was to plan everything: the play library would provide a list of all plays in categories: pre-war and post-war plays already adapted and ready

---

63 Barry, *From the Palace to the Grove*, 22–3.

64 Val Gielgud caused additional problems for the television drama department. His own play *Party Manners* was originally broadcast in June 1950 on the Home Service; it was transferred to television in October that year for a Sunday night performance, produced by Gielgud and Kevin Sheldon. The plot of *Party Manners* concerned the attempt by the British government to win an election by giving away the secret of the atomic bomb. As with the controversy over *Nineteen Eighty-Four*, this play tapped into Cold War anxieties of the time. The play was perceived as 'anti-Labour' by the press and politicians (Labour was in government), and Lord Simon of Wythenshawe, chairman of the BBC Board of Governors and a Labour sympathizer, banned the Thursday repeat transmission, planned for 5 October. Ironically, Gielgud had included the play in the schedules as a response to the criticism that there was too much 'gloom and brutality' in recent BBC television drama. After the play was banned there was much discussion as to who would be sacked as a result. As Gielgud says:
> Public speculation became rife as to whether the author–producer should, or would, be dismissed; whether Sir William Haley should resign; whether the BBC monopoly should be destroyed, as having proved by this instance that it was exercising its power through a censorship repugnant to the British Way of Life, to the British Tradition of Freedom of Expression. The *furore* was increased when at the height of the controversy Norman Collins resigned from the headship of the Television Service . . . (*British Radio Drama*, p. 177)

In fact Gielgud was to leave in far less spectacular circumstances, and Collins's resignation had more to do with George Barnes's appointment over him as Director of Television (in fact Collins's memos to producers on the *Party Manners* instructed them not to speak to the press, unless they used the standard reply that 'no representations from the Government were made'). The BBC were keen to demonstrate that they were not prone to state control, so much so that when similar controversy erupted around *Nineteen Eighty-Four* the BBC repeated the play in the face of considerable parliamentary criticism. It was this repeat which was telerecorded.

65 Spicer was appointed Television Programme Organizer in 1952, and Head of Programme Planning in 1955. See Leonard Miall, *Inside the BBC: British Broadcasting Characters* (London: Weidenfeld and Nicolson, 1994).

66 Memo, Joanna Spicer to Cecil McGivern and Val Gielgud, 5 Dec. 1950, BBC WAC T5/325.

for repeat production without further work on the script; commissioned scripts ready for production; proposals from drama producers submitted to the script unit for consideration and subsequently vetted by McGivern. Recently appointed[67] Director of Television, George Barnes recommended that Spicer's planning strategy be implemented immediately.[68] McGivern was unhappy with this: he still wanted the flexibility of last-minute schedule changes, but Spicer's plan became policy, although continued financial difficulties made it a difficult one to implement successfully until the mid-1950s.[69]

One of the more striking things about the late 1940s drama schedules is the tendency to produce plays of the Gothic, supernatural, or thriller genres, generically known by Television management as 'Horror Plays'. Given the proximity of the Second World War, and the involvement in that war of most of the Service staff, perhaps the high level of such material is not surprising. Charles Barr maps a similar fascination with fantasy, crime, and the macabre in the immediate post-war output of British cinema: a 'spectacular shift from the public sphere to the private sphere, with a stress on vision and fantasy'.[70] The choice of this material was also linked to the need to save money and rationalize production and planning. In 1948 McGivern suggested the serial drama as a solution: the same sets could be used on each occasion and the actors hired on long-term contracts. Mac-Dermot responds with the suggestion that dramatized ghost stories (M. R. James, E. F. Benson, and Algernon Blackwood) would provide good material:

> as far as I know this hasn't been done before, either in sound or television, and would make a good contrast to our dramatic output of drama, comedy and straightforward mystery thrillers. I believe that television could create a very effective eerie atmosphere in this way and suggest that, if you agree, the plays are placed at the end of the evening transmission only and are advertised as being unsuitable for children.[71]

67 Norman Collins resigned in autumn 1950 when Haley appointed Barnes who was a 'radio man'. See Briggs, *Sound and Vision*, 452–3.

68 Memo, Joanna Spicer to George Barnes, 'Drama Scheduling', 13 Dec. 1950. Barnes writes his response to McGivern at the foot of this memo. BBC WAC T5/325.

69 Memo, 'Drama scheduling', Cecil McGivern to George Barnes, 19 Dec. 1950. BBC WAC T5/325.

70 Charles Barr, 'Introduction', in Barr (ed.), *All Our Yesterdays* (London: British Film Institute, 1986), 16–18.

71 Memo, 'Serial plays' Robert MacDermot to Cecil McGivern, 17 Feb. 1948, BBC WAC T5/325. In fact the BBC later produced adaptations of M. R. James stories on *film*— 'Whistle and I'll Come to You' directed by Jonathan Miller in 1968; and, amongst others, an excellent adaptation of 'Lost Hearts' (1973). see Tise Vahimagi (ed.), *British Television: An Illustrated Guide* (Oxford: Oxford University Press, 1994), 196.

The interest in mystery and macabre thrillers concerned Norman Collins, as some content contravened the 'Sunday Programmes Policy' which prohibited themes 'likely to be considered blasphemous; luridly melodramatic or sadistic; sexually gross, suggestive or impudent.'[72] As the audience for television expanded, the questions about the choice of this material in terms of BBC 'suitability' were accentuated. The sense of 'intimacy' as 'getting closer' began to take on a different colour:

> It would be footling to say that we should never do any horror plays in television, but I think that, on the other hand, we have got to be careful not to overdo the terror and to recognise that what is seen on the screen in a person's home makes a very different impact from the impact made in a cinema when a stridently advertised horror film is being shown. Not only have we the initial responsibility that comes of knowing that our productions may be seen by children . . . but we must remember that there will always be large numbers of unsuspecting persons who, as in Sound radio, simply turn to their set during transmission to see what is on.[73]

The penchant for mystery-murder and 'horror' productions segues with the production in the immediate post-war years of drama with wartime themes. The claim that early television drama did not address contemporary issues is made nonsensical when one considers this selection of post-war material. The play shown on the opening day of the restored Service in June 1946, *The Silence of the Sea*, concerned the relationship between a German soldier (played by Kenneth More) and an elderly farmer and his daughter in occupied France; More returned to play an RAF officer the next week in *They Flew Through Sand*; two weeks later Jan Bussell produced *Sea Fever* set on a corvette, again during the war.[74] Michael Barry's production of Charles Terrot's *Adventure Story* in July 1946 was described by the *Radio Times* as 'the adventures of a young couple adjusting themselves to their new life after the husband's return from six years of war, in which he has reached a rank and has done work beyond the scope of civilian life he knew in 1939'.[75] Because these plays concerned

72 Memo, 'Sunday programme policy', Norman Collins to all television Heads, 5 July 1948, and 'Drama: Sunday Policy', Collins to McGivern, 14 August 1948, BBC WAC T5/325.

73 Memo, 'Horror Plays', Norman Collins to Cecil McGivern, 24 March 1949, BBC WAC T5/325.

74 For a discussion of the genesis of the production of *Silence of the Sea*, see Barry, *From the Palace to the Grove*, 46–6 and 54–6. The script of *Sea Fever*, written by Jan Bussell is included in his book *The Art of Television* (London: Faber and Faber, 1952).

75 *Radio Times*, 26 July 1946. For details on *Adventure Story* see Barry, 59–62.

themselves with contemporary or very recent events, they were usually new, and written for television. Malcolm Baker-Smith's play *The Traveller Returns* (September 1946) was billed by the *Radio Times* as a 'Television Play', and concerns a 'near-death' experience during the Blitz. In December there was a production of *The Web* written for television by Derry Nelson, a play about a RAF pilot who is blind (played, again, by Kenneth More).[76]

The emergence of a crime/thriller genre begins with a series of 15-minute dramatizations called *Telecrimes*, where a Scotland Yard inspector would introduce true crimes from the casebook.[77] The 'Scotland Yard' genre continued a month later with a production of *The Murder Rap*, described as a 'full-blooded Scotland Yard piece'.[78] In June 1947 Robert Barr, one of the originators of the 'drama-documentary' television genre, produced *Armed Robbery*, a reconstruction from a real-life Scotland Yard arrest.

Later in January 1947 came the first post-war production of *Rope*, followed in February by a production of *The Two Mrs Carrolls*, billed by the *Radio Times* as, 'A brilliant poisoning drama . . . with a setting in the South of France, concerns a husband's deliberate and cold-blooded plan to murder his unsuspecting wife by slow poisoning. He is discovered in the attempt and commits suicide' (The *Radio Times* is not reluctant to reveal plot details.)[79] Drama output by 1948 was such that one viewer felt compelled to write the following protest at television's 'lurid' output:

> As a family of viewers, may we please make a request that the plays televised may in the future take a less lurid turn? On Sunday evening *Mungo's Mansion*, billed as a comedy, turned out to be a most harrowing drama, ending in the cutting of a woman's throat. We do not object to a certain amount of drama, and realise that actors and actresses like to have 'close-ups' of registered horror, but are there no normal, happy plays left, and does no actress sometimes get sick of horror dramas and thrillers?[80]

Collins reports to McGivern a similar response:

> we must continually give attention to the production in terms of the amount of visual horror that is shown. *Dear Murderer* on

---

76 The *Radio Times* notes that, 'The theme is purely personal. Thus the play tells the story of a psychiatrist who endeavours to cure a blinded RAF pilot. The "tie-up" is that the psychiatrist is in love with the ex-pilot's sister, but she, being a very loyal sister, refuses to leave her brother while he is still blind.' More stars in a later RAF 'rehabilitation' drama, *Reunion*, written for television by John Pudney, and broadcast in November 1948.

77 *Radio Times*, 18 Oct. 1946.

78 *Radio Times*, 1 Nov. 1946.

79 *Radio Times*, 31 Jan. 1947.

80 Letter from H. M. Orchard, *Radio Times*, 30 April 1948.

Tuesday night might be taken as a case in point. Two perfectly intelligent, educated, representative women, both of whom had seen television many times before, found the episode which occurred quite early on where the victim had his head inserted in the lethal pillowcase too 'nasty' (their word) to watch. One of them, moreover, said that in her house she wouldn't have television simply because she could not ever 'feel sure' what would come on and certainly wouldn't let her two children, aged 9 and 12 respectively, go to the cinema to see the same kind of thing.

. . . we must be careful that nothing we do could provoke any action by the Lord Chamberlain to assume control of television plays by analogy with the control which he already exercises in the theatre.[81]

Collins did not object in principle to horror on television, but its visual representation, and the possibility that graphic depictions of horror might provoke censorship. Drama producers' interest in the 'horrific' continues into the 1950s, with the serials and plays such as *Quatermass* and *Nineteen Eighty-Four*.

Changes in programme content and scheduling were accompanied by technical and stylistic changes. Almost as soon as the post-war Service reopened, the engineers had solved the problems of camera transition: it was now possible to cut directly and instantly between two or more cameras, or between cameras and telecine. The *Radio Times*, always willing to signal visual developments, makes much of this in an article headed 'Cutting Speeds Up Action':

How many viewers of pre-war days have noticed an important technical advance in camera work since the service re-opened? The improvement is due to the new ability to 'cut' from one picture to the next. Up till a few weeks ago, scene transitions could be achieved only by 'mixing' from one camera to another, rather in the manner of the old magic-lantern 'dissolving views.' The effect was often quite a lovely one, but it tended to slow the action and was unsuited to quick-moving drama or variety acts.

Now the producer can snap into a new scene as fast as he can say 'cut'. Cutting not only speeds up the action but also suggests some tempting camera tricks.[82]

---

81 Memo, 'Horror Plays', Norman Collins to Cecil McGivern, 24 March 1949, BBC WAC T5/325.

82 *Radio Times*, 14 June 1946, 24. As late as 1958 the television 'cut' was still perceived by some as distinct from the film cut: 'A "cut" on film is made immediately and without jolting the eye. For technical reasons, a television cut is quite a jolt and the producer needs to use it more cleverly if the audience is not to notice it—and a good cut is one you do not see.' Michael Elliott, 'Television Drama, The Medium and The Predicament', *Encore*, 4/4 (1958), 34.

The combination of fast cutting and filmed inserts offered possibilities for stylistic development. Some drama producers took advantage of these, others did not. For example, the *Radio Times* television commentator, known as 'the Scanner', trailed Eric Fawcett's production of *Mother of Men* (8.30–10.00, Sunday 15 December 1946), based on the recent production at the Comedy Theatre, in the following way:

> Eric Fawcett, who is producing, says he is adapting the piece to what might be called 'true television'. That is, there will be far more dialogue than in a film version and more action than a stage presentation. I gather he will adopt almost a film technique and introduce a greater variety of scenes than was possible on stage.[83]

Fawcett was to further develop the 'cinematic' possibilities of television in a stylistically opposite direction to Fred O'Donovan's 'single-camera technique'. For example, Fawcett's production of *The Bunyip*, written for television by Henry C. James:

> In his new play, written specially for television, James has adopted film technique, necessitating rapid 'cuts' from one character to another at speed rarely attempted in the television studios. 'I have tried,' he says, 'to make it a fast-moving story, and I am afraid it is going to give some of the camera crews a headache. The emotional quality of the play will depend mainly on vision—rapid changes of scene—rather than on dialogue.' It is the scenery of this tense, character-revealing play that gave the producer his first worries. 'To begin with,' Fawcett told me, 'I couldn't film any of the action beforehand. There are no places that I know of where one can find countryside resembling the Australian Bush. So I must re-create the scene in the studio. I have fifty feet of Australian bush and scrub almost completed. The cameramen will have to be on their toes for the eerie night scenes . . . we hope to make as many rapid scene changes in ninety minutes as some film studios make in a month.[84]

By now the ability to cut is seen as an essential component of the television technique:

> On Friday Eric Fawcett will produce Frederick E. Weatherby's English adaptation of *I Pagliacci*, a story which, because of its intimacy, can be portrayed vividly by the multi-camera technique of television. Fawcett intends to use the film technique used so admirably and economically in many of the smaller French films such as *Carmen*. The camera will act as the eyes of the visitor to the fairground in which the action takes place, reflecting its life and movement.

83 *Radio Times,* 13 Dec. 1946, 33.

84 *Radio Times,* 5 Dec. 1947.

> Television has an advantage over other media in that four or
> five shots of the same incident can be taken in rapid succession,
> thus giving the viewer the feeling that he is actually at the
> fairground.[85]

Contrast this with the 'theatrical' Fred O'Donovan and his production of *Hindle Wakes*:

> As with other of his productions, Fred O'Donovan will use a
> technique of his own . . . Instead of cutting or 'mixing' from one
> camera to another, following the artists as they move about, he
> prefers to stick to one camera for any set scene.
>
> 'Mind you,' he says, 'this means much more work at rehearsals
> and it is more exacting in that the cast have to be grouped to suit
> the camera position, but I do contend that this method makes for
> a smoother and sometimes more polished performance.'[86]

For O'Donavan cutting vitiated the smoothness of performance
because the actors needed to be aware of when and where a camera
was covering them. The single camera technique allowed them to play
to one camera for a sustained period. Fast cutting and film inserts
were seen by others to rob the television drama of the authenticity of
'being there'. In 1950 O'Donovan continued to resist the use of film
and extensive cutting within scenes:

> *The Scarlet Pimpernel* to be produced twice this week by Fred
> O'Donovan, will be one of the most ambitious productions yet
> televised from Alexandra Palace. The cast numbers about forty
> players and the whole of the action will be contained in two
> studios. Use will not be made of film. The designer James Bould
> will aim at vista-like effects by rapid scene changes while the play
> is in progress.[87]

This implies a complex staging of the performance as an alternative to
rapid cutting and film inserts. Each drama producer had a different
'storytelling technique' that allowed variation in the way that the live,
continuous nature of television studio drama production was segmented by the variation in image scale and angle, the manipulation of
time and space. As drama producers' 'storytelling technique' became
more ambitious, some wanted to transcend the live studio time and
space by using film. As we have seen, one way to overcome the constraints of live production—the limits imposed by getting actors
from set to set, costume to costume in time for the next scene—was to
use film inserts. John Swift uses the example of Royston Morley's
1947 production of *Mourning Becomes Electra*:

85 *Radio Times*, 6 Nov. 1949.

86 *Radio Times*, 4 July 1947. *Hindle Wakes*, 8.30—10.00 p.m., Sunday 6 July 1947.

87 *Radio Times*, 5 Feb. 1950.

Early in the play it was essential to establish the illusion that everyone entering the house appeared almost at once in the hall. The planning in the studio made it necessary for the two sets— the outside porch and the hall interior—to be at opposite ends so that there was bound to be a time lag of anything up to half a minute to pass through a door. For the first time this happened it was arranged to shoot a short sequence on film showing one of the characters entering the hall and walking into the study. The film was shown immediately after the first entry into the house. It lasted about 45 seconds and gave the character reasonable time to move to the study scene ready to take over in 'live' action as soon as the film sequence had been seen.[88]

This issue of using film in live drama became hotly debated around in the late 1940s and the 1950s, as the use of film inserts was perceived by some critics and producers as a way of introducing impurities into the live aesthetics of television drama. I consider this debate in detail in the next chapter. However, there were other developments in television style that were not dependent on the use of film, in particular the development of shot scale and reframing. The two versions of *Rope* produced at this time demonstrates the development of technique.

Case Study

■ **Rope (1947 and 1950)[89]**

Rope was first broadcast on BBC radio in January 1932, and first produced for television in 1939, a 90-minute production by Dallas Bower, billed as 'A TV Horror Play'[90] It was repeated twice during the 1940s, both productions by Stephen Harrison; first in January 1947 and then again in 1950.[91]

88 Swift, *Adventure in Vision*, 160.

89 Patrick Hamilton's *Rope* was first performed on stage in 1929. It is set in a Mayfair first floor room, and the action is continuous. Two Oxford undergraduates, Wyndham Brandon and Charles Granillo, strangle a student 'friend', Ronald Kentley, with a rope and put his body in a chest. That evening they invite Kentley's father and Brandon's former teacher and mentor, Rupert Cadell, for a dinner party. Whilst eating supper from the chest that contains Ronald's body, Cadell, provoked by Brandon, argues that the concept of murder is a relative one, dictated by the hypocrisy of society, and that he would find a motiveless murder 'engrossing'. Granillo's revealing drunkenness, Brandon's interest in the perfect murder, and Ronald's absence from the party, lead Cadell to suspect something is seriously wrong. Kentley's father, concerned by his son's disappearance, leaves and the party breaks up. Cadell returns and asks to see inside the chest: horrified by its contents and ashamed by the consequences of the philosophy he outlined earlier, Cadell tells the murderers that society will judge them and that they will hang.

90 *Rope*, 9.05–10.35 p.m., Wednesday 8 March 1939; repeated 3.00–4.30 p.m., Monday 13 March. With Oliver Burt (Brandon), Basil C. Langton (Granillo), and Ernest Milton recreating his stage role as Rupert Cadell. Val Gielgud gives an account of the controversy and 'offence' that the radio production of *Rope* caused *British Radio Drama*, 165–8.

91 *Rope*, 8.40–10.00 p.m., Sunday 5 Jan. 1947; repeated 3.00–4.20 p.m. Tuesday 7 Jan. *Rope* 8.30–9.50 p.m., Sunday 8 Jan. 1950; repeated 8.30–9.50 p.m. Thursday 12 Jan. Harrison produced another version in 1953 (8 Dec.). Dirk Bogarde plays Granillo in the 1947 version, and Peter Wyngarde plays it in the 1950 version.

The stage play *Rope* is divided into three acts, but the action of the play is continuous. It is best known for the Hitchcock film version made in 1948.[92] Hitchcock had decided to experiment with the technical possibility of filming an adaptation of the play in continuous action:

> The stage drama was played out in the actual time of the story; the action is continuous from the moment the curtain goes up until it comes down again. I asked myself whether it was technically possible to film it in the same way. The only way to achieve that, I found, would be to handle the shooting in the same continuous action, with no break in the telling of a story that begins at seven-thirty and ends at nine-fifteen. And I got this crazy idea to do it in a single shot.[93]

For film this presented difficulties: the capacity of the 35mm film camera was at that time approximately ten minutes, and each shot in *Rope* lasts close to the full length of the reel of film in the camera.[94] Hitchcock aspires to replicate the continuous nature of a live theatrical production, and also restricts the space of the action to what would be the confines of a stage. In this virtually continuous film, variation in shot-scale is provided by elaborate camera choreography filmed over several weeks; for the television versions this variation is achieved by cutting between multiple cameras on the night of transmission during a live continuous performance. As the *Radio Times* explains:

> There is an exciting revival in the programmes this week— Stephen Harrison's production of Patrick Hamilton's thriller *Rope*. Harrison produced the play three years ago and showed how effectively the close-up technique of television could be applied to a presentation of this kind in which the *reaction* of the characters is as important as their action and speech. His technique will be similar this time, and we should notice some subtle camera work.[95]

As we have seen, this is not the first time that the BBC's listing magazine seeks to draw its readers' attention to stylistic aspects of

---

92 *Rope* (directed by Alfred Hitchcock for Transatlantic Films, 1948).

93 François Truffaut, *Hitchcock* (London: Secker and Warburg, 1968), 216–17.

94 Robin Wood corrects the assumption that Hitchcock's *Rope* contains a strict succession of 10-minute shots: 'Including the credit shot (roughly three minutes . . .), there are eleven shots. Only three of these are over nine minutes long; one is under five minutes; the last is under six. The remainder are all between seven and eight minutes.' Robin Wood, *Hitchcock's Films Revisited* (New York: Columbia University Press, 1989), 349.

95 *Radio Times*, 8 Jan. 1950. The billing for the earlier version also emphasizes this technique, *Radio Times*, 3 Jan. 1947.

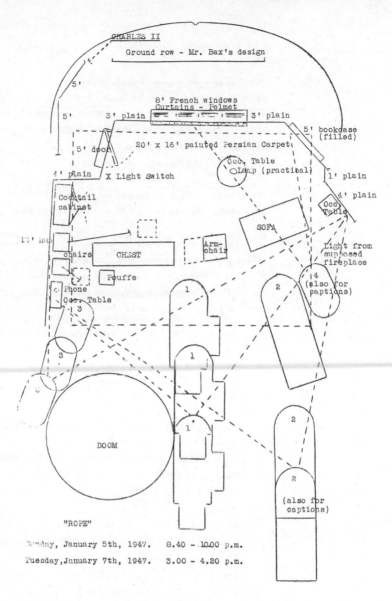

Fig. 6. Studio plan and camera positions for *Rope* (1947). *Source*: BBC Written Archives Centre, T5/439

The shapes of the camera symbols here reflect different camera mountings. Camera 1 is mounted on a crane, 2 on a smaller crane ('Baby Transatlantic'), and cameras 3 and 4 on conventional dollies. It is no longer the case, as in the late 1930s, that two cameras would have to move between shots: now all cameras could be mobile on air.

television drama production.[96] To argue that television drama's visual style is self-effacing or visually limited is to ignore the way in which it is often foregrounded in publicity and critical reception. In this case, however, the 'precise subtlety' of the camera work is difficult to establish, as no audio-visual record survives. The *Rope* programme file contains the running order for the 1939 version, a studio plan for the 1947 version (Figure 6), directions for each of the four cameras,

96 The trend continues: in 1994 the BBC's prime-time weekend medical drama, *Casualty*, started to use a video technique to make the image more 'cinematic', in a self-confessed attempt to ape the visual 'feeling' of the US 'style-saturated' cop-show,

CAMERA I (contd.)

SCRIPT Page	SHOT	DESCRIPTION

~~55~~ ~~L.S.~~ ~~Holding sideboard, door & chairs~~

34 M.S. Whole group at chest, *ending on C.U. of Brandon during first*

36 M.S. Whole group between chest and chair

37 C.U. ~~Group~~ *Rupert* in chair ~~from low angle~~, *tracking back on 4-shot in again to Rp.*

40 CS. ~~favouring~~ *from L.* BRANDON on arm of sofa, *tracking back in 2-shot.*

41 M.S. RUPERT, with two ~~xxx~~ others behind him, panning with him *L. in sideboard*

42 M.S. SIR J., BRANDON and RUPERT
43 M.S. *whole group, tracking in to lose Rupert on R.*

45 M.S. GRANILLO by door, panning with him to chair

46 2-shot, starting with GRANILLO in chair and leaving space for BRANDON to enter *on* left.

47 M.S. GRANILLO in chair, with space for BRANDON to enter behind him
"   C.S. *Rupert* ~~Chair members~~, *tracking back in 3-shot.*

48 3-shot ~~BRANDON with group in chair~~, *tracking in to C.U. Rupert in chair*

49 M.S. RUPERT in chair, with room for BRANDON to enter *to* left.

50 *CLOSE SHOT* ~~_____~~ RUPERT in chair, *tracking back to 2-shot*

51 C.S. RUPERT in chair, *tracking in to C.U. of bookshelf.*
"   M.S. RUPERT at window; he walks into C.U. by chest

53 2-shot RUPERT & BRANDON behind chest ~~tracking back in 2-shot~~

54 2-shot as before, *tracking back in M.S*

56 M.C.S. ~~Cut to~~ RUPERT & BRANDON between chest and chair

58 C.U. ~~from low angle of BRANDON~~ *Rupert* in chair, *tracking back in to full again*

Fig. 7: *Rope* (1950): script for camera 2 showing revisions. Source: BBC Written Archives Centre, T5/349.

and three camera cue-cards (these were reference notes for the cameramen detailing position and shot-order, which were placed above their viewfinders during rehearsals and transmission).[97] It is possible to match the camera directions with their positions on the studio plans, which provides a partial reconstruction of the transmission as it was planned.

However, the camera script for the 1947 version has many ink alterations. This indicates two possibilities: that Harrison extensively revised his shooting script for the 1947 production during camera rehearsal and that these sheets constitute his revisions for that transmission; or that Harrison's production three years later used the same basic sets and camera set-ups and the same basic camera script which he then extensively modified in ink (Figure 7). In the first scenario we have an interesting example of a revision in mid-production; in the second we have an equally interesting example of the way in which television drama production style had become relatively standardized (the same basic script) and yet had developed *visually* in some

NYPD Blue. The *Radio Times* reported this and that the technique had now been abandoned because, 'Viewers . . . felt distanced from the action, preferring the sharpness and immediacy of untreated video.' 15–21 Oct. 1994.

97 *Rope*, BBC WAC T5/438.

interesting ways: type of shot, use of close-ups, camera mobility. The second scenario would allow a provisional mapping of stylistic changes.

In fact the second scenario is the correct one. The script for camera 2, which was to transmit the captions, has an altered cast list: Dirk Bogarde's name is crossed out and replaced in ink by the initials 'P. W.'. As it is known that Bogarde played Granillo in the 1947 version, and Peter Wyngarde took the role in the 1950 version, these camera scripts are certainly ink revisions of the 1947 script for the 1950 production. The reconstruction of the camera shot order from the scripts available is particularly difficult, not simply because of the messy nature of the ink revision, but because each page is a camera cue card that lists shot changes for that particular camera. I have combined the scripts based on certain guiding assumptions about the nature of live production—crucially the fact that every camera change must be a change to a different camera, and that if a camera has to move or reframe on air this will be indicated in the script.

Three cameras covered the main action, and a significant stylistic change between the 1947 and 1950 version is the specification of some shots as *low* angled shots, and one as a *high* angled shot. There is also a revision of nomenclature: some shots labelled 'C.U.' (close-up) become 'C.S.' (close-shot) so that the 1950 script has a distinction between close-shot and close-up. Close-*shots* are usually mobile shots, whereas close-*ups* are either static or constitute the beginning or end of a shot.

Camera movements are also modified: the majority of revisions add movement to the shot. The 1947 script indicates that camera movement is motivated by character movement, but the 1950 revision adds movement even when the characters are static.

The apparent 'theatricality' of the script for the 1950 version of *Rope* conceals another, very different, approach to the staging of narrative space. This version contains 114 separate shots, typically alternating between medium two-shot and close-shots, giving an average shot length of around 42 seconds. This arithmetic suggests long takes, but it does not account for the variation of shot-scale afforded by a style that favoured frequent camera movement and reframing to follow actors or emphasize dialogue and reaction (hence the limited value of average shot length calculations for television analysis). Over 35 per cent of the shots in *Rope* contain some form of camera movement: tracking, panning, reframing. The movements indicated by the studio plan do not suggest any complex camera choreography, but each camera position demarcates a movement closer to the set, and to the characters. 26 of the 114 shots are in close-up, with a further dozen tracking into a close-up of a character, typic-ally at a dramatic moment of crisis (the majority of them planned for the play's climax). What would appear from the studio plans to be a highly theatrical television production is also a highly segmented one, and one which approaches the television style that was to become standard by the early 1950s. Comparing the two versions illustrates the shift to a more mobile and variously angled *mise-en-scène* between 1947 and 1950.

The changes in drama planning, organization, and production completed during this time—the script library, a more standardized drama schedule, new studios and equipment, telerecording—were to come to fruition and full use during the early 1950s. It was this period which saw the consolidation of a drama standard, and the routinization of work practices, which would only face restructuring again when the competition arrived in the form of ITV in 1955.

As drama productions developed at the end of the 1940s so that transitions between cameras and camera movement to adjust shot-scales became more common, there is a temptation to rationalize this in terms of a stylistic development towards the 'cinematic', where cinematic means editing and theatre means 'stasis'. This is not to suggest that television drama developed in autonomous isolation above and beyond film, theatre and radio. In fact television drama productions increasingly performed a stylistic dialogue with film forms and styles, and this continues into the 1950s.

4

'Lost not cosy': Expanding the Screen of Television Drama, 1951–55

Basically, Television is a by-product of the theatre . . . it requires of an author much the same discipline as does the theatre. It asks him to tell a story. And it asks him to tell it by means of credible and interesting characters, into whose mouths he has put dialogue which rings true and which conveys his meaning clearly. A Television play . . . is live, continuous, consecutive. Its only cutting-room is in the director's head . . . once the play begins, it cannot stop. That is the way of the theatre, not of the cinema. For stage plays and Television plays are living things, whereas films are in cans.

Basil Bartlett, BBC Television Drama Script Supervisor[1]

To get the ultimate out of any medium, it must be possible to define its limitations. And the limitations were indefinable. They changed almost week by week, both at the transmission and reception ends . . . Already it is becoming clear that there is no technique, but a thousand. Increasing mechanical resources should make style as individual to the story and teller of it as in any other medium . . . Television drama at its best will be almost identical with film at its best.

Nigel Kneale, Staff Writer, BBC Television Drama[2]

DEBATES ABOUT TELEVISION'S ANCESTRY and its familial relationship with other media continued in the 1950s, even where (as Kneale correctly notes) its essential characteristic was its mutability. In the late 1930s the limits and ambitions of the new medium were debated and delineated; the rapid expansion of the television service and its audience during the early 1950s and the increasing *visibility* of television for the public, press, and state, meant that a similar process of definition and redefinition began to take

---

1 Basil Bartlett, *Writing for Television* (London: George Allen & Unwin Ltd., 1955), 11–14.

2 Nigel Kneale, 'Not Quite So Intimate', *Sight and Sound*, 28/2 (Spring 1959), 86.

place. By 1955 the 'lusty, demanding infant' had to grow up fast as its television audience expanded and it faced competition in the form of the network of ITV companies.[3] Television's maturation was also exhibited in the increased ease with which film and television camera image sources were combined, in the recording of programmes, and in the further debates about stylistic technique.

The expansion of the television coverage was facilitated by the establishment of new transmitters: Sutton Coldfield (serving the Midlands) in 1949, Holme Moss (North) and Kirk o'Shotts (Scotland) in 1952. The BBC plan was to serve at least 70 per cent of the population by 1952 and 80 per cent by 1954.[4] By 1953 the number of television receivers produced exceeded the number of sound receivers, and this was also the year when television coverage of the Coronation reached an audience of 20 million.[5] The expansion of the television audience coincided with the expansion of television's production base: new studios and equipment, an increase in staff, and a longer and more varied schedule.

The BBC bought the Lime Grove Film Studios from the Rank Organization in November 1949, and began production in May 1950.[6] Lime Grove was intended as a stop-gap solution between the significant inadequacies of Alexandra Palace, and the realization that the planned purpose-built Television Centre at the White City site (announced in March 1949) would take several years before it could be operational.[7] There were five dedicated studios at Lime Grove, as well as space for dressing rooms, a dubbing theatre, film editing rooms, and scenery storage.[8] The total floor space of the studios was six times the total area of the two studios at Alexandra Palace. This increased floor space allowed larger sets and room for uniform lighting.[9] The larger studios also meant more space for camera and boom microphone mobility (also helped by running their cables

---

3 The phrase is Derek Horton's in *Television's Story and Challenge* (London: George Harrap, 1951), 13.

4 See Herbert Morrison, 'Television: the Plan and the Timetable', *Radio Times*, 9 Oct. 1949 and Noel Ashbridge, 'Television Comes to the Centre of England', *Radio Times*, 9 Nov. 1949.

5 See Asa Briggs, *The History of Broadcasting, iv. Sound and Vision* (London and Oxford: Oxford University Press, 1971), 241–2.

6 M. J. L. Pulling, 'The Lime Grove Television Studios', *BBC Quarterly*, 5/3 (autumn 1950), 173.

7 The White City site was originally the space where the Franco-British Exhibition of 1905 took place. The circular building planned to house 200 offices, 9 television studios, an expanded Film Unit, and storage and scenic construction space.

8 For details of the transition between Alexandra Palace and Lime Grove see, 'TV Premises, Studio Equipment', File 1, BBC Written Archives Centre (WAC) T17/91/1.

9 For more detail see H. O. Sampson, 'Television Lighting Technique', *Proceedings of the Institute of Electrical Engineers*, 99/3a/17 (April–May 1952), 150–8.

from the ceiling). The studios were equipped with six mobile cameras, each with a four-lens turret, a caption camera, a ten channel mixing unit (i.e. up to ten separate camera or telecine images could be mixed together simultaneously), and twelve monitors in the control room. Improved cameras, and updated camera mountings, motorized cranes, crab dollies, back-projection systems, overlay and inlay techniques were also developed during this time.[10]

By March 1953, most drama productions were transmitted from Lime Grove studio D, although there were teething problems with the move.[11] The transfer of staff, equipment, and production necessitated a rationalization of production organization and planning. The division of labour became more stratified: the main departments were now served by a variety of ancillary departments (make-up, telerecording, costume, etc.), and communication between departments and these services were codified in a range of coloured forms (previously, the Producer would simply write a memo).

For drama production, the process of 'making a play' was separated into component units which would supply the overall production: a white form was used for 'Wardrobe and Make-Up Requirements' (Actor/Character/Costume/Details/Hair and Make-Up); an orange form for 'Caption Requirements', a pink form for 'Film Sequences', and so on. The routinization of production required staff who were familiar and competent with this process. The necessity for trained staff meant that a training wing was established, and Royston Morley was put in charge of TV training in November 1951.[12] The distinction between drama 'producer' and 'director' was also established during the early 1950s, as part of a training process where the 'director is responsible for the casting, rehearsal, and transmission of the piece under the overall responsibility of the producer whose hand, probably more experienced in television practice, may be seen helping in the background'.[13] In 1951, Basil Bartlett was appointed Television Script Supervisor and the Play Library and catalogue was formally renamed the Television Script Section; at the same time the first staff writers, Nigel Kneale and Philip Mackie, were hired.

The departmentalization, subdivision, and routinization of the production process was matched by the consolidation of the drama schedule. Sunday night dramas continued to be the main drama event the week, repeated on Thursday night. Serial forms, adapted

---

10 Ian Atkins, 'Inlay, A Development in Television Technique', 14 Oct. 1952, BBC WAC T17/91/1.

11 See various minutes to TV Drama Producers' Meetings, March–Nov. 1952, TV Routine Meetings, Drama Producers' Meetings, File 1, 1948–53, BBC WAC T26/11/1.

12 See Briggs, *Sound and Vision*, 286.

13 Michael Barry, 'Producer and Director', *Radio Times*, 9 Jan. 1953.

from radio programming, provided a regular identity for certain time slots during the week, such as the Saturday serial drama. In contrast to the single drama 'event', the Saturday serial was in the form of 30-minute thrillers, detective serials, or adaptations such as *The Warden* (six parts, May 1951) and *Pride and Prejudice* (six parts, February 1952).[14] In 1951 a six-part serial, *The Inch Man*, followed 'the adventures of a house detective in a London Hotel'; C. A. Lejeune adapted six Conan Doyle stories under the rubric, 'Sherlock Holmes in . . .'[15] Lejeune subsequently adapted John Buchan's *The Three Hostages* into a six-part serial, and the first Francis Durbridge serial written for television, *The Broken Horseshoe*, was produced in March 1952.[16] The best-known examples of this Saturday night serial written for television are *The Quatermass Experiment* (July 1953) and *Dixon of Dock Green* (July 1955).

Written by BBC staff writer Nigel Kneale, *The Quatermass Experiment* was billed as 'a thriller in six parts' and demonstrates how serial production functioned as an extremely economical means for providing regular drama.[17] *Quatermass* was allocated a budget of £4,000 for all six episodes. A breakdown shows that the majority of this went on artists' fees (£2,500), with £570 allocated to design and £380 to filming (i.e. film inserts). In comparison, a Sunday night play, with one repeat, typically cost between £2,000 and £3,000. A Sunday night production would last perhaps 90 minutes, but there was only one repeat production, and props and settings would often be too specialized to use again for another production. The serial was a cheaper form of drama production: a significant factor in the development of television drama.

In July 1954 the first *filmed* serial was scheduled. Until now all the serial productions had been broadcast live, but *I Am the Law* was a US twelve-part import shot on film.[18] Billed as 'The first in a new series of American television films', it is an early example of the US cop show genre; in November, an indigenous filmed detective serial *Fabian of Scotland Yard* began ('the first in a new series of detective films based on the methods of Scotland Yard, specially produced for television'). Using made-for-television filmed material meant that programmes such as *Fabian* could be moved with relative ease from Saturday to

---

14 For a discussion of the principles of early television adaptation, see Cedric Wallis, 'What would Miss Austen have done?', *Radio Times*, 25 Jan. 1952.

15 See C. A. Lejeune, 'The Case of the Undying Detective', *Radio Times* 12 Oct. 1951. Lejeune was film critic for *The Observer*, and occasionally reviewed television.

16 See Francis Durbridge, 'My First Television Serial', *Radio Times*, 7 March 1952.

17 *The Quatermass Experiment*, 8.15–8.45 p.m. (then various times 8.00–9.00 p.m.) Saturday 18 July–22 August, 1953. The first two episodes, 'Contact Has Been Established' and 'Persons Reported Missing' survive as 35mm telerecordings.

18 *I Am The Law*, 8.55–9.25 p.m. (then various times), Saturday 10 July 1954. Twelve episodes were transmitted.

Wednesday; an episode of *I Am the Law* could be replaced or delayed without cancelling actor's bookings or having to reorganize studio time and storage space. Serial drama on film allowed a greater flexibility with schedule organization. Film material in general had a greater presence in the schedules with an increase in film shorts in the afternoon (Laurel and Hardy for example) and feature films on non-drama evenings.

Another change in the 1954–5 period is the scheduling of tele-recorded plays instead of live repeats. Live repeats of drama produc-tions did continue, but the telerecording of a live drama production and the subsequent repeat of *the telerecording* became more common. Maurice Gorham's insight in the late 1940s that telerecording could transform drama production by saving time, space, and money was only now being realized. There were problems with telerecordings: during the production of *The Quatermass Experiment*, the producer, Rudolph Cartier, had wanted to film trailers for the series, and it was suggested that this could be done during rehearsals as they were obvi-ously needed before transmission. However, Joanna Spicer warned Cartier:

> We have no agreement with Equity for repeat in recorded form of performances by Equity Artists and we are therefore precluded from telerecording any live performance by actors for subsequent use, even in the form of a trailer to another live performance by the same actors.[19]

The performances of actors were already being filmed as inserts to be telecined into the live studio action, which seemed to offer a solution. The television booking manager Holland Bennett advised Cartier:

> say that the filming of trailers is an integral part of the live transmission. Our agreement with Equity allows us to use film in this way, and as the film sessions will take place during the normal rehearsal period, no extra payment is necessary.[20]

The series was due to be telerecorded for sale to the Canadian Broadcasting Company, and afterwards Equity agreed with the BBC that a telerecording could be made, but only of the *repeat performance* (e.g. a recording of the Thursday night repeat of a Sunday play), which guaranteed actors two performances.[21] In August 1953 a single

19 Memo Joanna Spicer to Rudolph Cartier, 16 June 1953, BBC WAC T5/418.

20 Memo Holland Bennett to Rudolph Cartier, 17 June 1953, BBC WAC T5/418.

21 Although some actors found the repeats difficult: 'Speed the day, I say, when actors' union regulations will permit the telerecording of plays, especially for the "repeats". To work like a black for three weeks, give one performance, have three days off, and then do the repeat, causes something of a mental shock to the actor.' 'Peter Cushing Talks Shop', *TV Annual for 1955* (London: Odhams Press, 1955), 62. For some excellent accounts of acting in early television drama see Jim Pines (ed.), *Black and White in Colour: Black People and British Television Since 1936* (London: BFI, 1992).

play, *The Broken Jug*, was transmitted in telerecorded form, and there is no evidence that the original live performance was transmitted; it is an early example of a play being pre-recorded for later transmission.[22] As there was only one transmission of the play, it would involve no problems with Equity. Three months later, another play was broadcast in the same way, *The 23rd Mission*.[23] In April 1954 *Martin's Nest* was transmitted as a telerecording, as was a 15-minute adaptation of a Chekov short-story, *The Baby*, in July.[24] The *Radio Times* always signals a telerecording, without any explanation of why the original live performance was not transmitted. There are two reasons: the practical convenience of recording, so that actors and staff were not rigidly confined to transmission time and the telerecording could be stored and used if necessary at a point when there was a shortfall in drama output for the week. In 1955 there was the first use of telerecording to repeat the original live transmission. A new policy had been agreed with the talent unions, now also in negotiation with the new ITV companies. At first, there was a long gap between original transmission and recorded repeat. In April a 60-minute play, *Noah Gives Thanks*, was broadcast live on Tuesday evening and telerecorded; the telerecording was transmitted a month later.[25] Rudolph Cartier's production of *Midsummer Fire*, also broadcast and telerecorded in April, was repeated in mid-May.[26] This was a main Sunday night play which followed the Thursday night repeat pattern, albeit a Thursday three weeks later.[27]

The four-week gap was a condition made by Equity for the recorded repeat transmission, with repeat fees equalling 100 per cent of the performance fee if the repeats took place within the first month; 75 per cent of the combined fees for performance and rehearsal for repeats that take place within the first year. Repeats could only take place *within* that year: causing problems with the later repeat of prestige series.[28] For the BBC it was also a way to avoid the 'loss' of a night's viewing for the audience by the *immediate* repeat of

---

22 *The Broken Jug*, 9.00–10.25 p.m., Monday 18 Aug. 1953.

23 *The 23rd Mission*, Wednesday, 11 Nov. 1953.

24 *Martin's Nest*, 9.15–10.45 p.m., Tuesday 27 April 1954. *The Baby*, 8.35–8.50 p.m. Wednesday 7 July 1954.

25 *Noah Gives Thanks*, 9.30–10.30 p.m., Tuesday 5 April 1955; telerecorded repeat, 9.30–10.30 p.m., Thursday 5 May 1955.

26 *Midsummer Fire*, 8.45–10.15 p.m. Sunday 17 April 1955; telerecorded repeat 9.05–10.35 p.m. Thursday 12 May 1955.

27 Other examples: *The River Line*, 8.50–10.20 p.m. Sunday 8 May; telerecorded repeat 9.30–11.00 p.m. Thursday 9 June 1955; *Alibi Children*, 5.00–6.05 p.m. Sunday 15 May; telerecorded repeat 5.00–5.50 p.m. Thursday 9 June 1955.

28 This agreement continued until the 1960s. See 'The Age of Kings' programme file, BBC WAC T5/610/1.

the Sunday play on the following Thursday. As television audiences increased, and the prospect of competition loomed, the possibility of alienating the audience by repeating plays was treated with considerably more gravity than it was in the late 1940s.

Throughout the summer of 1955, all Thursday night plays were telerecorded repeats of live transmissions from a month before. The autumn schedule changed significantly as a direct result of the new ITV companies beginning transmission in September. For the first time since McGivern's reorganization in the late 1940s, Sunday night plays were not repeated on Thursday: instead, each of these evenings was devoted to a new drama production, and these were rarely repeated. In an era of competition, the BBC drama department was wary of the accusation of repetition and homogeneity, particularly since it was clear that ITV drama departments had no intention of scheduling repeat showings of their dramas in the same week, if at all.

Repeats now had a different function. Before, they had been convenient material used to double the life of a costly production, and to relieve pressure on the need to fill evening and afternoon schedules. In 1955, the use of telerecordings and serial production allowed a new flexibility by which the BBC could respond to the attack of ITV drama output.

The rate of serial repeats increased for different reasons. Attacking the programming weakness of early ITV schedules, the BBC commissioned *Quatermass II* in 1955, a sequel to the popular 1953 serial *The Quatermass Experiment*. The first live transmission was scheduled for (what could now be called) 'prime-time' Saturday night; it was telerecorded and repeated on the following Monday evening, and the pattern continued for all six episodes.[29] Until this point, scheduling of Saturday night serials had been variable, with episodes of the same serial shown perhaps half an hour later or earlier from one week to the next. Now that the BBC schedule was in competition with ITV this inconsistent approach to transmission times was inappropriate: *Quatermass II* was always shown and repeated at the same times.[30]

The increase in seriality in television programming was enabled by telerecording and the filmed series, but also impelled by the necessity to differentiate the BBC product from ITV programming. This meant that the schedules started to be organized around precise and consistent patterns that viewers could become familiar with. Establishing familiarity in the repetition of patterns of programming

29 *Quatermass II*, 8.30–9.00 p.m. Saturdays 22 Oct.–26 Nov. 1955; telerecorded repeats, 10.15–10.45 p.m. Mondays.

30 The pattern of Saturday night serial and Monday repeat was established by the serial *As I Was Saying* ('six portraits in crime.'), although the Saturday transmission times were variable: 8.15–8.45 p.m. (various) Saturdays 10 Sept.–15 Oct.; repeated Mondays 10.15–10.45 p.m. (part five repeated on Tuesday and part six not repeated).

was an aspect of television's intimate address, as well as an exercise in product differentiation.[31] Familiarity through repetition was also an internal feature of the series or serial, as Martin McLoone argues:

> The intimacy results from the context of viewing—the home, most commonly imagined at the family home. But intimacy also comes from the continuity of the television series or serial, the recurring characters, locales and situations that become part of the habituated viewer's domestic experience.[32]

A new sense of intimacy as a familiar pattern—external, in the order and timing of programmes, internal in the weekly repetition of situations and characters—was strengthened.

However, while television remained primarily live, the potential for drama productions to transcend those patterns and repetitions through improvisation or accident remained. Improvisation by the drama producer at the micro-level of reframing and cutting in response to the performance was always a possibility. A producer might digress from the planned order of shots in the camera script, perhaps because an unanticipated development in the intensity of a particular performance required that the view remained *this angle* and *this close* rather than cutting or tracking to another view as planned.[33] The coverage of unplanned micro-events such as this—and less positive things such as an actor forgetting his lines—were anticipated as part of the danger of live production. The function of the producer, in his own style, was to communicate the sense of the performance as it developed live in the studio, and this determined the style of presentation, as John Caughie argues:

> For early television . . . the artistic values were those of the theatrical event or studio performance, and the values of form and style were the functional values of relay: how well, or with how much immediacy and liveness, the technology and the technique communicated the event.[34]

---

31 Seriality is a fundamental aspect of modern broadcasting: 'For output to have the regular, familiar routine character that it has, seriality is crucial throughout the range of output. It creates that difference-in-sameness which is the hallmark of radio, television and newspaper production.' Paddy Scannell, *Radio, Television and Modern* (Oxford: Blackwell, 1996), 10.

32 Martin McLoone, 'Boxed In?: The Aesthetics of Film and Television', in John Hill and Martin McLoone (eds.), *Big Picture, Small Screen: The Relations between Film and Television* (Luton: John Libbey Media, 1997), 89.

33 This means that the reconstruction of drama in a historical study will always be a provisional account of what was planned to be but might have been better—or worse on the night.

34 John Caughie, 'Before the Golden Age', in J. Corner (ed.), *Popular Television in Britain* (London: British Film Institute, 1991), 40.

Television critics and producers considered the drama event as not simply relayed by the technology but created by it. Live drama perform-ance and the mediation of it by television were not separate events in the way that a game of football and its coverage on television are separate. If the live performance on the night retained a sense of danger, and the possibility of improvisation, this was precisely in recognition that things may not go to the rigorously rehearsed plan. As indicated in the previous chapters this meant that television was not seen as a passive agency in the production of drama—the desire by programme-makers to flaunt stylistic innovation and experiment with novel sound–image combinations very often transcended the-atrical or literary values. The development of television drama is not a story of the steady emancipation from theatrical values toward the cinematic, but one where producers were able to choose from a range of stylistic features, some of them associated with theatre, some with film styles, and some with the narrative forms of literature, such as the serial or novelistic.[35] Instead, it is possible to identify two tendencies in the production of early television drama in Britain by the 1950s: the intimate and the expansive.

The meanings of intimacy—closeness, penetration and familiarity— continued to be applied by critics and producers to television drama production in the 1950s. The nearness between the television appar-atus and the actor, for example, was seen to establish and foster a new performance technique:

> actors had to cope with three cameras. They needed to be aware of which camera was taking the picture, which might well be taking the close-up, be in exactly the right prearranged position to deliver a particular line as well as delivering it in a natural but, for them as stage performers, wholly unnatural way. Here was a whole new technique of acting—a technique different from stage, different from film, different from radio, which first had to be evolved and then learnt.[36]

Acting on television meant that actors had to perform in spaces that were being imaged by multiple cameras. They needed to be aware of when and where aspects of their performance were being covered: is my face in close-up now? Where do I turn next? Performers new to Alexandra Palace recalled the way that rehearsals meant positioning

---

35 Ben Brewster and Lea Jacobs make a similar point in regard to early cinema. *Theatre to Cinema: Stage Pictorialism and Early Feature Film* (Oxford: Oxford University Press, 1997), 212–16.

36 Bruce Norman, *Here's Looking At You: The Story of British Television, 1908–1939* (London: Royal Television Society/BBC, 1984), 158–9.

the actors in the right place at the right time. Knowing when the camera was on you (and on which part of you) was a crucial part of a successful performance. Although the actor needed to be aware of which camera was shooting what and where, this did not interfere with the advantage of *continuous* performance that live television drama offered. In 1939 Grace Wyndham Goldie reported an interview with Sybil Thorndike, who had recently made her first television appearance in a play called *Sun Up*:

> We saw her almost continually in close-up and her face became a window through which she let us see into Widow Cagle's mind ... After the performance I talked to her about it. She said, 'Oh but television's splendid for actors. It's far better than films or broadcasting. For an actor a film's like a mosaic, all separate pieces that you have to try to hold together in your mind. But acting for television or the stage is like painting a picture.'
>
> [GWG:] 'But don't you have to alter your methods for television? for the close-ups, for instance?'
>
> 'Well, I do decrease the size. It's like the kind of acting you do in your own sitting room when you're working on a part, and that's always the nicest kind. You think and breathe things and they come over.'
>
> ... Television is going to give us an entirely new kind of acting. Different from stage acting because the nearness of the camera makes it more intimate. But even more different from film acting because the acting is continuous and the emotional pattern of the character is decided by the actor as he acts and not by the director on the floor or by the cutter in the cutting room.[37]

Being 'let into' Widow Cagle's mind is not the same as thinking and feeling like Widow Cagle: instead of cinematic identification (seduction) here, this account indicates something more like close—intimate—observation. It suggests the intimacy of 'nearness' to Thorndike's performance, but one that is always observational so that, even when inside the mind of the character, there is separation of 'the window'. It is as if Thorndike does the work of identification for us in her 'sitting room', deciding on the 'emotional pattern', and then showing it to the attentive, monitoring television cameras.

Karen Lury has described the 'theatrical' form of television acting that is 'on display' *as acting*, and where the pleasures for the viewer lies in the fact that we can appreciate the actors acting.[38] Lury is talking

---

37 Grace Wyndham Goldie, 'Television: A New Acting Technique?', *The Listener*, 1 June 1939.

38 See Karen Lury, 'Television Performance: Being, Acting and "Corpsing" ', *New Formations*, 26 (1995–6), 123. See also John Adams, 'Screen Play: Elements of a Performance Aesthetic in Television Drama', in Jeremy Ridgman, *Boxed Sets: Television Representations of the Theatre* (Luton: The Arts Council of England/John Libbey Media/University of Luton, 1998).

about contemporary television drama, but we have already seen the explicit showcasing of actors in pre-war plays, where they were introduced in character at the beginning of the play (*Clive of India*).

The close-up observation of the television camera also meant that it revealed weak performances. As W. E. Williams, television reviewer for the *New Statesman* put it in 1949:

> I get the impression from many recent productions that
> Television may help to arrest the decadence of acting in this
> country. The camera is ruthless in its exposure of those facial
> forgeries of emotion which get by in the auditorium; the
> proximity of the actor to his audience imposes upon him a severe
> discipline of integrity in all he does with a smile or an eyebrow.[39]

The nearness of the television camera militates against the long-distance laziness in the theatre that might permit 'forgeries of emotion', and meant the necessity for total control of the micro-gestures of performance (moving eyebrows, for example). This new acting was concentrated on the face, a distillation and concentration of the expansive, projective gestures required by the stage.

But what comes first: the acting style or the camera style? The 'close-up' could be a part of the acting technique as well as a technical instruction to the cameraman:

> The value of the close-up is immeasurable. The actor, emotionally
> and mentally, can sweep his scene along to a grand climax without
> any interruption . . . Anyone who has seen a really well-lit close-
> up in the television receiver will agree that it has a beauty of its
> own . . . There is a peculiar intimacy that belongs to television
> alone.[40]

Who is doing the 'close-up' work here? Both the actor (without interruption) and the (well-lit) production process. W. E. Williams also uses 'close-up' as both a technique and an acting style:

> Television singles out . . . capacities in the actor, notably his
> powers of concentrated expression and, above all, of close-up
> revelation. Many actors of the stage who are effective at long range
> on the stage do not succeed in the point-blank dimensions of the
> miniature screen. The test which television imposes upon the
> actor is dictated by the narrow field of action that the cameras can
> command—a mere fraction of the wide open spaces on which a
> play can be deployed in the theatre. The image transmitted to our

39 W. E. Williams, 'Television Notes', *New Statesman*, 27 Aug. 1949. The London Academy of Music and Dramatic Art offered the first course in television acting in the early 1950s. See G. H. Garrett, 'Acting Ambition—Lime Grove', *TV Mirror* 2/9 (Feb. 1954).

40 George More O'Ferrall, 'The Televising of Drama', *Radio Times*, 19 March 1937.

little screen allows no elbow-room for opulent gesticulation or brisk sallies of action; indeed, most strenuous bodily activity is a wasted effort in a medium that thrives best on a minimum mobility. Economy, reticence, intimacy are the qualities the actor must seek to apply, and these, mainly, through his fluent command of facial expressions.

These considerations were brilliantly demonstrated a week or two ago by Roger Livesey and Ursula Jeans in a new play which revealed a rare fidelity to the basic principles of television. . . . The dialogue was given the subordinate role of disclosing what was at issue between husband and wife, but the motives and emotions involved were entrusted for interpretation to the powers of facial expression which Ursula Jeans and Roger Livesey so sensitively command. As a sound broadcast *The Canvas Rainbow* would have sounded banal, for its language was thin and unevocative. But by virtue of delicate, intimate, visual acting, it scored finely on the screen. It was true television.[41]

In this interpretation television's virtues lie in the limitations of its 'narrow field of action' and its status as 'a medium that thrives best on minimum mobility.' Television's agency is not its ability to visualize 'motives and emotions', but to *observe* or *monitor* closely the interpretation of 'motives and emotions' through the 'powers of facial expression which Ursula Jeans and Roger Livesey so sensitively command'. For Williams, television plays to its best advantage when it is gently observing the small scale, delicate, and sensitive revelation of feeling by the actors.

Michael Barry, the Head of BBC Television Drama in the 1950s, also interprets television's limitations as virtues, or 'challenges' as he calls them. Barry compares television to a microscope in order to demonstrate that television's observational powers are appropriately and objectively directed at the level of the micro-gesture and expression:

Let us consider the acting first. As the cameras move in to the 'actor's shots' the volume of expression is emphasised, and the result upon the screen becomes a harsh caricature of reality. The actor and the producer who are prepared to accept the small screen as a challenge instead of a limitation can turn this fault to an advantage and explore an exciting new field. As the microscope reveals a world in which everything is still as large as its own life, but subtler in perception to the intruder from outside, so the television camera closes in beyond the physical projection of the actor upon the stage until the major movements of arms, legs, and body are of no account. The camera is concerned with the human

41 W. E. Williams, 'Television Notes', *New Statesman*, 22 Oct. 1949.

face and the microcosm of thought and feeling that can be expressed by the eye and mouth.[42]

Seen in this way, the television 'microscope' was an instrument that, when properly controlled, revealed the hidden small scale life of the dramatic performance, concentrated in the face of the performer. Such a close observation of performance detail required a responsive production technique that privileged the close-up style. The responsive production technique meant that the producer functioned as a 'stand-in' live audience, mediating performance through his creative and responsive consciousness, and choice of camera style. Live drama production had to be sensitive to—be intimate with—the rhythm and tempo of the performance itself. This meant an intimate response to an intimate style. George More O'Ferrall in conversation with R. K. Neilson Baxter, argued television production allowed him to control the urgency of the creative moment:

NB: . . . Why do you prefer producing television plays to producing plays in the theatre or directing films?

GMOF: Because I have a more direct and immediate control of the medium than I have on the first night of a play. . . . you know you are enabling other people to be creative. Now this is like the theatre, and even more exciting because for the first time you see the actor in close-up, you see him thinking. I sometimes say to actors: 'I don't want to hear what you say: I want to see what you think.'

NB: Well that brings you slap up against the direct comparison. The cinema does that too.

GMOF: No, no, no. Not with the same continuity or urgency. Fundamentally it is quite, quite, different.[43]

In some anecdotal accounts the excitement of producing live drama sometimes seems to overwhelm any consideration of broadcast product, and here too O'Ferrall seems to rue the fact that his own 'performance of production' is not visualized:

It's only by feeling the scene with the actors that the producer can get the correct rhythm into the movements of the cameras. Ideally, there is one split second which is the right time to cut or 'mix' . . . It is rather like conducting an orchestra. In fact, the producer gives a performance, too. It's unseen.[44]

---

42 Michael Barry, 'Problems of a Producer', *BBC Quarterly*, 3/3 (Autumn 1951), 168.

43 George More O'Ferrall, Mary Adams, Michael Gough, R. K. Neilson Baxter, Roger Manvell, 'Television's Challenge to the Cinema', in *The Cinema 1950* (Penguin Books, 1950), 173–4.

44 Quoted in John Swift, 'Who Would be a Producer!', *Radio Times*, 14 Jan. 1947.

For O'Ferrall and other producers and critics, live studio television was a monitor that allowed the producer to be sensitive to the rhythms of a live performance in a way that no other media form could.

This responsive production style was combined with valorization of the close-up as the appropriate stylistic choice for dramatic television. If television drama was based on close observation, and a close-up acting style, then the television camera's close-up seemed the natural stylistic choice of good drama producers. This fetishization of the close-up style in television drama was based on the assumption that the nearness to the actor's face was analogous to nearness to thought. While this is understandable as a recognition of the universal potency of the human face as a communicative and expressive agency, it says little about the artistic worth of a close-up image of it in a television drama. Critical valorization of 'close-up technique' was an attempt to promote a particular camera style that was appropriate to television. The television close-up for television critics meant observation and analysis of the actor's acting face,[45] and was motivated by a sense that the television camera could 'see better' into the performance:

> Graham Greene's *The Living Room* is another play in which,
> by means of close-ups, the television cameras were able to
> reveal more than one saw in the play when it was performed
> in the theatre. Because it is a play of thought and argument it is
> particularly well suited to television. In the close-ups the cameras
> seem to penetrate into the very minds of the characters; so much
> so that one had the feeling that what they were photographing
> was not the faces of the characters but their innermost thoughts.[46]

Perhaps it is because the close-up visualises a mediation of distance, and also tends to reveal surface textures that may be obscure in normal vision, that it is called upon to perform a wide range of symbolic functions (revealing thoughts, unmasking insincerity, etc.). Film theorists also invoked the sense of the close-up's mystical abilities, regarding it as the image that, 'produces a psychic distance specific to the cinema'. Jean Epstein in the 1920s said that the close-up was the 'soul of cinema', transforming the spectator's sense of distance and 'leading the spectator to extreme psychic proximity or

---

45 As Noël Carroll has noted, 'The metaphor in "let's have a closer look" is not literally univocal with the spatial conception of "close" in "close-up".' Noël Carroll, *A Philosophy of Mass Art* (Oxford: Oxford University Press, 1998), 135.

46 Norman Marshall, 'Are Stage Plays Suitable for Television?', *World Theatre*, 9/4 (1960), 307. It is useful to compare the sense of 'interrogation' here to the literal interrogation that Andy Medhurst describes in the *Face to Face* interview with Gilbert Harding: 'Every Wart and Pustule: Gilbert Harding and Television Stardom', in John Corner (ed.), *Popular Television in Britain: Studies in Cultural History* (London: BFI, 1992).

intimacy'.[47] Of course, the television close-up is usually smaller in terms of absolute image size than the film close-up, even to the extent that the image size of a face might be congruent with its actual dimensions. It is probably the case that the proximity of the television close-up in a domestic space encouraged a sense of possession and control over it on the part of the audience. However, given that members of the television audience already owned and controlled their television sets, any feelings of possession correctly expressed their relationship with *all* television images whatever their scale on the screen.

These 'intimate' aspects of television drama—close-up acting, its interpretation and observation by the producer, and the close-up as the primary style of visualization—were really expressions of the limited critical thinking about television, rather than the actual limits of the medium. The problem with these critical accounts was that they took a particular set of stylistic and thematic choices in television drama as indicative of the limits of aesthetic and stylistic ambition. They also tied the essence of the medium to a static conception derived from its technology: television had a 'small' screen so, naturally, this demanded a 'close-up' style. What really makes these characterizations of television problematic is that they contained some element of truth. Michael Barry's use of the 'microscope' as analogous to the scrutiny of some television programmes is accurate to the extent that television is at its best when it is a medium that monitors, that observes and visualises information.[48] There might well be aesthetic value in the way that it does this, but the value cannot be derived from the technology of the medium itself.

This thinking about television is similar to the critical theorizing about cinema that was current with critics like Rudolph Arnheim, Paul Rotha, and Ernest Lindgren.[49] These writers evaluate film according to the limitations of its material and technological base: the photographic image, the ability to edit celluloid. As V. F. Perkins points out:

> The idea that form and style are made possible by the observance
> of limitations is common to most theories of art. But theory
> must distinguish a discipline freely accepted by the artist from

---

47 Jacques Aumont, *The Image* (London: British Film Institute, 1997), 105–6. See also Béla Bálazs, 'The Close Up, from *Theory of the Film*', in Gerald Mast, Marshall Cohen, and Leo Braudy (eds.), *Film Theory and Criticism*, 4th edn. (Oxford: Oxford University Press, 1992), 261.

48 See Stanley Cavell, 'The Fact of Television', in *Themes Out of School* (Chicago: University of Chicago Press, 1984).

49 e.g. Rudolph Arnheim, *Film as Art* (London: Faber & Faber, 1958), Paul Rotha, *The Film Till Now* (London: Vision Press, 1949), Ernest Lindgren, *The Art of the Film: An Introduction to Film Appreciation* (London: George Allen & Unwin, 1948).

inhibitions dictated by external forces. Restraints imposed on the filmmaker by mechanical contingencies are not helpfully defined as 'the natural limitations of his medium', even when those restraints are most artfully exploited.

. . . I do not believe the film (or any other medium) has an essence which we can usefully invoke to justify our criteria. We do not deduce the standards relevant to Rembrandt from the essence of paint . . .[50]

The critical assumptions about television drama production and criticism in the 1930s and 1940s were similar, but at that time drama production was still seen as exploratory, drawing upon a range of styles that meant that the uncertainty of 'somewhere between them all' was also a permission to draw upon a range of stylistic and thematic choices from radio, theatre, film and literature. By the 1950s critical thinking set around the proscriptive formulation of the 'intimate screen' threatened to close down stylistic experiment and thematic range in television drama.

Fortunately, the technological 'limits' of television were not fixed, and were already being transcended. For example the standard 9-inch television screens were gradually being upgraded to 15-inch screens, which provoked Cecil McGivern to argue that the demand for a television style based on the close-up resulted from the temporary small size of the television screen itself:

Very recently a well-known critic produced the remark that good television meant close-up and begged television producers to accept this truth and act upon it. Television producers have been acting on this since television began in 1936 . . . it is vital to see that this statement must be qualified. Good television *with screens as they are today* means close-up. Television of the future, I sincerely hope, will not need to accept this limiting law.[51]

McGivern also suggested that the necessity to get the actors close to the camera in order for them to be seen at all eliminates aspects of the script which cannot be served by this close-up style:

he [the television producer] manoeuvres his cast, he steers his cameras, he twists the action and arranges his groupings, he gets up to all kinds of dodges and wheezes in order to get his actors into close-up, so that their heads and shoulders fill the screen and they are, at this size, intelligible and satisfying. Unfortunately . . . he eliminates passages from the script which prevents his doing

---

[50] V. F. Perkins, *Film as Film: Understanding and Judging Movies* (Harmondsworth: Penguin, 1972), 54.

[51] Cecil McGivern, 'The Big Problem', *BBC Quarterly* 5/3 (Autumn 1950), 146.

this . . . If the television producer knew he was producing for 20-inch screens, his work would be easier . . . And when that happens, there will be no more nonsense about good television being close-up. Already a full close-up on a 15-inch screen can be as ugly as a full close-up on the cinema screen. And a play shot mainly in close-up and seen on a 15-inch screen would be ludicrous. Television today is not television but small-screen television, a very different matter.[52]

The characteristics of the medium itself were extrapolated by critics like Manvell and Williams from what was a *trend* in post-war television drama production, the small-scale interior drama. But these critics did not represent the totality of thinking about television drama. In 1949, the resident *Radio Times* television drama critic, Lionel Hale, recognized that the limitations of the 'interior drama' were really limitations connected with British stage writing that television often relied upon. For Hale, television had the ability to transcend interior spaces:

> What people are some ninety per cent of plays about? The upper-middle class. And what is the scene of ninety per cent of plays? Why, the drawing room or that curious habitation, the 'lounge hall'. Television seems to be doing its best to get away from this convention. It was excellent to be taken in *The Director* to the street of an Irish village and the back rooms of a pub. New writers for television may seize every chance of showing us scenes unfamiliar to a theatre—a corner of a street market, the jetty of a seaport, the bell tower of a church.[53]

The appetite for a television drama that would exploit its visual mobility and transcend the drawing room was evident at the BBC in early 1950s, but it was to meet critical and managerial resistance.

For many critics in the 1950s, the greatest mistake that television drama could make was to imitate film style. In fact, 'film style' was really a code-phrase for flashy and exhibitionist television, one that drew attention to its visuality. Roger Manvell, for example, argued that the demands of the television drama performance overwhelmed any personal style of the drama producer, and televisuality was subordinate to performance:

---

52 Ibid. 147.

53 Lionel Hale, 'Away with the Drawing-Room', *Radio Times*, 13 Nov. 1949. In 1962 Hugh Greene, the BBC's Director-General similarly argued that 'One must get away from the middle-class "Who's for tennis" type of drawing-room drama to show the problems of poverty, lack of housing, what have you.' Cited in Glen Creeber, *Dennis Potter Between Two Worlds: A Critical Reassessment* (Houndmills: Macmillan, 1998), 40.

The director of a television play works largely in terms of small groups of actors; he uses group shots and close-ups, cutting from camera to camera according to a carefully rehearsed series of 'set-ups' for which the actors have been prepared in rehearsal. As far as the actor is concerned, the television 'live' production provides an ideal medium. He has all the advantages of the theatre in being able to go straight through the play as a single creative whole, and all the advantages of the cinema in being able to interpret his character intimately through close-up. The director is therefore very much more the servant of the actor in the television 'live' production than he is in the cinema-film. Although his personal style may emerge in the way he plans his production and directs his actors, in the end he will depend almost wholly on them to sustain the atmosphere of the final performance.[54]

'All the advantages' of theatre and cinema therefore serve to restrain any personal visual stylistic contribution. Indeed, for Manvell television style is mostly irrelevant:

On the small screen tempo must be reduced and dialogue comes to the fore in the place of photographed action. Shots which would seem intolerably long and dull on the large screen are acceptable without any strain on the small screen. The late Fred O'Donovan became highly skilled in handling complete acts of stage plays with a single camera, amounting to twenty minute or even half-hour 'takes'. Alfred Hitchcock's experiments with ten-minute 'takes' in his film version of the play *Rope* seemed in contrast tedious and unimaginative in the cinema, largely because they involved the rejection of editing, which is the main principle behind film-making for the cinema. In a television 'live' production the rate of 'cutting' may well average about one-fifth or one sixth that of the cinema film.[55]

For Manvell, then, the style of Fred O'Donovan (who died in 1951) was most appropriate for intimate television drama: 'On reflection, I think the one-camera technique suits best a play where the pace is slow of the tension very deliberately built up, or where an insistent use of close-up is dramatically desirable.'[56] Film-making requires editing, and the visibility of editing (if it is not to be 'tedious'!); for television continuity and observation are appropriate visual strategies.

But what if television drama wished to get outside the interiors, to move around in space? Live studio spaces were relatively small: only

---

54 Roger Manvell, *The Film and the Public* (Harmondsworth: Penguin, 1955), 279.

55 Ibid. 279.

56 Roger Manvell, *New Statesman*, 4 Aug. 1951.

the film insert, telecined into the live action could provide the large contrast in scale between interiors and exteriors. However, film inserts interfered with television's 'intimacy' in two ways, temporally and spatially. They vitiated the live co-temporality between performer, audience and producer, and expanded the production beyond the smaller spaces of the studio:

> having to use film at all is a confession of failure. . . . Television with its small screen and intimate presentation does not lend itself—and I question whether it ever will—to the same vastness of approach that the film can achieve. You could not put, say, *The Covered Wagon* on television because those long wonderful shots of the wagons winding across the plain just wouldn't mean a thing . . .
> . . . You have to come back every time to the benefits and limitations of intimate presentation, the small canvas, the limited field.[57]

Another, more technical, complaint about the use of film inserts was that they rarely matched the lighting and tempo of the studio scenes. The visibility of different source textures was seen as 'unprofessional'.

Technically, the exact matching of telecine film with studio performance should not have presented any problems. Improvements made during the late 1940s and early 1950s to the variable-speed, continuous motion telecine projector allowed great flexibility for producers.[58] As we have seen, film inserts in live studio drama had three uses:

1. When looped, the film could supply 'effects' footage: rain, fog, fire. The film source from the telecine channel was then superimposed over one or more camera channels.
2. Specially filmed for location shots or other scenes which it was impractical to set up in the studio: battle scenes, outside scenery or as establishing shots, or to indicate the transition between locations/settings.
3. To break up studio transmission allowing space and time for scenery/make-up/lighting/set/costume changes.

By the early 1950s film inserts, interior and exterior, were *specially filmed* by the BBC Film Unit, using actors and settings from the play. Although the join between television and film was sometimes

---

57 O'Ferrall *et al*.'Television's Challenge to the Cinema', 183.

58 See D. C. Birkenshaw, 'Television Programme Origination: The Engineering Technique', *Proceedings of the Institute of Electrical Engineers*, 99/3a/17 (April–May 1952).

visible,[59] the film was seen by many, not as a confession of failure, but as a way to extend television's visual range: 'Television can not only do everything that film can do, but can do it better by introducing film sequences to improve a "live" performance in the studio.'[60] Others suggested inserts introduced impurities into the relationship between performance and audience:

> There is a mongrel-element in television drama. In order to economise in scene shifting, convenient passages of production are sometimes filmed beforehand and subsequently worked-in to the studio-performance. Almost invariably the differences between these prefabricated sections and the main body of the play are distressingly plain to the viewer—in pace, perspective, lighting, and even in the actor's make-up.[61]

The difficulties in matching the style, tempo and technique of live multi-camera studio production with the single camera pre-recorded film insert—especially when pre-filming interior scenes—were a regular cause for concern at the drama producer's monthly meetings. The Film Department supplied equipment and stock to drama producers who had little experience of film-making.[62] But drama producers shooting film inserts were not provided with continuity staff, and film editors rarely liaised with the producers who shot the film. Producers agreed to shoot their film to match the studio style 'rather than completely film-wise'.[63] According to Basil Bartlett, the limit on film inserts for a play was around six minutes to 'open it up and give it spaciousness'.[64]

Furthermore, using film signalled a creative ambition that some critics felt was inappropriate for television drama. W. E. Williams argued that television should learn its place, know its limitations and stick to them:

---

59 See Shaun Sutton, *The Largest Theatre in the World: Thirty Years of Television Drama* (London: BBC, 1982), 88–9. This visible difference was noticeable in the image texture, but not *necessarily* distracting: the frequent use of the film insert in, for example, *Whatever Happened to the Likely Lads?* (BBC, 1973–4) is pleasantly visible.

60 Derek Horton, *Television's Story and Challenge* (London: George Harrap, 1951), 92.

61 W. E. Williams, 'Television Notes', *New Statesman*, 26 Aug. 1949, 228. See also, Roger Manvell, 'Drama on Television and the Film', *BBC Quarterly*, 1/1 (1952), 26–7 and Royston Morley, 'The Television Drama', in Paul Rotha (ed.), *Television in the Making* (London: Focal Press, 1956), 36.

62 Minutes, 23 Feb. 1953, BBC WAC TV Routine Meetings, Drama Producers' Meetings, File 1 1948–53, T26/11/1.

63 Minutes, 15 Feb. 1954, BBC WAC TV Routine Meetings, Drama Producers' Meetings, File 2 1954, T26/11/2.

64 Bartlett, *Writing for Television*, 36.

Its proper métier, in drama, is to transmit the intimate, one-set, four-or-five character plays, and it should leave plays of major scope to the more abundant and resourceful art of the cinema. [65]

A few lines later, the same critic can find nothing but praise for the Outside Broadcasts Department's ambitious coverage of the Cup Final: 'At Outside Broadcasts generally and sporting events in particular, Television is triumphant . . . In dexterity and range finding the cameramen were faultless . . . we seemed as close to the play as the referee.' It was television *drama* that would embarrass itself by over-reaching its ambitions, rather than the thrillingly mobile outside broadcasts: it was not that television itself could not be mobile, rather it was that television drama should be still. Williams again:

> *Charles and Mary* . . . was another example of that intimate,
> miniature drama which goes so much better on television than
> the thronging play of movement. Seldom were there more than
> three characters on the scene, out of a modest total of a dozen.
> There were no vistas, no elaborate sets, no extensive deployment
> of action. In its small domestic interiors there was enough elbow
> room for the poignant story to be developed without seeming
> to be forced through the eye of a needle. It is to be hoped that
> television will increasingly accept the scale and conventions of its
> medium, instead of whoring after Lyceum panoramas seen
> through the wrong end of a telescope.[66]

This is an 'intimacy' of *scale*: a small-scale production, few characters, concerned with emotional drama rather than spectacle, separate from the art of film. Williams's purism comes at a time when, paradoxically, some television producers were becoming more ambitious with their use of film, attempting to *expand* the space of television rather than limit it. Technical development had benefited both trends—composing in depth and observing in detail—and by 1954 they could be identified as alternative schools of television drama style:

> One such school of production thought has applied itself to the
> enrichment of the screen, to pushing it backwards in depth and
> outwards in space by the use of film inserts and the important
> use of *décor*. These producers have answered the criticism that
> scenery is erected in the studio but not seen upon the screen.
> Another school of thought has explored the possibilities of
> 'closing in' and obtaining the utmost effect from the observance

65 W. E. Williams, 'Television Notes', *New Statesman*, 7 May 1949.

66 W. E. Williams, 'Television Notes', *New Statesman*, 4 June 1949.

of detail. . . . the trends described in these productions would not
have been so clearly defined without the cameras that drama has
used since March 1952. The variable lenses on these cameras
broke through the shallow field of focus. They allowed the
camera-man to compose in depth instead of restricting his clear
vision to a narrow alley running at right angles before his lens. He
was enabled also to reach in to observe detail without thrusting a
bulky vehicle across the foreground of the other apparatus on the
floor.[67]

Barry seems to be the disinterested arbiter between these two schools
of thought, but his loyalty belonged in the camp of the intimate
screen. This is not to denigrate or belittle his achievements. When
Barry succeeded Val Gielgud as Head of Television Drama, he believed the potential of television that was more than 'illustrated radio',
arguing that television drama had to rely less on dialogue, more on
the 'power of the image': that television had to be visibly 'televisual'. It
is one of the injustices of television history that Barry's achievements
in this respect have been denigrated by comparison with the self-
aggrandisement of Sydney Newman.

However, as we have seen, Barry's idea of televisuality was closely
associated with the metaphor of 'observation' (the microscope). This
conception of an observational visuality really favoured the less ambitious and more intimate dramas. It was the arrival of Nigel Kneale
as BBC staff writer, and Rudolph Cartier as a new drama producer
with a background in writing and directing German crime-thrillers
of the 1930s, that challenged the intimate drama directly. Cartier is
rightly recognized as a major influence on the visual development of
British television drama. He joined the BBC Drama Department in
1952, after an early career as a scriptwriter and director in the German
film industry in the late 1920s and early 1930s.[68] By the mid-1960s he
had directed over 120 separate productions, most of them live studio
plays.

Cartier has been seen as the most significant and innovative of the
early television producers. When he died in April 1994, his obituaries
stressed his pioneering impact on early television drama:

> At a time when studio productions were usually as static as the
> conventional theatre, he was widely respected for a creative
> contribution to British television drama which gave it a new
> dimension. Breaking out of this static straitjacket presented
> Cartier with an irresistible challenge . . .

67 Michael Barry, 'Shakespeare on Television', *BBC Quarterly*, 9/3 (1954), 143.

68 See Jason Jacobs, 'Rudolph Cartier', in Horace Newcomb (ed.), *The Encyclopedia of Television*, i (Fitzroy Dearborn, 1996).

[*Nineteen Eighty-Four*] was also a production in which Rudolph Cartier displayed fully his technical skills. He had 28 sets and included six sequences that were shot on film. 'These sequences,' he said 'came between the main studio sequences and they gave me the chance to move artists and the cameras from one set to another.' These innovations were an important development in the age of live television drama.[69]

As I have indicated, the use of film inserts to allow camera and scenery changes was a standard feature of some television dramas in the 1940s and even the pre-war years, hence hardly innovative in 1954. This estimation of Cartier's pioneering work is to show that his innovation in television drama was to increase mobility and to overcome spatial limitations, primarily by using a combination of material derived from film inserts and live studio performance:

> what actually made them work so well [the *Quatermass* serials] was their essentially televisual quality in an era of filmed theatre . . . Particularly impressive and unusual at the time, is the effective use they make of location-shot film inserts . . .[70]

It is true that Cartier's matching of film and live studio in his productions was exemplary and innovative for the time, but for more complex reasons than the fact that he used film at all. Film enabled a 'wider canvas' only because Cartier wanted to push the 'limits of the medium' outward rather than toward the intimate drama. As the veteran television critic Philip Purser notes:

> I think he was terribly important because he was the first man to expand television, to make it big, to get out of the little sets and the little three or four shot confrontations, he really had unfettered ambition. He did it in the studio right up to and including *Quatermass and the Pit* in which he destroyed half of London. He did use a lot of film, he was a brilliant director of film inserts—nobody ever matched the studio production so perfectly, and nobody ever got such instant quick quality which he got. He used a lot, more than the average director was allowed to use. But he only used it when he had to. Ahead of Sidney Newman he had this depth, he went inside the drama, instead of just viewing it as a series of boxes. He had enormous ambition . . . The bigger and more difficult it was, he did it.[71]

Barry interviewed Cartier for a post as drama producer in 1952, and asked his opinion of British television drama:

---

69 *The Times*, 10 June 1994.

70 Julian Petley, *Guardian*, 11 June 1994.

71 Philip Purser, interview with author 29 June 1992.

I told him I thought it was dreadful. I said that the BBC needed new scripts, a new approach, a whole new spirit, rather than endlessly televising classics like Dickens or familiar London stage plays.[72]

It says a lot about Barry's prescience that Cartier was given the job, and the opportunity to develop his own approach to television drama. One way of changing traditional approaches to television drama direction was to look at different source material, and Cartier selected and directed more unconventional, modernist European drama: Brecht, Sartre, and Anouilh. Before he produced *Nineteen Eighty-Four* in 1954, Cartier produced thirteen plays for the BBC, and the six episodes of *The Quatermass Experiment*. The plays varied from supernatural and fantasy stories to historical costume-drama and 'classic' adaptations such as *Wuthering Heights*.[73]

Cartier's conception of the television's address to the domestic space of the home is a familiar one:

How does television differ from films . . . ? The television end-product is different from a film or stage one because it is destined for a very small audience, sitting secluded in a semi-darkened room and trying to look through a small sheet of glass into the world of realism, fantasy, and so on we are trying to create.[74]

However, this fact of television's delivery in the home does not require a particular mode of television address. This was the theoretical mistake made by producers and critics alike: extrapolating the characteristics of television's production style from its mode of reception. Jan Bussell, a drama and children's programme producer, takes the technical and reception components of television and represents them in terms of a 'cosy' relationship between producer and audience:

The television screen . . . normally shows things approximately actual size, and there is nothing unpleasant or unnatural in a TV

---

72 Rudolph Cartier quoted in Lynda Myles and Julian Petley, 'Rudolph Cartier', *Sight and Sound*, 59/2 (Spring 1990), 126.

73 Cartier's producer's credits up to *Nineteen Eighty-Four* (Dec. 1954): *Arrow to the Heart*, 8.55–10.40 Sunday 20 July 1952; *The Dybbuk*, 8.30–10.10 Tuesday 21 Oct. 1952; *Portrait of Peter Perowne*, 8.15–9.15 Tuesday 2 Dec. 1952; *L'Aiglon*, 8.40–10.40 Sunday 12 April 1953; *The Quatermass Experiment* (six episodes), 8.15–8.45 Saturdays beginning 18 July 1953; *Operation Northstar*, 8.30–9.55 Sunday 25 Oct. 1953; *Wuthering Heights*, 8.40–10.35 Sunday 6 Dec. 1953; *Sacrifice to the Wind*, 9.00–10.00 Tuesday 26 Jan. 1954; *Such Men Are Dangerous*, 8.10–10.10, Sunday 28 Feb. 1954; *Sorry-Wrong Number*, 9.20–9.50 Saturday 27 March 1954; *That Lady*, 8.40–10.20 Sunday 2 May 1954; *Count Albany*, 9.20–10.00 Tuesday 25 May 1954; *Captain Banner*, 8.25–10.00 Sunday 8 Aug. 1954; *Rebecca*, 9.15–11.00 Sunday 10 Oct. 1954. All productions p.m.; all the Sunday productions were repeated on Thursday, none of the others were repeated.

74 Rudolph Cartier quoted in 'The Man Who Put *Nineteen Eighty-Four* on Television: A Producer with a Personal Style', *The Times*, 1 Dec. 1958.

close-up of a face. The artist is brought to your fireside just the size he would be if he were really there. This permits extremely intimate acting. With a larger screen the viewer would need to sit at the other end of his room for comfort, and the intimacy would be lost.

Furthermore, the fact that the audience consists of the family circle, twos or threes in their own homes, again calls for this special intimacy which is so much a feature of television. They do not want to be lectured or harangued, but to partake, and to be chatted with. The sort of playing necessary in the theatre or lecture hall is just as unsuitable as that required for the cinema. Finally, the consciousness that it is all happening now this minute, that one is witnessing actual creation—that might even go wrong—adds tremendously to the feeling that one is a part of it, that it is something personal between oneself and the artist, and makes television what can only be described as a 'cosy' medium. It is the producer's art to exploit these assets to the full, and obviously the performer has to adjust his technique accordingly.[75]

This 'cosy' medium was an anathema to Cartier and Nigel Kneale, but it was the logical and banal conclusion to a set of assumptions that depended on tropes about 'nearness' in order to differentiate television as a medium. Bussell insists on the 'cosy' address to the family circle, in a way that is reminiscent of the ideas around Nation as a Family in the early 1950s, exemplified by the official film of the 1951 Festival of Britain, Humphrey Jennings's *Family Portrait*, and later the televising of the Coronation itself (despite the fact the BBC were not allowed an intimate close-up of the new Queen).

A way of escaping the 'intimate' and 'cosy' drawing room-style of drama production was to explore different genres that demanded imaginative visualization of fiction worlds. As Joy Leman notes:

Science fiction as a genre in literature, film and television offers the possibility of moving beyond the dominant narrative constraints of realism and naturalism in exploring political ideas, visions of an alternative reality and dramas of fantasy.[76]

75 Jan Bussell, *The Art of Television* (London: Faber & Faber, 1952), 20. In a similar way Alan Bennett describes the difference in tone between film and television: 'In terms of writing I don't think that one can talk of feature films and TV films in the same breath, and it's not a simple question of scale or scope. It seems to me to have something to do with the space between an audience and the screen. On television one does not have to raise one's voice. The relationship with the audience is intimate, the tone conversational. A cinema audience is physically further away from the screen, so that one's tone, and the tone of the writing has to be different, projected more.' 'Life before Death on Television', *Sight and Sound* 53/2 (1984), 122.

76 Joy Leman, 'Wise Scientists and Female Androids: Class and Gender in Science Fiction', in John Corner (ed.), *Popular Television in Britain: Studies in Cultural History* (London: British Film Institute, 1991), 108–9.

Kneale and Cartier shared a common desire to invigorate television with a faster tempo and a broader thematic and spatial canvas, and it was no coincidence that they turned to science-fiction in order to get out of the dominant stylistic trend of television intimacy.[77] Looking back at *The Quatermass Experiment* (1953), Kneale remembers:

> I desperately wanted to do something different, something fast-moving and adventurous. We wanted to get right away from the usual talky piece set in a couple of rooms in which people said things like 'put down that gun, it might be loaded' or 'let's not go to the police', and so on.[78]

But their ambition was beginning to outstrip BBC budgets. In 1954 Barry sent Cartier a warning that his productions were becoming too expansive and, more importantly, expensive:

> After *Captain Banner* we had a long talk about the danger of your productions becoming too big both in terms of the load upon the service and the effect upon television performance. The performance of *Rebecca* seems to me to have taken us further into the danger area instead of showing any improvement. I am unable to defend at a time when departmental costs and scene loads are in an acute state the load imposed by *Rebecca* on Design and Supply and the expenditure upon extras and costumes . . . the leading performances were stagey and very often the actors were lost in the setting.
>
> There has already been a television performance of this play in which the accent was placed upon the actors and the play stood out upon the screen in a way which it never did on Sunday. Occasionally there were fine shots such as when Max was playing the piano with his wife beside him, and the composition of figures, piano top and vase made a good frame, but the vast area of the hall and the stairway never justified the great expenditure of effort required in building and one is left with a very clear impression of reaching a point where the department must be accused of not knowing what it is doing.[79]

---

77 Kneale worked on six adaptations for the drama department before writing the six episodes of *The Quatermass Experiment* in 1953. Kneale worked with Cartier on his first BBC drama production, an adaptation of *Arrow to the Heart* (20 July 1952) and between 1952 and 1962 Kneale wrote the three *Quatermass* serials and two original dramas, and adapted ten other single plays. He worked with Cartier on three further adaptations (*Wuthering Heights*, 1953; *Nineteen Eighty-Four*, 1954; *Wuthering Heights* again, 1962) and the *Quatermass* serials.

78 Nigel Kneale, quoted in Julian Petley, 'The Manxman', *Monthly Film Bulletin* 56/662 (March 1989), 91. Kneale's adaptation of *Nineteen Eighty-Four* includes his own sequence where the mechanical production of pornographic fiction is mocked. O'Brien (André Morell) reads out the line, 'put down that gun, it might be loaded'.

79 Michael Barry to Rudolph Cartier, memo, 12 Oct. 1954, BBC WAC T5/424.

Barry is judging Cartier's production in terms of the 'intimate style' espoused by the critics W. E. Williams, Roger Manvell, and Jan Bussell—'cosy', small scale, few characters, with attention paid to the actors not the setting, and favouring close shots (Barry notes 'fine shots' such as 'Max playing the piano with his wife beside him'). Cartier's television style was different—it attempted to *expand space*, using long shots, large sets *and* close-ups.

Cartier responded to Barry's criticisms by saying that 'the set should be large enough so that the small Mrs de Winter should feel "lost" enough and not "cosy" '.[80] This observation reveals the contrast between the early intimate BBC drama style associated with producers such as O'Donovan, O'Ferrall, and Bussell (longer-running shots, close-ups, the study of one or two characters), and Cartier and Kneale's conception of a wider canvas of shooting styles, a more integrated mixture of studio and film, larger sets, multi-character productions.

Kneale sums up his frustration at the early styles and essentialist discourses he saw as restricting the possibilities of television:

> there were various mystiques about What Television Should Be . . . One fellow felt that TV drama should be produced like a radio play, where the actors line up and then come to the microphone one by one peeling off left and right once they'd said their lines. Somebody else shot everything in close-up; at least the faces were in focus but it was all dreadfully monotonous and uninteresting— all you were getting was cut, cut, cut.[81]

Kneale exaggerates here (there is no other record of the 'radio' idea, although it sounds like a Haley or Gielgud thinking), but it is important to realize that the stylistic alternative that Kneale and Cartier offered did not simply lie in a greater use of film. It was their refusal to confine television within one style that required constant reference to its material base (intimate because the screen was small, the audience was at home, urgent because it was live, etc.), that made them important. Using film extended the range of stylistic choices. Film was just the source material, a technological opportunity to transcend the spatial and temporal limitations of live studio drama. It does not imply a 'cinematic' style (whatever one decides that is), any more than television's delivery to the home viewer demanded the frequent use of the 'cosy' close-up. It was more a use of film as material that could expand the space of the production. Kneale again:

80 Rudolph Cartier to Michael Barry, memo, 13 Oct. 1954, BBC WAC T5/424.

81 Nigel Kneale quoted in Julian Petley, 'The Manxman', *Monthly Film Bulletin* 56/662 (March 1989), 91. I suspect that Kneale intended something more like, 'cut . . . cut . . . cut . . .'.

> The idea of putting in bits of film linkage was quite an old one,
> but they tended to be a shot of someone walking into a house. It
> was reckoned to be rather a status symbol to haul out a camera
> crew on location, shoot garbage like cars going round a corner
> and then shove it in the programme at random.[82]

Kneale and Cartier used film in a way that was integrated into the
story and provided more than simple linkage. Kneale (and certainly
Cartier is in agreement) despised what he saw as the cult of 'intimacy'.
Writing in 1959, just after the production of *Quatermass and the Pit*,
he outlines what he saw as the confusion of the early 1950s amongst
drama producers:

> when I came to it [the Television Service] I found people
> were still baffled. Plays in particular—what should they be?
> I watched sad radio men trying to turn it into illustrated radio
> using still photographs to keep that infernal screen occupied.
> And disappointed men from films despairing at limitations of
> time and space that confounded their too-loose scripts. In
> canteens and conferences I have heard arguments about the
> missing mystique, the TV Philosopher's Stone that would confer
> legitimacy on a bastard medium, and make it an art-form
> overnight.
>   The favourite bet was on Intimacy. 'It's a small screen, so it
> stands to reason you have to get in close.' This appealed strongly.
> One producer made a cult of it, and shot play after play entirely
> in close-up, regardless of the monotony of a series of almost
> identical compositions. We heard reports of intimate TV writing.
> But apart from one or two like Chayefsky, their scripts turned
> out disappointing, their gimmick a weird, tiny rhetoric. Self-
> important and repetitious. Dead end. The probing for the heart
> of television's mystery went vaguely on.[83]

This cosy intimacy is contrasted against Kneale's praise of his own
work in terms of its contemporaneity, its recognition of change and
the consequences of change. Kneale is drawn to science-fiction because it is a genre which allowed him to explore the possibilities,
dangers and consequences of a changed world, particularly if that
imagined world relates, in however extended and amplified a form, to
the present-day world:

> All the *Quatermass* films have been very much tied to their time;
> they are all extrapolations from the present . . . I always feel that
> the most interesting strange thing was to have an ordinary setting.

82 Kneale quoted in Petley, 'The Manxman'.

83 Nigel Kneale, 'Not Quite So Intimate', *Sight and Sound*, 28/2 (Spring 1959), 86.

I like the blending of the ordinary and the extraordinary, the funny and the horrific.[84]

I don't like the term 'science-fiction' but if we're going to bandy it about, it could be applied just as well to the world we live in. The form is appropriate, if taken seriously. And that is the way I do take it. I try to give those stories some relevance to what is round about us today. The last one [*Quatermass and the Pit*], for instance, was a race-hatred fable that broke through to an encouragingly large and intelligent audience. On the technical side, it went about as far as possible towards exploding the 'intimacy' fallacy. Huge sets, long shots, crowd scenes were the order of the day. One critic remarked: 'Not only does it sweep away detachment, but it obliterates also the feeling of being a solitary spectator; one reacts to it with enlarged response as a member of a communal audience.'[85]

In a way this is a return to Gerald Cock's sense of television drama as topical and contemporary, a relay of information (we might locate Sydney Newman's ideas about 'agitational contemporaneity' in the same light). The new dominant aesthetic for television drama, which continued into the 1960s, was that it offered an authentic national theatre, for and about working class concerns, majority concerns—a far cry from the bourgeois drawing room, the intimate 'cosy' sets. However, we must be careful when assessing the caricature of earlier BBC dramas that Kneale, in 1959, outlines above (a caricature which has a continuity through the 1960s and 1970s up to Gardner and Wyver's 'The Single Play'). Kneale and Cartier's drama productions are as much a culmination of what went before as a departure from it. Kneale's critique has some validity: in the early years television drama was live and immediate: and yet its subject matter was often (but not always) contained, either set in the past or closed-off in the small-scale 'drawing room'. Cartier and Kneale had the ambition for their productions to have an impact on a mass audience, and the scope of their attention was not confined to the 'cosy' aesthetics of intimacy. Cartier uses the close-up both to reveal emotions and as a shock device: a more threatening—and perhaps exhilarating—method than was used before. 'Intimacy' is reformulated by Cartier in terms of his power and control over the viewer—no longer a part of the family, but isolated in his home. For Cartier, this is a special 'power' which television possesses, and one that gives it a superior impact over film:

84 Nigel Kneale, in Petley, 'The Manxman', 91. Some comment is needed here on Kneale's use of the words '*Quatermass* films': it is unlikely he is referring to the later Hammer film versions; perhaps it is in recognition that the serials were telerecorded on film, or a slippage in terminology which reflected his desire to make television drama more like film . . . ?

85 Kneale, 'Not Quite So Intimate', 88.

Having established the necessity of bringing the story 'close'
to the viewer, the next thing to consider is the condition under
which he views. He will probably be sitting at home, in a darkened
room, together with other people; or, of course, he may be alone.
If the TV director knows his medium well and handles it skilfully,
he can wield almost unlimited power over his mass audience; a
power which no other form of entertainment can give him—not
even cinema.

I can only quote a few examples of this, from my own
personal experience, which may serve to illustrate the point.
The Quatermass Experiment, its sequel *Quatermass II*, and *The
Creature*, were more successful on the small TV screen than in the
cinema, mainly because of the 'hypnotic' quality emanating from
the TV screen to the viewer sitting *isolated* in his darkened
room.[86]

It is particularly ironic that the director of *Nineteen Eighty-Four*
should use notions of control, over an isolated, privatized, individual
audience. Cartier goes on to explain the superior impact on the audience of the television version of *Nineteen Eighty-Four* over the film
version made a year later:[87]

When Orwell's novel was made into a film . . . all the directional
skill of Michael Anderson could not recapture the impact of the
TV transmission . . . the main reason was that the subject could
only frighten spectators who were 'conditioned' to experience
fear by sitting alone in the darkness, and unable to find help or
comfort by looking around the mass audience in a modern
cinema—where they would feel safe from 'Big Brother'. It was
decidedly different in the TV viewer's own home, where cold eyes
stared from the small screen straight at him, casting into the
viewer's heart the same chill that the characters in the play
experienced whenever they heard his voice coming from *their*
'watching' TV screens.[88]

Intimacy remains in Cartier's plays in terms of 'nearness' to the
performance, and to the anxieties and concerns of 'present-day'.
Establishing nearness to the contemporary was the job of new writers
for television. For early television style, Cartier was to rethink the idea
of 'intimacy' as a close-up style taken in the drawing-room, to an important component in a *range* of stylistic choices. What the close-up
revealed was still 'observed', the performance of emotion:

86 Rudolph Cartier, 'A Foot in Both Camps', *Films and Filming*, 4/12 (Sept. 1958), 10.

87 *1984*, directed by Michael Anderson (GB, 1955).

88 Cartier, 'Both Camps', 10.

The main weapon of television is the close-up because it gives the viewer a chance to watch emotion as portrayed from a distance of less than a foot. Because it is the main weapon it must be used sparingly. Music at a continuous fortissimo would make dull listening . . . My practice is to save it until the final scene, so that the viewer can see the agony of decision, twitching in the hero's cheek muscles from as close as possible during the crisis of the play.[89]

In Cartier's production of *Nineteen Eighty-Four* expanded and intimate space are combined in some novel ways.

Case Study

■ **Nineteen Eighty-Four (1954)**

Nineteen Eighty-Four, was adapted by from Orwell's novel by Kneale and produced by Cartier. It was first broadcast in the prime Sunday night drama slot between 8.35 and 10.35 p.m. on 12 December 1954, and repeated live on the following Thursday.[90] It was a large-scale, high-profile production: the budget was the most expensive of any drama production at the time (there were 22 sets and 28 actors).[91] The main stars, Peter Cushing (Winston), Yvonne Mitchell (Julia) and André Morell (O'Brien), were already well known on television. Cushing was a television star, gracing the cover of the *Radio Times*, and taking the leading role in several BBC dramas. He had recently starred in the Saturday night serial *Epitaph for a Spy* (March 1953), in *Rookery Nook* (a Ben Travers farce, 23 May 1953), *Anastasia* (12 July 1953—this play won the Daily Mail 'Best TV Play of the Year' award), had played the title role in *Beau Brummell* (14 March 1954), and would return to the Kneale/Cartier partnership in 1955 in the production of *The Creature*.[92]

A significant part of the budget, after actors' fees, was taken up by the cost of film. The inserted film sequences took two forms: stock library shots, and pre-filmed scenes, both interior and exterior. The planned library shots were:

(a) Atomic explosion (6 different shots).
(b) CU sheep's face [not used].
(c) Crowds in Trafalgar Square on VE night.
(d) A thrush in a tree [not used].
(e) Stock shots taken in summer, for wood sequence.

---

89 Rudolph Cartier quoted in 'The Man Who Put *Nineteen Eighty-Four* on Television: A Producer with a Personal Style', *The Times*, 1 Dec. 1958.

90 This repeat performance is the version which was recorded on 35mm and survives today.

91 See *Nineteen Eighty-Four* programme files, BBC WAC T5/362/1–2. The final budget was £3,250.

92 *The Creature*, 9.15–10.45 p.m. Sunday, 30 Jan. 1955. Repeated the following Thursday.

The library shots were combined with pre-filmed material that was telecined into the live studio action. In all this makes fourteen film sequences in the production, some of them lengthy, some merely 2–3 second inserts. They were as follows:

1. Opening sequence: the atomic switches are pressed; model shot of London in 1984.
2. Cubicles in Ministry of Truth.
3. Two Minutes Hate: Goldstein's speeches; a Eurasian soldier.
4. Winston and Syme queuing in the canteen.
5. Winston leaving Ministry of Truth and entering Victory Mansions.
6. Close up of Winston's diary; he is writing 'Down with Big Brother'.
7. Winston entering Prole Sector.
8. Winston leaving Prole Sector; model shot of Chestnut Tree cafe.
9. Corridor outside Pornosec.
10. Paper with 'I love you' written on it.
11. Winston and Julia meet in the wood.
12. Singing prole woman.
13. Parsons hanging bunting for Hate Week.
14. Rats.

Several of these sequences linked spaces (2, 5, 7, 8) showing Winston moving from one area to another; others are for close-ups of written text (6, 10) where moving the live camera to find focus on text would be awkward; other exterior scenes (11, 12, 13) are also filmed, as are the (always unpredictable) rats.

In the 1936/7 period 'scenes' from current West End plays, meant just that: the relay of a theatrical scene mediated by two or more cameras. By 1938 a 'scene' in the television play no longer corresponds to the 'scene' of the stage play which has been adapted. The meaning of the word 'scene' for early television is thus a loose and historically varied one. Here 'scene' is defined as having the elements of continuous duration and locale, and the end of each 'scene' corresponds either to the transition to another set, or to a film sequence.

Table 3 outlines the running time of each scene; the number of shots in each; narrative information. I have included the opening and closing title sequences. I also indicate where film inserts are used.

The first column, 'Time' lists the running time of the play through each scene; the figure in square brackets below shows the total running time of each scene. For example, scene 4 begins 10 minutes 53 seconds into the play, and lasts for 8 minutes 9 seconds.

The second column gives the shot count for each scene; the figure below this gives the total number of shots for that scene. For example, scene 20 begins with shot 288 and contains 31 shots in total.

The third column indicates whether the scene is filmed, live studio, or a composite. The studio/film mixture is sometimes complex

TABLE 3: Nineteen Eighty-Four breakdown

Time	Shots	Studio/Film	Scene	Commentary
00.00		film	Titles	
00.35 [01.20]	1–10 [10]	film	1 Establishing narration	Narrator's voice-over; stock shots of atomic explosions; pan along a model shot of ruined London in 1984; tilt up model of Ministry of Truth; Winston looking out of window.
01.55 [04.09]	11–29 [19]	studio/film	2 Ministry of Truth	Introduces Winston and his work; introduces O'Brien.
06.04 [04.49]	30–74 [45]	studio/film	3 Two Minutes Hate	Party members watch propaganda on a telescreen; Julia is introduced; Winston shows secret disloyalty to Big Brother.
10.53 [08.09]	75–94 [20]	studio/film	4 Canteen	Winston and Syme discuss Newspeak; Parsons sits down and discusses Hate Week; a ration announcement on the telescreen; Winston realises it is a sham.
19.02 [00.52]	95–102 [8]	film	5a Winston walks home	Exterior shots of a desolate landscape, and Victory Mansions
19.54 [01.50]	103–109 [7]	studio	5b Winston's flat	He opens his diary, but is interrupted by Mrs. Parsons.
21.44 [04.34]	110–131 [21]	studio	5c Parsons' flat	The sink is unblocked by Winston; the children accuse him of spying; Parsons returns.
26.18 [03.44]	132–143 [12]	studio/film	5d Winston's flat	Parsons is enthuses about the Party; Winston writes 'Down with Big Brother' in his diary.
30.02 [01.13]	144–149 [6]	film	6a Prole Sector	Winston wanders into the forbidden prole sector.
31.15 [03.15]	150–154 [5]	studio	6b Prole Bar	Proles discuss pornographic fiction and the lottery; Winston talks to an old man about the past.
34.30 [05.52]	155–168 [14]	studio	7 Mr. Charrington's Shop	Winston buys a paperweight and Charrington shows him the room upstairs.
41.22 [00.29]	169–172 [4]	film	8 Prole Sector (night)	Winston walks back; sees a sign for the Chestnut Tree cafe.
41.51 [04.30]	173–190 [18]	studio	9 Chestnut Tree café	Winston meets Syme in cafe; Syme reveals he has been suspended from all his duties; Winston leaves, the police arrest Syme.
46.21 [00.37]	191 [1]	studio	10 Winston's flat	Winston plans to murder Julia

TABLE 3: (cont'd)

Time	Shots	Studio/Film	Scene	Commentary
46.58 [00.35]	192–198 [7]	film	11 Ministry of Truth corridor	Winston watches Julia enter 'Pornosec'
47.33 [03.51]	199–216 [18]	studio	12 Pornosec and Winston's cubicle	Julia injures her hand whilst using the fiction-writing machine; she manages to hand Winston a note 'I love you'.
51.24 [1.20]	217–219 [3]	studio	13 Canteen	Winston and Julia arrange to meet in a wood.
52.44 [04.46]	220–238 [19]	studio/film	14 Wood	Winston and Julia declare their mutual love for each other, and their hatred for the Party.
57.30 [01.27]	239 [1]	studio	15 Mr. Charrington's Shop	Winston arranges to rent the room upstairs.
58.57 [00.27]	240–252 [13]	film	16 Hate Week	Montage of preparations and crowds.
59.24 [07.15]	253–278 [26]	studio/film	17 Mr. Charrington's Shop (upstairs room)	Julia and Winston: Julia changes into a dress; Winston is terrified by a rat.
66.39 [01.43]	279 [1]	studio	18 Ministry of Truth (chess club noticeboard)	O'Brien tells Winston to come to his house.
68.22 [02.57]	280–287 [8]	studio	19 Mr. Charrington's Shop (upstairs room)	Julia agrees to come with Winston to O'Brien's house.
71.19 [07.37]	288–318 [31]	studio	20 O'Brien's flat	Julia and Winston agree to join the Brotherhood against the Party.
78.56 [06.26]	319–340 [22]	studio	21 Mr. Charrington's Shop (upstairs room)	Winston reads from Goldstein's book; the Thought Police arrest both of them.
85:22 [00.12]	341–342 [2]	film	22a Cars arrive outside Ministry of Love	Winston is driven to Ministry of Love.
85.34 [03.40]	343–358 [16]	studio	22b Cell in Ministry of Love	Winston meets Parsons, who has been betrayed by his children; O'Brien enters and reveals he has tricked Winston
89.14 [11.32]	359–396 [38]	studio	23a Torture room	Winston is tortured
100.46 [01.33]	397–407 [11]	studio/film	23b Room 101	Winston betrays Julia
102.19 [04.32]	408–432 [25]	studio	24 Chestnut Tree café	Julia and Winston reveal they betrayed each other. Voice over Winston: 'I love Big Brother.'
106.51			End Titles	

(scene 3), sometimes simple (scene 5d, the film sequence is a close-up inserts of Winston writing in his diary).

The fourth column lists and describes each scene. Some are clearly discrete scenes, taking place within one set; others such as scenes 5a, 5b, 5c, and 5d take place in the same locale (in this case Victory Mansions) in continuous time, but each takes place in a different set, or returns to a previous set (5b and 5d). 5a, although it takes place outside Victory mansions, is clearly the establishing shot for this sequence. Generally, punctuation devices informed my demarcation of scenes: a fade to black or a dissolve in this production always indicated the passing of time and usually a change of locale (extradiegetic music also provides some cues). Cuts between locales (for example, 6a to 6b) indicate temporal continuity.

Before all this begins to sound like a basic film studies textbook, it should be remembered that the conventions of television—especially live television—*could* differ significantly from film. For example, a cut to black in scene 21 is a camera error, and long gaps of black between some scenes are in order to allow costume and scenery changes to be completed. For example, between scenes 22b (the prison cell) and 23a (Winston lying in a 'torture coffin') there is a 30-second black-out which allows Cushing to change into rags, and make-up to be applied to his face. In fact, during the beginning of scene 23a there is some delay, as O'Brien is shown questioning Winston, before we are given a shot of Cushing lying in the coffin. The delay seems 'unnatural' in terms of classical Hollywood spatial continuity, because it is over a minute before we are shown who O'Brien is talking to. Again, the practical limitations of live drama (Cushing is considerably changed when we see him again) have definite stylistic consequences.

The fifth column contains a brief description of each scene. This table, unlike previous ones, is not intended as a reconstruction of, or a substitute for, a viewing of the play itself.[93]

The average shot length (ASL) for *Nineteen Eighty-Four* is around 15 seconds; for the film sequences alone the ASL works out at 6 seconds; for studio/film composite scenes the ASL is around 13 seconds; counting the studio scenes alone, the ASL works out at 17 seconds. It is no surprise, therefore, that film inserts, reduce the overall ASL significantly, although this is partly a result of a fast montage scene (16).

It is important to remember that there is no *simple* relationship in television drama of the 1940s and 1950s between the number of shots and the play's theatricality or 'cinematic' style. Some shots (10 and 18) last over a minute, and some are coterminous with 'scenes', but there is no sense that they have a theatrical style. In other studio sequences which contain long shots there is no sense of stasis or

93 A 35mm print is available for viewing at the National Film and Television Archive.

tedium. This is because cameras frequently reframe according to the movement of the actors, for reaction or dialogue shots, varying the shot scale by movement rather than by the use of editing.

This mobility has two modes. First there is the stylistic tendency to reframing that is subordinate to the movement of performance. This aspect of reframing is signalled in a paper written by Ian Atkins in the early 1950s.[94] Atkins outlines a television style that is subordinate to performance and therefore requires constant reframing.[95] According to Atkins, the frequent reframing of on-air cameras is motivated by both actor movement, and the scale of the shot:

> To be of significance the background must be established. Let us consider the essential difference between the medium or long shot and the close-up. In a long shot the composition will be determined by the static scenic elements in the picture, and the characters will move within them without materially altering the balance of the composition and will therefore give no reason for the camera to pan. Similarly, it is possible, although not quite so easy, to compose a medium shot that can remain static whilst allowing the action considerable movement. When we come to medium-close-up and close-up shots, however, the bodies of the actors occupy so much of the picture that the composition now depends on their position. They are in motion, and this requires a continuous although imperceptible movement of the camera in order to keep a correct composition throughout the scene. To move from medium shot to close-up we must cut, track-in or bring the actors forward.[96]

Or as Michael Barry puts it, 'They [producers] handle an apparatus that requires continuous, live action viewed through a constantly moving 'frame'.'[97]

The other mode is exhibitionistic camera movement, a mobility on display as mobility, and not motivated by performance, but *is* the performance. The performance of camera mobility is, of course, precisely the mobility associated with the dramas of 'Armchair Theatre' and Sydney Newman's order to his directors that 'the cameras must definitely move on air'. Take, for example, a late 'Armchair Theatre' (ABC Television, 1956–62) production from 1961, *Afternoon of a*

94 Ian Atkins, 'Television Programme Production Problems in Relation to Engineering Technique', *Proceedings of the Institute of Electrical Engineers* 99/3a/17 (April–May 1952), 77.

95 See David Bordwell, Janet Staiger, Kristin Thompson, *The Classical Hollywood Cinema: Style and Mode of Production to 1960* (London: Routledge, 1985), 56–9 for a description of the historical basis of this convention.

96 Atkins, 'Television Programme Production', 79–80.

97 Michael Barry, 'Problems of a Producer', *BBC Quarterly* 3/3 (Autumn 1951), 167.

Nymph. The broadcast play contains 177 separate shots, giving an average shot length of around 18 seconds. And yet the pace of the play is very rapid. The intense sensation of visual mobility is largely the result of continual—often very complex—camera movements.[98] Rather than camera movement being subordinate to performance, in this production the cameras in motion occasionally get in the way of performers.

It is wrong to suppose that the performance of camera mobility was invented with 'Armchair Theatre': in the comparisons of the two versions of *Rope* (1947, 1950) we can see that camera movements are added to the later version. *Afternoon of a Nymph* represents an *extension* of an earlier multi-camera studio style rather than a total transformation of it.

Nineteen Eighty-Four uses both modes of camera mobility, and also demonstrates some penetration by the cameras into the sets, more so than *Rope*, but not as extensively as *Afternoon of a Nymph*. I will limit my attention to the opening scenes here; they exemplify the overall style throughout the production.

The first scene establishes the time, locale, and context of the story, using a narrated montage: atomic war and the destruction of the old order; in its place a new order, Big Brother, the Party. A panning shot over a model of a ruined London in 1984 establishes a bleak locale, before we cut to a shot of Winston looking out over the landscape from a window in the Ministry of Truth. We cut from this filmed sequence to an interior shot, live from the studio, of Winston staring from the window. It is the first of many cuts between film and live studio performance which appears effortless, and one which demonstrates the way in which film could be employed to 'expand' the space of the action.

Scenes 2, 3, and 4 take place in the Ministry of Truth, sequentially, and hence form a group; however, they are separated by dissolves (here indicating a brief passage of time), and scenes 3 and 4 constitute two major 'set-pieces' (the Two Minutes Hate, the Canteen). In twenty minutes these three scenes establish the nature of Winston's work in the Records Department (restructuring the past according to the Party's requirements), introduce all the main characters (Julia, Syme, Parsons, O'Brien), and demonstrate Winston's secret disloyalty to the Party. Each of them has a discrete function however, and that is the rationale for separating them.

Scene 2 introduces Winston's work for the Party. We see him first staring outside the window, and then challenged by the iron voice of

---

98 For the camera script of *Afternoon of a Nymph*, see John Russell Taylor, *Anatomy of a Television Play* (London: Weidenfeld & Nicolson, 1962), 175–203; for the studio plan, see 139.

the Telescreen, and ordered to resume work. Winston returns to his cubicle, but meets O'Brien on the way: they exchange glances. Here Cartier matches interior film inserts and studio. As I noted above, the previous scene ends on a shot of Winston looking out at the bleak landscape of London. The next scene continues directly from this film sequence, in the studio. As Winston is ordered to return to work, and exits frame left, we cut to a filmed shot of him walking left to right past a Party member working in a cubicle. We then cut to a shot of O'Brien coming out of a door marked 'Inner Party Members Only.' Another shot of Winston walking along a corridor past a cubicle (in fact the same one with a different actor) before we return to the live studio and Winston sits down at his cubicle—in fact the very same set as was used in the two film shots.

Film is used here to expand space (Winston seems to walk a long way, past two cubicles and a doorway—the corridor looks long), to supply narrative information (O'Brien is an Inner Party Member; he shows an interest in Winston; other people work at the Ministry, just like Winston). It is also used to supply time (live studio transmission is halted) for Peter Cushing to move from one set to another. Of course, filming also saves expense on set construction: three cubicles are seen here whereas only one needs to be built.

Scene 3, the Two Minutes Hate, demonstrates a more complex use of film and studio. The scene dramatizes the use of Party propaganda, and the mass hysteria it provokes among Party members. Assembled in a hall, they watch on the telescreen a speech by the enemy of the party, Goldstein. As he berates the Party, the audience rise in a shrieking mass to denounce the enemy. As the crowd shout, 'I hate him!' a track in to Winston visualizes his 'thoughtcrime' and we hear him secretly chanting 'I hate Big Brother'. This is the moment when the central character reveals his secret treachery.

The transitions from audience to Goldstein, from film to live studio, have to be rapid: they are reacting to his taunts. The cutting between studio shots is very quick, often under a second per shot, as we are given a selection of hysterical denouncements. Here is an example of scene dissection—not simply cutting within a space using multiple studio cameras—but between multiple cameras *and* film inserts supplied by a telecine machine.

We move to the canteen (scene 4), via a mix from a close-up of Julia's face, watching Winston and Syme (Donald Pleasance) exit, to a sign in the canteen ('Regulation Meal'). The camera tilts down to reveal prolewoman serving the food, and then tracks back to reveal a queue of Party members. A cut to Winston and Syme in the queue, and Syme asks Winston if he has any razor blades. They collect their food and Winston indicates to Syme that there is 'a free table under that telescreen'. The film insert ends as Syme exits the frame right.

We then cut to the live studio action, canteen interior. It is difficult (without further information) to identify definitively the purpose of the insert, but I have two suggestions. First, the queue and the canteen food table requires extra space, and it makes sense to save this space by pre-filming it (after all, it is a short sequence). The canteen set in the studio, on the night of transmission, then requires little more than two tables and some chairs. Second, as we have seen, a film insert allows actors to disperse and prepare for the next scene; it may even be that the canteen set—because it is very simple—was set up during the film insert in the same space the Two Minutes Hate sequence was staged.

What follows will illustrate the way in which Cartier draws upon a range of television styles. As Winston and Syme discuss Newspeak at the table, the camera reframes slightly to follow performance. Winston sits at the table, the camera following his movements closely, reframing as he sits, and pulling back to cover Syme's entrance into the shot. These constant, often minor, adjustments to the frame continue throughout the scene (indeed I would argue that they are a characteristic visual signal of the 'urgent' style of live television).

The narrative point of the sequence is to demonstrate Syme's fanatical enthusiasm for the destruction of old language and its replacement by thought-controlling Newspeak; this is contrasted with Winston's uncomfortable attempts to feign interest.

Performance is everything here. Winston is a man fighting to hide from the Telescreen his revulsion at the picture of the future Syme is enthusiastically describing. Peter Cushing's performance has to reveal a man who is acting for the telescreen; we have to witness his disloyalty to the Party when he is overtly attempting to conform for the telescreen:

SYME: Did you go to see the prisoners being hanged yesterday?
WINSTON: No, the Telescreens [*looking up at the offscreen Telescreen*] are bound to show it soon.
SYME: Very inadequate substitute. [*pause*] How's the stew today?
WINSTON: [*mumbles*] Alright. [*looking up, louder*] Oh, it's very good!

During the pause we see Winston eating two mouthfuls of his stew and grimacing as he swallows, indicating that it is repulsive. What the exchange teaches the audience is that the constant surveillance of the Telescreen demands constant self-surveillance (of performance). When in front of the telescreen we often see the actors performing their character's fake interest or conformity.

The conversation between Syme and Winston is covered by two cameras, at 90 degrees to each other, both giving two-shots; one camera gives a profile of Winston and a frontal view of Syme, the other reverses this composition. Cutting between the two views is usually motivated by dialogue (cut to frontal view Winston, when Winston speaks, etc.).

The two cameras also change position between shots. For example, one camera is preparing for the next close-up of Syme, whilst a two-shot is being transmitted on the other camera. The flexibility of the two camera set-up is partly about the ability to improvise around the performance; as Syme leans close to Winston, the camera is adjusted to follow his movement and finds Winston's profile (a close-up of one actor becomes a two-shot) before reframing again to a close-up of Syme. There is a real sense here (whether it was actually planned or not) that Donald Pleasance's performance becomes so enthusiastic, so fanatical, that he loses the precise sense of the camera's position, and Cartier has to keep up with him, ordering the cameraman to re-frame, before choosing the other camera. This is where the 'mastery' and 'control' of the drama producer in the gallery has to be combined with the rhythm of the performance in the sense that George More O'Ferrall refers to, that 'It's only by feeling the scene with the actors that the producer can get the correct rhythm into the movements of the cameras. Ideally, there is one split second which is the right time to cut or 'mix'.[99]

This reciprocal sensitivity between performers and cameras continues as Julia appears and sits at the table behind Winston. When Parsons arrives and sits opposite Syme, one camera adjusts to frame a profile of Parsons, Winston frontally, and Julia behind. This disrupts the composition on this and the other camera, as Syme is obscured by Parsons.

We then cut to a close-up of a Telescreen, and an announcement about the 'increase in the chocolate ration'. This is presumably a film insert; the 'reverse' angle gives a static shot of Parsons, Winston, and Julia looking up to where the Telescreen would be as the announcement continues. Their facial expressions convey keen interest in what is being said (although, in fact all of them, Julia, Winston, and Parsons are later arrested for disloyalty). We are watching them watching the Telescreen.

Winston breaks the strong grouping of eyelines in confusion: earlier we saw him at work modifying a note which indicated a *decrease* in the chocolate ration. He turns to Parsons, 'Increase?' Parsons is extra-happy, 'My kids will be pleased!' We see Winston looking shaken and again looking away from the Telescreen.

What follows is the clearest visual recording of what I think the intimate style of 'getting closer' was supposed to be. We cut to a close-up of Winston and track-in to an extreme close-up of his face; as in

---

the Two Minutes Hate, studio sound is cut and we hear a voice-over of his thoughts:

> The chocolate ration was *reduced* to only twenty grams yesterday
> . . . Yes, they believe it. Doublethink. They make themselves
> believe it. 'Our new happy life' . . . grease and grime, the smell
> of dirty clothes and synthetic gin . . . and that stew!—careful—
> Facecrime.

Cushing's face fills the entire screen during this shot; we are drawn as close as possible to his disgust and unease. The ambition of the shot is to show, in a televisual 'aside', Winston's secret revulsion at the Party lies and lifestyle. It also illustrates Cartier's argument that:

> The TV viewer always wants to be as close as possible to the artist,
> and feels cheated, or disappointed, if the director does not give
> him a chance to study emotions in close-up.[100]

The microscopic observation of emotion here is not simply 'discovered' by the camera. The movement of the camera from close-up into an extreme close-up of Cushing's face is clearly a moment of technical performance: the movement of getting closer, achieving nearness, is visualized.

The 20 second close-up also allows us to 'study emotion' by showing us a performance of the visualization of the character's thoughts that we can hear being spoken in voice-over. The tiny movements in Cushing's face in response to the voice-over, are actually quite large movements in extreme-close up. Those movements do more than illustrate the spoken words, they embody and amplify his 'innermost thoughts'. A more detailed transcript of the shot reveals that the attempt to visualise Winston's thoughts transcend the literal meaning of the words:

> *[Camera tracks in on Winston in profile. As the camera tracks in,
> Winston turns toward camera slightly.]* The chocolate ration was
> reduced to only twenty grams yesterday . . . *[Camera stops track
> in.]* Yes *[slight nod]* they believe it. Doublethink. *[Frowns]* They
> make themselves believe it. *[Eyebrows slightly raised]* *[Sudden
> frown]* 'Our new happy life' . . . *[disgusted disbelief]* grease and
> grime, the smell of dirty clothes and synthetic gin *[winces]* . . .
> and that stew! *[closes eyes in disgust]*—careful—*[assumes 'blank'
> vigilant expression]* Facecrime.

The shot begins with Winston looking down, and moving his eyes from side to side in apparent bewilderment. There is the slight quality of a jump cut to this transition because the change in angle from the previous shot is nearly 90 degrees, from a virtually frontal shot of

100 Cartier, 'Both Camps', 10.

Cushing's face to a profile (turning his head to the right slightly brings him out of profile.) Bright key and fill lighting remove most of the shadow from his face, but model its shape strongly. As the camera tracks in Winston lifts his head as if in a moment of remembering and realization ('. . . chocolate ration was reduced . . .') which quickly becomes 'noble' and superior ownership of the truth, signalled by the further raising of his chin at '. . . yesterday.' At this point he is looking slightly up, screen left. On 'They believe it . . . Doublethink' he looks up further up as if in momentary wonder at the power or authority that could impose such an overwhelming concept as 'Doublethink'. On 'They make themselves believe it' the eyebrows are raised briefly in surprise (Why would they? How do they do it?), before a sudden hardening of the face in childlike resentment at the lie of the slogan 'Our New Happy Life'. The eyes move down as he lists the physically repugnant objects, each item marked by an increasingly hardened frown, and slight rocking movement from the (unseen) torso below, before the big reaction (eyes closed) for 'that stew!' 'Careful!' stops the lower body movement, and a sly flash of eyes to the left accompanies 'Facecrime'.

My stress on the physical and visual aspects here is not to underplay the significant impact of intonation in the voiceover: 'Double-think' is spoken with a tone of awe, a pedagogic address signalled by the separation of its words (two things), a respect that becomes tinged with surprise and—perhaps—disgust with the subsequent, 'They make themselves believe it.'

What Cushing is trying to convey by his acting is what it would look like if Winston really was thinking those thoughts. Despite the care with which it is performed, there is never a suggestion that Cushing is not acting, or that he is 'really' feeling this—how could there be when the technical performance of camera movement and the separation of voice from body so obviously signal the mediation of the television apparatus. The shot also feels artificial because it is clearly a cutaway to a close-up that is for *us*, the viewer sitting at 'home in his semi-darkened room'. When Cushing turns his head to the right, slightly toward the camera, it is as if to offer a theatrical aside, a feeling emphasized because no residual signs of the set (for example the slogans 'Ignorance is Strength and War is Peace') are visible in the background. The turning away is emphasized because the previous shot has Parsons, Winston, and Julia all looking off screen right. By breaking this eyeline, Winston signals his separation, and a willingness to look elsewhere—towards the viewer—in order to make sense of what is happening and to tell us what he thinks and show us how he feels about it. There is a double moment of interrogation, for Winston is also being watched by the Telescreen: the close-up is both a relay of his resistive reading of what the Telescreen announces and a study of his literal 'facecrime', which, apparently, only we can see.

Compared with Rod Steiger's Method-addled performance in the US early television drama classic, *Marty* (NBC, 1953), the gestural clarity of Cushing's performance does seem 'theatrical', in the sense that even in close-up it seems to be 'projecting'. Steiger's Marty directs performance energy inward towards his entire body, whereas Cushing is able to perform in close-up on command in a controlled manner (this is British-style acting); Steiger lumbers around in poorly lit areas, with the inarticulate demeanour of a child. It is a style that is appropriate to the limited abilities of his character, but the mannered and inarticulate nature of the performance (similar to that of Brando, Dean, and Clift in the 1950s), and the vulnerability that is supposed to evoke, is no match for the visual pleasure of seeing a skilled actor like Cushing in control of his performance.

This is the distinction between the face that is spontaneously reflecting mental states and the face that is 'puppeteered'.[101] The pleasure in watching Cushing's performance is seeing the puppeteers (Cushing and Cartier) at work together. If this reading reiterates the clichéd view that the difference between American and British acting is that the former has raw emotional power and the latter a 'theatrical' control, then so be it.[102] Both performances are concerned with reflecting interior states, but *Marty* pretends that the poor low tech world it is set in doesn't exist; Cushing knows he is in the middle of the most expensive and ambitious television drama in Britain to date, and does not wish to hide it.

Cushing himself articulated the codes of 'intimate acting' under scrutiny in an article written around the time of *Nineteen Eighty-Four*:

> Television is so intimate a medium, and so 'quiet'—it is like acting in a small room—that you dare not let up for one moment. You are, as it were, under microscopic attention; whereas the greater size of stage playing does allow you now and then to take it less intensely. This means that in TV absolute concentration is needed, and really hard thinking has to go into your part during rehearsal.[103]

There is also some self-referential game playing in the canteen scene. At one point interrupting Syme, Winston begins reciting, to

101 This terminology is taken from Lawrence Shaffer, 'Reflections on the Face in Film', *Film Quarterly*, 31/2 (Winter 1977–78), 6–7.

102 See Carole Zucker, 'British Film, Stage and Television Performance: Training, Praxis, and Culture', in *CineAction*, 49 (July 1997).

103 Peter Cushing, 'Peter Cushing Talks Shop: This favourite TV actor speaks here as a specially interested play-viewer', *TV Annual For 1955*, 63–4.

himself, the 'To be or not to be . . .' soliloquy from *Hamlet*, while staring blankly ahead. He trails off at 'Or to . . . or to . . .'. Cushing de-
livers the part-soliloquy with a blank expression, as if groping for
memory. The completion of the line he cannot remember is '. . . to
take arms against a sea of troubles, And by opposing, end them' the
irony being that the thought control through language that Syme is
enthusing about has already removed the memory of the line, and its
rebellious implications, from Winston's recall. On the other hand, we
know full well that Peter Cushing, the actor knows how the line
finishes, as we all have to if we are to understand the irony; he will get
to finish Winston's soliloquy soon enough anyway.

Cartier, the drama producer who is associated with *expanding* the
canvas of television drama, was also comfortable when drawing
on the 'intimate' style of the close-up visualization of thoughts—
although this is hardly a 'cosy' close-up. Cartier introduces a spatial
mobility into television drama—the sense that 'outside' is as access-
ible as 'inside'—with skill and fluency.

At the end of the canteen scene—after a tracking shot where the
television camera itself hits the table where Winston is sitting (inad-
vertent exhibitionism!)—we get a film insert of Party members leaving the (BBC) building, and Winston in long shot, walking past a
large sign with the face of Big Brother and a slogan 'Big Brother Is
Watching You' underneath. It is a miserable day and, again in long
shot, we see Winston hop over a puddle, exiting screen left. This is an
exterior space that could not be staged live in the studio, so a film
insert is necessary. Although the texture of the sequence is slightly
different (the image is sharper across a wider depth of field), the
tempo and sense of the shots perfectly complements the studio shot
of Winston's soliloquy. Here the contrast in scale between the big,
iconic face of Big Brother and the long shot of Winston's everyday action in avoiding wet shoes, rhymes with Winston's turning
away from the Telescreen as much as it reinforces the ubiquitous presence of Big Brother's face (it is outside, therefore everywhere too).
Other film sequences draw attention to themselves as exercises in
pure style: Winston's arrival in the Prole sector at night has the con-
trasts in shadow and bright directed light behind 'Big Brother' signs,
that one associates with Hollywood's reworking of German Expres-
sionist lighting styles in film noir.

One of the most visually exhibitionistic aspects of the production
is the representation of the Telescreen itself: a screen within a screen,
with most shots framing the apparatus alone, filling the television
screen.[104] Cartier argues that the effect of this was:

---

104 Screens were in the news: the recent development of widescreen in the cinema was
seen as a response to the popularity of the smaller television screen.

in the TV viewer's own home . . . cold eyes stared from the small screen straight at him, casting into the viewer's heart the same chill that the characters in the play experienced whenever they heard [Big Brother's] voice coming from *their* 'watching' TV screens.[105]

Nineteen Eighty-Four dramatized a type of authoritarian control that used the media as a weapon. Cartier shrewdly chooses a small-sized telescreen[106] as the futuristic form of media control—in fact it is one that corresponds exactly to the size of 1950s television models:

This instrument has two components: the upper one similar to a large-size television screen of 1954; the lower a large, protruding 'bullseye' lens with a spot of light travelling constantly around the circumference like the rolling pupil of an eye.[107]

The dual function of the telescreen—to display and to threaten—perhaps has some affinity with Cartier's reformulation of the intimacy aesthetic. Instead of 'chatting' with the viewer the address of this production reveals emotion and psychology in order to challenge and disturb. In the play, the Telescreen apparatus is used for intimate surveillance: they are everywhere, in public spaces and in the home as part of the wall. The Telescreen has multiple functions: it is a form of narrowcasting (only available to Party members), it functions as a radio, spewing out propaganda sound, it can transmit films and relay live events (such as public executions). Most importantly, it can receive and transmit simultaneously, it is a perverse form of interactive television, picking up voices and minute details of facial expressions ('facecrime'). While the actors have to know where the television cameras are they also need to show their awareness of the diegetic mode of surveillance. The Telescreen functioned as a figurative reconstruction of the less 'cosy' ideas of nearness, observation, visibility, and control.

The televising of *Nineteen Eighty-Four* had considerable public impact, chiefly because it tapped into one of the most significant ideological discourses of the Cold War: the threat of totalitarianism.[108] As Nigel Kneale noted, on the eve of the BBC production:

105 Ibid.

106 Compare to the large, cinema-screen sized Telescreens in Michael Radford's film *1984* (GB, 1984).

107 Bartlett, *Writing for Television*, 120. This book also contains selections from other television scripts from the early 1950s.

108 Tise Vahimagi notes that *Nineteen Eighty-Four* also popularized the 'psychology of indoctrination' television subgenre, also dependent on Cold War anxieties, and evident in series such as *The Prisoner*, *The Man From U.N.C.L.E.*, *The Guardians*, *1990*, etc. Tise Vahimagi, 'TV Zone', *Starburst*, 1/11 (1981), 50–1.

When Orwell published the brilliant novel five years ago, it had the shock effect of saying aloud something which people had been afraid to do more than think. It was the setting down of a nightmare—our own age gone mad, gone bad. In *Nineteen Eighty-Four* the worst has happened: dangerous tendencies have become monstrous facts; the very nature of human thought has become distorted; standards, morals, laws, have been twisted upside-down. Science is the slave of power, for power's sake. Satirically, savagely, with an ominously fact-founded inventiveness, Orwell demonstrated the techniques that might be used to perpetuate this fearful way of existence. Some of the words he coined in the process—'thoughtcrime,' 'doublethink,' 'unperson,' 'facecrime,' 'Newspeak' and others—have passed warningly into the language of the fifties.[109]

That *Nineteen Eighty-Four* was so controversial had much to with the way in which its representation of totalitarianism matched contemporary ideological discourses. *The Times*, in an editorial after the repeat performance, sees *Nineteen Eighty-Four* as confirming the power of television, and linked this power to an endorsement of Cold War ideology:

> If anything had been needed to underline the tremendous possibilities of television the reactions of the last few days have provided it . . . until last Sunday's broadcast it could be said that the impact of *Nineteen Eighty-Four* on the British public had been only marginal. That is no longer the case. Despite their use hundreds of times in newspapers, in broadcasts and in other ways such phrases as 'totalitarianism', 'brain-washing' and 'dangerous thoughts' and the Communist practice of making words stand on their heads have for millions of people suddenly taken on a new meaning. The BBC is to be congratulated on its coverage.[110]

For *The Times* the production had graphically focused and clarified the horrors of totalitarianism, endorsing Cold War ideology largely through simplification. As an earlier *Times* review put it, 'What we saw was not so much Orwell's vision but a pictorial simplification of it . . . concentrating on the action.'[111] It is interesting that the editorial refers to the BBC's 'coverage' rather than production, as if the play were like the Coronation, an event of national importance that the BBC team merely relayed. The *New Statesman* also praises the BBC for its 'actuality', although the editorial cites the play in a more critical context than *The Times*:

109 Nigel Kneale, 'The Last Rebel of Airstrip One', *Radio Times*, 10 Dec. 1954, 15.

110 *The Times*, 16 Dec. 1954.

111 *The Times*, 13 Dec. 1954.

Last Sunday's television version of *Nineteen Eighty-Four* drew the intended squeals of horror at George Orwell's picture of what life might be like just thirty years on. Yet when the BBC this weekend reports on the nightmare deliberations of the Nato Council in Paris, the British public will remain placid and unmoved. The reason for the contrast is obvious. Of course the real war preparations of the present are far more horrific and demented than the fictions of George Orwell's invalid imagination. But this fact must be carefully concealed from the British public. So the BBC diverts our emotions with fictional fears. We are to be shocked by the Orwellian fantasy of what life might be like under Big Brother into believing that reliance on the H-Bomb and the A-Bomb is a sensible way of keeping Big Brother at a distance.

If only we had the capacity to give the Nato deliberations in Paris the kind of actuality with which the BBC producers endowed their play last Sunday![112]

The audience reaction, based on letters sent in to the BBC,[113] was mostly hostile. Many criticized the production for its 'highbrow' aspirations, but most criticized the play on the grounds of obscenity: the clearly adulterous relationship between Julia and Winston, the torture scenes, and the various references to pornography and sexual activity. It is interesting that the letters—however unrepresentative letters to the BBC might be—are also concerned with the effect of the production on the audience: 'unsuitable for the vast audience', or talked about it in terms of 'pollution': such productions could be *bad* for people. If the Coronation proved that television had access to a mass national audience, *Nineteen Eighty-Four* demonstrated that television could also frighten and perhaps harm that audience. A new, less cosy, but more visually daring form of intimacy had been recognized.

The paradox is that whilst the press coverage stressed the contemporary relevance of the play, and recent critics (including myself) continue to praise it for its technical innovation, the television audience at the time seemed very unhappy with it. Cartier reports that he received death threats, and the BBC had to hire bodyguards to protect him. Perhaps this indicates that the shift from less 'cosy' drama to that which pulled no punches in its representation of intense distress and discomfort, had ramifications beyond the internal debate about technical etiquette: the audience could no longer trust the intimate screen.

112 Editorial, *New Statesman*, 18 Dec. 1954.

113 These letters can be found in the *Nineteen Eighty-Four* programme files, BBC WAC T5/362/2.

5
Conclusion

TELEVISION DRAMA has been self-conscious from the beginning. In the late 1930s drama producers were developing their own styles of television technique, experimenting with studio design, script layout, and film-studio combinations. New lightweight camera mountings were bought because of an unanticipated desire for a more mobile 'Programme Technique.'[1] The hunger for innovation and visual mobility was a defining characteristic of early television drama as much as its dependence on some theatrical source material, which television drama was able 'to light to its own needs'. Although theatre provided the source material for early television drama, it did not define its limits.

The history of television drama in the immediate post-war years provides another surprise: that television drama actively resisted the influence of radio drama on its form and content. The attempt to integrate sound and vision during the late 1940s meant that the aesthetic and formal differences between both were made explicit, and 'radio men' such as Val Gielgud failed to subsume the visual ambitions of television under the traditions of sound drama.

In the 1950s when a move to new premises at Lime Grove required the formalization of working practices and standards, critical ideas about the 'true' aesthetic limits of television also began to be rigidly applied. New writers and producers such as Nigel Kneale and Rudolph Cartier transcended the emerging rules of the 'intimate screen', and demonstrated that the close observation of emotions could be as visually exciting as the liberation of space through the expansion of dramatic spaces on film and in the studio.

The history of early television drama as a self-aware rather than aesthetically dependent practice means that some of the old television drama history needs revision, and further elaboration. For example, the role of Michael Barry as Head of BBC Drama in the 1950s

---

1 'Tel. PM said that he would like it recorded that he would have preferred the "Fearless Dollys" for Studio no.2 instead of the two Iron Men which had been provided. Programme technique is not now advancing in the use of Iron Men, but Dollys are used instead.' Minutes of the Meeting of Television equipment Liaison Committee at Broadcasting House, 19 Jan. 1938. A year later a new lightweight dolly was ordered 'in view of the increasing number of tracking shots'. Source: Alexandra Palace Television Society.

would benefit from a balanced assessment that was more careful about the contrast with Sydney Newman. The idea that early BBC television drama relied on theatre rather than encouraged new writers suggests that new writers were shunned by the BBC, until ITV and Newman came along, liberating them, and the television cameras, from their theatrical chains. But as we have seen Denis Johnston, Robert MacDermot, and Barry himself were always interested in attracting new writers for television. As veteran television critic Philip Purser recalls:

> By the time I started to watch in the mid-1950s the outside broadcasts were still, in the eyes of the pioneers, the most exciting and interesting: I found these greatly overrated and rapidly becoming corrupted in the sense that it was being set-up, managed, and that television drama had replaced it as the most vital and spontaneous, really, live manifestation of television. Drama was live, and it was so adventurous. I think the judgement on Michael Barry has been a little unfair: he did so much more in the way of visual drama than he's been given credit for. He commissioned new plays as well.[2]

The changing fashions of the British theatre itself during the mid-1950s may have contributed to a new 'sell' for ITV television drama that was coincident with Newman's arrival as head of 'Armchair Theatre'. Ironically, it was Michael Barry who, in 1956, took Sydney Newman to a production of John Osborne's *Look Back in Anger* at the Royal Court Theatre:

> That play with its unusual worm's eye view of society and its derisive radicalism, seemed to Newman the dazzling light on the road to Damascus; more accurately it summed up what he had come to believe about the drama.[3]

Inspired by the theatre, Newman set out to change television. Ironically, it was the televising of an extract—in a manner reminiscent of 'Theatre Parade' in 1936—from *Look Back in Anger* which transformed it into a popular and critical success:

> Despite notices that suggest that something exciting was afoot, *Look Back in Anger* had not done notably better than its fellows in the first repertory season; when it took over by itself it coasted along for the first eight weeks just below the taking at which it would break even. Then, at the beginning of the ninth week, an

---

2 Philip Purser, interview with author, 29 June 1992.

3 Bernard Sendall quoted in David Self, *Television Drama: An Introduction* (Houndmills and London: Macmillan, 1984; 1988), 49.

extract was shown on television, and takings jumped at once from about £950 for the week to over £1,300, and in the following week to over £1,700 . . .[4]

The image of Barry and Newman watching this play together encapsulates the subsequent cross-fertilization of drama personnel, and therefore style and technique, between ITV and BBC. Even when ITV companies began their first drama broadcasts, and with an increased scheduling of filmed material, the production standard remained modelled on the BBC mode because much of the early ITV drama output was managed and made by migrants from the BBC:

> There was a wholesale exodus of staff from the BBC to ITV. For example, from Lime Grove entire studio crews left. Everybody, together, the floor managers, the directors, the cameramen. It was for money. ITV was offering a £1000 a year, and the BBC was paying £500–£600.[5]

The migrants included BBC drama producers such as George More O'Ferrall, Alvin Rakoff, Dennis Vance, Desmond Davis, Royston Morley, and Julian Amyes. These drama producers, perhaps working with familiar personnel from the BBC, would have translated their styles and techniques (albeit in modified forms, according to the demands of different studios, formats and organization) for ITV drama. This translation was also one which had to account for the new technological changes which were beginning to come on line, in particular videotape and the techniques of editing videotape which were developed later.

This 'second wave' of drama directors, trained at the BBC but eventually working for ITV provide a continuity between the early period of television drama and the 'golden age' of the 1960s. This is why *Nineteen Eighty-Four* and the year 1955 marks the beginning of a transitional period. It is important not to collapse early and transitional periods together, just as much as it is vital to recognize the various continuities they share. A full understanding of the changes that were to come, in the form and scope and audience and impact of television drama, is only possible if it is based upon an informed and uncaricatured sense of the early development of television drama.

Jean Renoir and Roberto Rossellini were interviewed by André Bazin for *Sight and Sound* in 1958; after Rossellini questions the centrality of montage (editing) for cinema, Renoir goes on to make a distinction between the cinematic and television close-up:

4 John Russell Taylor, *Anger and After: A Guide to the New British Drama* (London: Methuen, 1962), 35.

5 Mike Savage, BBC engineer, interview with author, July 1994.

I ought to say that the television shows I've found most exciting have been certain interviews on American TV. I feel that the interview gives the television close-up a meaning which is rarely achieved in the cinema. The close-up in the cinema is essentially a reconstruction, something prefabricated, carefully worked up—and, of course, this has yielded some great moments in the cinema. This said, I believe that in thirty years we have rather used up this type of cinema and that we should perhaps move on to something else. In America I've seen some exceptional shows . . .

I remember for instance, certain interviews in connection with some political hearing. Here, suddenly, we had a huge close-up, a picture of a human being in his entirety. One man was afraid, and all his fear showed; another was insolent, insulted the questioner; another was ironical; another took it all very lightly. In two minutes we could read the faces of these people: we knew who they were. I found this tremendously exciting . . . and somehow an indecent spectacle to watch. Yet this indecency came nearer the knowledge of man than many films.[6]

Getting closer to the subject is the historical function of television, and because of that it is part of the definition of the subject. The television close-up was felt to have such potency that during the BBC's live televising of the Coronation of 1953 in Westminster Abbey, the television cameras were restricted to the nave so that they would not violate 'the frightful intimacy of the service'; closeness had no respect.[7]

But the desire to reveal interior landscapes provides the continuity from the early period of television drama to the 1960s, and up to the present day. Getting inside the head, revealing the interior psychological dramas, was the ambition of modernist writers such as Dennis Potter.[8] But the visualization of interior subjective states is a part of the intimate—drawing room—address of some television drama from the beginning.

It seems to me that whatever the paternalistic address of public service broadcasting, the BBC treated its audience as adults, if 'culturally challenged' adults. Barry and Cartier granted their audience autonomy: the chance to study dramatically enhanced emotions. Perhaps Renoir has something when he notes the indecent power of the close-up in terms of political interview. What changed in the late 1950s and early 1960s was the increase in news and current affairs programming, from virtually nothing in the early 1950s. What early

6 *Sight and Sound*, 28/1 (winter 1958–9), 27.

7 Quoted in Paddy Scannell, *Radio, Television and Modern Life* (Oxford: Blackwell, 1996), 81.

8 See Glen Creeber's excellent study, *Dennis Potter: Between Two Worlds* (Basingstoke: Macmillan, 1998).

television drama producers discovered in an era before current affairs and news were 'in vision', was the importance of 'getting close'. After 1955 television drama was to develop its styles and interests not towards film modes, but instead towards politics, documentary, and current affairs (some of it shot on film). In this way the visualization of 'getting close' was part of a public look, of a looking at the world rather than the stage. It is that sense of the personal image of the political that is encapsulated in the title of Grace Wyndham Goldie's account of the relationship between British television and British politics, *Facing the Nation*.[9] The close-up visualization of the face is the place where we can check the face against the words that the participants have to find for their lives, and for ours.

'Where is the distinctive art form? Where is that which *is* TV?' asked Sir Michael Balcon, head of Ealing Studios, itself responsible for some 'intimate' British films.[10] As this book demonstrates he was not the first or the last to ask that question. Noël Carroll notes that 'a theoretical concern with essences is philosophical'[11] and it is my feeling that the thinking about intimacy by critics and practitioners points the television historian towards questions that might properly be addressed by a philosophy of television. This would mean thinking about the medium as a medium whilst attending to the difficulty of the question, What is a medium? Uncovering the history of early television drama, then, is also a revelation about other ways of thinking about television. It should be possible to think about 'television as television' without having to divert our attention to something else that we feel is deserving of it.

This account has also shown that television drama became self-conscious early on, that it was mobile as well as static and that it mattered to those involved in its production and in its criticism. My intention was to demonstrate that early television drama can be written about, and that it is worth thinking and writing about. Questions about the form and look of early television drama that this book has covered, raise further questions about the nature of the television medium as a whole, issues that concern thinking about what a medium *is*.[12] If that implies a philosophy of television, then I can only point to the fact that these questions, as I have shown, were asked by early drama producers themselves.

9 Grace Wyndham Goldie, *Facing the Nation* (London: Bodley Head, 1977).

10 Quoted in Jonathan Giles, 'I Won't Make Films for TV', *TV Mirror*, 2/7 (1954), 14.

11 Noël Carroll, *A Philosophy of Mass Art* (Oxford: Oxford University Press, 1998), 110.

12 These comments are inspired by reading Stanley Cavell, *The World Viewed* (Enlarged edition, Harvard University Press, 1979), 163–5 and 'The Fact of Television', *Themes Out of School: Effects and Causes* (Chicago: University of Chicago Press, 1984).

Bibliography

ABC TELEVISION LTD., *The Armchair Theatre: How to Write, Design, Direct, Act and Enjoy Television Plays* (London: Weidenfeld and Nicolson, 1959).

ABRAMSON, A., *Electronic Motion Pictures: A History of the Television Camera* (Berkeley and Los Angeles: University of California Press, 1955).

—— 'A Short History of Television Recording', in R. Fielding (ed.), *A Technological History of Motion Pictures and Television* (Los Angeles, Berkeley: University of California, 1967).

—— *The History of Television, 1880–1941* (McFarland, 1987).

ALLEN, R. C. (ed.), *Channels of Discourse, Reassembled* (London: Routledge, 1992).

AMOS, S., and BIRKENSHAW, D. C., *Television Engineering Principles and Practice*, 4 vols. (London: Lliffe & Sons, 1953–8).

ARLEN, M., *The Camera Age: Essays on Television* (New York, 1981).

ARMES, R., *On Video* (London: Routledge, 1988).

ARMSTRONG, A. C., *Television Viewers' Handbook* (London: English University Press, 1954).

ASHBRIDGE, N., 'Television Comes to the Centre of England', *Radio Times*, 9 November 1949.

ASSOCIATED-REDIFFUSION LTD., *You Want to Write for Television* (London: 1959).

ATKINS, I., 'Television Programme Production Problems in Relation to Engineering Technique', *Proceedings of the Institute of Electrical Engineers*, 99/3a/17 (April–May 1952).

AUMONT, J., *The Image* (London: British Film Institute, 1997).

BADDER, D., 'Frears and Company', *Sight and Sound* (Spring 1978).

BAILY, K., *Here's Television* (London: Vox Mundi, 1950).

—— 'The Play has five Faces', *Radio Times*, 16 October 1953.

—— (ed.), *The Television Annual For 1955* (London: Odhams Press, 1955).

BAKER, H. W., 'Planning a Television Studio', *BBC Yearbook* (1951).

BAKER, H. W., and KEMP, W. D., 'The recording of television programmes', *BBC Quarterly*, 4/4 (1949–50).

BARNES, G., 'Is Television on the Right Lines?', in K. Baily (ed.), *The Television Annual For 1955* (London: Odhams Press, 1955).

BARNOUW, E., *A Tower in Babel* (New York: Oxford University Press, 1966).

—— *The Golden Web* (New York: Oxford University Press, 1968).

—— *Tube of Plenty* (New York: Oxford University Press, 1975).

BARR, C. *et al.*, 'The Making of *Upstairs, Downstairs*, a Television Series', *Movie* (Autumn 1975).

—— 'Criticism and TV Drama', in the special issue of *Broadcast* published as the Official Programme of the Edinburgh International Television Festival, (1977).

BARR, C. *et al.*, 'A Conundrum for England', *Monthly Film Bulletin* (August 1984).

—— 'Television on Television', *Sight and Sound*, 55/3 (1986).

—— (ed.), *All Our Yesterdays: 90 Years of British Cinema* (London: British Film Institute, 1986).

—— 'Broadcasting and Cinema: Screens Within Screens', in Barr (ed.), *All Our Yesterdays: 90 Years of British Cinema* (London: British Film Institute, 1986).

—— ' "They Think It's All Over": The Dramatic Legacy of Live Television', in J. Hill and M. McLoone (eds.), *Big Picture, Small Screen: The Relations Between Film and Television* (Luton: University of Luton Press/John Libbey, 1997).

BARRY, M., 'Problems of a Producer', *BBC Quarterly*, 3/3 (autumn 1951).

—— 'Producer and Director', *Radio Times*, 9 January 1953.

—— 'The Craft of Visual Storytelling', *Radio Times*, 1 May 1953.

—— 'From Script to Screen', *TV Mirror* 1/5 (September 1953).

—— 'Shakespeare on Television', *BBC Quarterly*, 9/3 (1954).

—— *From the Palace to the Grove* (London: Royal Television Society, 1992).

BARTLETT, B., *Writing for Television* (London: George Allen & Unwin Ltd., 1955).

BELL, E., 'The Origins of British Television Documentary: The BBC 1946–55', in J. Corner (ed.), *Documentary and the Mass Media* (London: Edward Arnold, 1986).

BETTINGER, H., *Television Techniques* (New York & London: Harper and Bros., 1947; 1955).

BIRD, C. K., *Ten Years of Television 1949–59* (London: BBC, 1959).

BIRKENSHAW, D. C., 'Television Programme Origination: The Engineering Technique', *Proceedings of the Institute of Electrical Engineers* 99/3a/17 (April–May 1952).

—— and CAMPBELL, D. R., 'Studio Technique in Television', *Journal of Institute of Electrical Engineers*, 92/19 (September 1945).

BLACK, P., *The Mirror in the Corner* (London: Hutchinson and Co. Ltd, 1972).

BLUEM, A., and MANVELL, R., *The Progress of Television: an Anglo-American Survey* (London: Focal Press, 1967).

BODDY, W., *Fifties Television* (Urbana and Chicago: University of Illinois Press, 1990).

—— 'Archaeologies of Electronic Vision and the Gendered Spectator', *Screen*, 35/2 (1994).

BOND, F., *You Can Write . . . Techniques for Television, Radio and the Theatre* (New York: Sentinel Books, 1959).

BORDWELL, D., STAIGER, J., and THOMPSON, K., *The Classical Hollywood Cinema: Film Style and Mode of Production to 1960* (London: Routledge and Kegan Paul, 1985).

BORDWELL, D., and THOMPSON, K., *Film Art: An Introduction*, 4th edn. (New York: McGraw-Hill Inc., 1993).

BOWER, 'Television and the Films', *Radio Times* (Television Supplement), 15 January 1937.

BRADBY, D., and JAMES, L. (eds.), *Performance and Politics in Popular Drama* (Cambridge: Cambridge University Press, 1981).

BRANDT, G. (ed.), *British Television Drama* (Cambridge: Cambridge University Press, 1981).

—— (ed.), *British Television Drama in the 1980s* (Cambridge: Cambridge University Press, 1993).

BRANSTON, G., 'Histories of British Television', in C. Geraghty and D. Lusted (eds.), *The Television Studies Book* (London: Arnold, 1998).

BRETZ, R., *Techniques of Television Production* (New York: McGraw-Hill Book Co., 1953).

BRIDGEWATER, T. H. *et al.*, 'Televising the Boat Race—1950: The Engineering Problems', *BBC Quarterly*, 2/1 (Summer 1950).

BRIDGEWATER, T. H., 'Television Outside Broadcasts', *BBC Quarterly*, 5/3 (Autumn 1950).

BRIGGS, A., *History of Broadcasting in the UK*, vols. i–v (London and Oxford: Oxford University Press, 1961–95).

BRYANT, S., *The Television Heritage* (London: British Film Institute, 1989).

BURTON, P., *British Broadcasting: radio and television in the U.K.* (Minneapolis: University of Minnesota Press, 1956).

BUSCOMBE, E., 'Broadcasting From Above', *Screen Education*, 37 (1980–1).

—— 'Thinking it Differently: Television and the Film Industry,' *Quarterly Review of Film Studies*, 9/3 (Summer 1984).

—— 'All Bark and No Bite: The Film Industry's Response to Television', in J. Corner (ed.), *Popular Television in Britain: Studies in Cultural History* (London: British Film Institute, 1991).

BUSSELL, J., *The Art of Television* (London: Faber and Faber, 1952).

CAIN, J., *The BBC: 70 Years of Broadcasting* (London: BBC, 1992).

CALDWELL, J., *Televisuality: Style, Crisis, and Authority in American Television* (New Brunswick, NJ: Rutgers University Press, 1995).

CARROLL, N., *A Philosophy of Mass Art* (Oxford: Oxford University Press, 1998).

CARR, E. H., *What is History?* (Harmondsworth: Penguin, 1981).

CAUGHIE, J., 'Progressive Television and Documentary Drama', *Screen*, 22/1 (1981).

—— 'Rhetoric, Pleasure and "Art Television"—Dreams of Leaving', *Screen*, 22/4 (1981).

—— 'Television Criticism: "A Discourse in Search of an Object" ', *Screen*, 25/4–5 (July–Oct. 1984).

—— 'Adorno's reproach: repetition, difference and television genre', *Screen*, 32/2 (Summer 1991).

—— 'Before the Golden Age: Early Television Drama,' in J. Corner (ed.), *Popular Television in Britain* (London: British Film Institute, 1991).

CAVALCANTI, A., BELFRAGE, C., DICKINSON, T., GRIERSON, J., and GREENE, G., 'Broadcasting and Television Manifesto,' *World Film News and Television Progress*, 1/1 (April 1936).

CAVELL, S., *The World Viewed*, Enlarged edn. (Harvard University Press, 1979).

—— 'The Fact of Television', *Themes Out of School: Effects and Causes* (Chicago: University of Chicago Press, 1984).

CHAPMAN, N. F., 'A Film Dubbing and Review Suite for Television Film Production', *BBC Quarterly*, 5/2 (Summer 1950).

CLARK, K., *What is Good Taste?* (London: Associated Television, 1959).

CLAYTON, D., *A Picture Book of Television, 1930–1950* (London: BBC, 1950).

COCK, G., 'Looking Forward, a Personal Forecast of the Future of Television', *Radio Times*, 29 October 1936.

COLLEY, I., and DAVIES, G., 'Pennies From Heaven: Music, Image, Text', *Screen Education*, no. 35 (1980).

CORNER, J. (ed.), *Popular Television in Britain: Studies in Cultural History* (London: British Film Institute, 1991).

—— *Television Form and Public Address* (London: Edward Arnold, 1995).

COVEN, F., *Daily Mail Television Guide* (London: Daily Mail, 1953).

CRISELL, A., *An Introductory History of British Broadcasting* (London: Routledge, 1997).

CROZIER, M., *Broadcasting Sound and Television* (London: Oxford University Press, 1958).

DAVIES, J. R., *Understanding Television* (London: Data Publications, 1963).

DAVIS, A., *Television: The First Forty Years* (London: Independent Television Publications Ltd., 1976).

DAVIS, D., *The Grammar of Television Production* (London: Barrie & Rockliffe, 1960).

DAY-LEWIS, S., *Talk of Drama: Views of the Television Dramatist Now and Then* (Luton: University of Luton Press/John Libbey Media, 1998).

DORTÉ, P., 'Television and the Cinema', *Radio Times*, 23 March 1951.

DRAKAKIS, J. (ed.), *British Radio Drama* (Cambridge: Cambridge University Press, 1980).

DRUMMOND, P., and PATTERSON, R. (eds.), *Television in Transition* (London: British Film Institute, 1986).

DURBRIDGE, F., 'My First Television Serial', *Radio Times*, 7 March 1952.

ELLIOTT, M., 'Television Drama, The Medium and The Predicament', *Encore*, 4/4 (1958).

ELLIS, J., *Visible Fictions: Cinema: Television: Video* (London: Routledge, 1982).

ELSAESSER, T. (ed.), *Early Cinema: Space, Frame, Narrative* (London: British Film Institute, 1990).

—— 'TV through the Looking Glass', *Quarterly Review of Film & Video*, 14/1–2 (1992).

—— *et al.* (eds.), *Writing for the Medium: Television in Transition* (Amsterdam, University Press, 1994).

ENGLANDER, A. A., *Filming for Television* (London: Focal Press, 1976).

ENRIGHT, D. J., *Fields of Vision* (Oxford: Oxford University Press, 1988).

FAIRLEY, P., *Television: Behind the Screen* (London: Independent Television Publications Ltd., 1976).

FAIRLEY, R., *The Small Screen* (London: Cassell, 1958).

FALLON, M., *Writing for Television* (Bristol: Fallon Publications, 1949).

FEUER, J., 'The Concept of Live Television: Ontology as Ideology', in E. A. Kaplan (ed.), *Regarding Television* (California: American Film Institute Monograph, 1983).

FIDDY, D., *Television: An Introductory Guide to its History* (London: MOMI Education pamphlet, 1994).

FIELDING, R. (ed.), *A Technological History of Motion Pictures and Television* (Los Angeles and Berkeley: University of California, 1967).

FURNIVALL, R., 'The Wall of Glass: Some Notes on the Writer in Television', *Encore*, 5/4 (1958).

GARDNER, C., and WYVER, J., 'The Single Play from Reithian Reverence to Cost-Accounting and Censorship', and 'The Single Play: An Afterword', *Screen*, 24/4–5 (1983).

GARNHAM, N., and BAKEWELL, J., *The New Priesthood: British Television Today* (London: Allen Lane, 1970).

GELMIS, J., *The Film Director as Superstar* (New York: Doubleday, 1970).

GIDDENS, A., *The Transformation of Intimacy: Sexuality, Love and Eroticism in Modern Societies* (Cambridge: Polity Press, 1992).

GIELGUD, V., 'Policy and Problems of Broadcast Drama', *BBC Quarterly*, 2/1 (1947).

—— 'Drama in Television and Sound', *BBC Quarterly*, 5/4 (Winter 1950–1).

—— 'Drama on the Television Screen', *Radio Times*, 12 January 1951.

—— *British Radio Drama 1922–1956* (London: George Harrap, 1957).

—— *Years in a Mirror* (London: The Bodley Head, 1965).

GOLDIE, G. W., *Facing the Nation: Television and Politics, 1936–1976* (London: Bodley Head, 1977).

GOLDSTEIN, N., *The History of Television* (New York: Portland House, 1990).

GOMERY, D., and ALLEN, R., *Film History: Theory and Practice* (New York: Alfred A. Knopf, 1987).

GORHAM, M., *Television: Medium of the Future* (London: Percival Marshall, 1949).

—— Television: A Medium in its own Right?', from *The Cinema 1951* (Penguin Books, 1951).

—— *Broadcasting and Television Since 1900* (London: Andrew Dakers Ltd., 1952).

GOULD, P., *The Structure of Television* (London: Pion, 1984).

GOWDA, A. H. H., *The Idiot Box: Early American Television Plays* (New Delhi: Stirling, 1987).

GRAY, A., *British Television Year Book 1947–8* (London, 1947).

GREENE, H., 'Television Transcriptions: The Economic Possibilities', *BBC Quarterly*, 7/4 (1952–3).

GREENFIELD, J., *Television: The First 50 Years* (New York: Abrahams, 1977).

GRIFFITHS, W. N., *A Guide to Radio Writing* (London: K. K. Tuition, 1950).

HAILEY, A., *Close-Up or Writing for Television* (New York: Doubleday & Co., 1960).

HAINAUX, R., 'Editorial', *World Theatre*, 9/4 (Winter 1960).

HALE, L., 'Away with the Drawing-Room', *Radio Times*, 13 November 1949.

—— 'A Tempest of a Tragedy', *Radio Times*, 28 March 1952.

HALLIWELL, L., and PURSER, P., *Halliwell's Television Companion* (London: Granada, 1982).

HALLOWS, R. W., *Television Simply Explained* (London: Chapman & Hall, 1947).

HARBORD, J., and WRIGHT, J., *Forty Years of British Television* (London: Boxtree, 1992).

HARE, D., *Ah! Mischief: The Writer and Television* (London: Faber and Faber, 1982).

HICKETHIER, K., 'The Television Play in the Third Reich', *Historical Journal of Film, Radio and Television*, 10/2 (1990).

HILTON, J., *Performance* (London: Macmillan, 1987).

HOBSON, H., 'What We Want in Television Plays', *BBC Quarterly*, 5/2 (Summer 1950).

HOOD, S., *Radio and Television* (London: David & Charles, 1975).

—— *On Television* (London: Pluto, 1989).

HORTON, D., *Television's Story and Challenge* (London: George Harrap, 1951).

HOUSTON, B., 'Viewing Television: the Metapsychology of Endless Consumption', *Quarterly Review of Film Studies*, 9/3 (Summer 1984).

HUBBELL, R. W., *Four Thousand Years of Television* (London: Harrap, 1946).

—— *Television Programming and Production* (London: Chapman and Hall, 1956).

HUDSON, R., 'Television Drama in Britain: Description and Dissent', *Theatre Quarterly*, 2/6 (April–June 1972).

HUTCHINSON, R. W., *Television up-to-date* (London: University Tutorial Press, 1935).

HUTTON, G., 'The Challenge of Television', *BBC Quarterly*, 5/4 (Winter 1950–1).

IGLÉSIS, R., 'First Steps in Television for the Stage Producer', *World Theatre*, 9/4 (Winter 1960).

JACOBS, J., 'No Respect: Shot and Scene in Early Television Drama', in Jeremy Ridgman (ed.), *Boxed Sets: Television Representations of Theatre* (Luton: Arts Council of England/John Libbey Media/University of Luton, 1998).

JONES, P., *The Technique of the Television Cameraman* (London: Focal Press, 1965).

KAUFMAN, W., *How to Write For Television* (New York: Hastings House, 1955).

KELLAWAY, F. W., *Television for Everyone: History and Practice* (Bognor Regis and London: John Crowther, 1944).

KENNEDY-MARTIN, T., 'Nats Go Home: First Statement of a New Drama For Television', *Encore* (March 1964).

KERBY, P., *The Victory of Television* (New York and London: Harper & Bros., 1939).

KINDEM, G., *The Live Television Generation of Hollywood Film Directors* (Jefferson, NC, and London: McFarland, 1994).

KING, C., 'The Influence of Documentary Methods on Television Drama (with particular emphasis upon the years 1946–1962)' (Unpublished Ph.D. diss., University of Hull, 1975).

KNEALE, N., 'Not Quite So Intimate', *Sight and Sound*, 28/2 (Spring 1959).

—— *The Quatermass Experiment* (London: Arrow Books, 1979).

—— *Quatermass 2* (London: Arrow Books, 1979).

—— *Quatermass and the Pit* (London: Arrow Books, 1979).

KREUTER, D. W., *British Radio and Television Pioneers, A Patent Bibliography* (Metuchen, NJ, and London: Scarecrow Press, 1993).

KRUGER, L., *The National Stage: Theatre and Cultural Legitimation in England, France and America* (London and Chicago: University of Chicago Press, 1992).

LANGLEY, N., 'The Nature of the Television Play', *BBC Quarterly*, 8/3 (Autumn 1953).

LAURITZEN, M., *Jane Austen's Emma on Television* (Göteborg: Acta Universitatis Gothoburgensis, 1981).

LEJEUNE, C. A., 'The Case of the Undying Detective', *Radio Times*, 12 October 1951.

LEMAN, J., 'Wise Scientists and Female Androids: Class and Gender in Science Fiction', in J. Corner (ed.), *Popular Television in Britain: Studies in Cultural History* (London: British Film Institute, 1991).

LEONARD, W. T., *Theatre, Stage to Screen to Television* (Metuchen, NJ, and London: Scarecrow Press, 1981).

LEVIN, R., *Television By Design* (London: Bodley Head, 1961).

—— *Television and Design* (London: BBC, 1968).

LEWIS, J., and STEMPEL, P., *Cult TV* (London: Pavilion Books, 1993).

LURY, K., 'Television Performance: Being, Acting and "Corpsing"', *New Formations*, 26 (1995–6).

MacCORMICK, I., 'An Experiment in Television Drama', *Radio Times*, 21 May 1955.

MacMURRAUGH-KAVANAGH, M. K., '"Drama" into "News": Strategies of Intervention in "The Wednesday Play"', *Screen* 38/3 (1997).

—— 'The BBC and the Birth of "The Wednesday Play", 1962–66: Institutional Containment versus "Agitational Contemporaneity"', *Historical Journal of Film, Radio and Television*, 17/3 (1997).

MACKIE, P., 'Six Hundred Hours a Week', *Sight and Sound*, 24/1 (July–September, 1954).

MADDEN, C., 'Television: Problems and Possibilities', *BBC Quarterly*, 2/4 (1948).

MADDEN, P. (ed.), *Keeping Television Alive* (London: British Film Institute, 1981).

MANVELL, R., 'Drama on Television and the Film', *BBC Quarterly*, 1 (1952).

—— *On the Air* (London: Deutsch, 1953).

—— *The Crowded Air . . . A Study of the Problems and Potentialities of American and British Television* (New York: Channel Press, 1953).

—— *The Film and the Public* (Harmondsworth: Penguin, 1955).

—— *The Living Screen, Background to the Film and Television* (London: Harrap, 1961).

MARETH, P., 'America's Public Broadcasting Service, Public Visions: Private Voices', *Sight and Sound* (Winter 1976–7).

MARLOW, E., and SECUNDA, E., *Shifting Time and Space: The Story of Videotape* (New York: Praeger, 1991).

MARSCHALL, R., *The Golden Age of Television* (London: Bison, 1987).

MARSHALL, N., 'Are Stage Plays Suitable for Television?', *World Theatre*, 9/4 (Winter 1960).

McCLEERY, A., 'The Theatre's Debt to Television', *World Theatre*, 9/4 (Winter 1960).

McGivern, C., 'The Big Problem', *BBC Quarterly*, 5/3 (Autumn 1950).

—— 'Let's Get it Moving Again', *Contrast*, 1/3 (Spring 1962).

McGrath, J., 'TV Drama: The Case against Naturalism', *Sight and Sound*, 46/2 (Spring 1977).

McLoone, M., 'Boxed In?: The Aesthetics of Film and Television', in J. Hill and M. McLoone (eds.), *Big Picture, Small Screen: The Relations between Film and Television* (Luton: John Libbey Media, 1997).

Miall, L., *Inside the BBC: British Broadcasting Characters* (London: Weidenfeld and Nicolson, 1994).

Millerson, G., *The Technique of the Television Producer* (London: Focal Press, 1961).

Moore, R. W., 'Television: A Cautionary Approach', *BBC Quarterly*, 5/1 (Spring 1950).

Morley, J. R., 'The Television Drama', in Paul Rotha (ed.), *Television in the Making* (London: Focal Press, 1956).

Morrison, H., 'Television: The Plan and the Timetable', *Radio Times*, 9 October 1949.

Murray, B., and Wickham, C. J. (eds.), *Framing the Past: The Historiography of German Cinema and Television* (Carbondale: Southern Illinois University Press, 1992).

Musser, C., 'Toward a History of Screen Practice', *Quarterly Review of Film Studies* (Winter 1984).

Myles, L., and Petley, J., 'Rudolph Cartier', *Sight and Sound*, 59/2 (Spring 1990).

Nelson, R., *TV Drama in Transition* (London: Macmillan, 1997).

Newnham, J. K., *Television Behind the Screens* (London: Convoy Publications, 1948).

Noble, P., *British Theatre* (London: Knap, Drewelt and Sons, 1946).

Norden, D. (ed.), *Coming to You Live! Behind-the-Screen Memories of Forties and Fifties Television* (London: Methuen, 1985).

Norman, B., *Here's Looking At You* (London: British Broadcasting Corporation and Royal Television Society, 1984).

O'Ferrall, G. M., 'The Televising of Drama', *Radio Times*, 19 March 1937.

—— Adams, M., Gough, M., Baxter, R. K. N., and Manvell, R., 'Television's Challenge to the Cinema', in *The Cinema 1950* (Penguin Books, 1950).

Perkins, V. F., *Film as Film: Understanding and Judging Movies* (Harmondsworth: Penguin, 1972).

Petley, J., 'The Manxman', *Monthly Film Bulletin*, 56/662 (March 1989).

Pick, J., *The West End: Mismanagement and Snobbery* (Eastbourne: John Offord, 1983).

Priestley, J. B., 'Television . . . the Danger', *Radio Times*, 31 August 1951.

Pulling, M. J. L., 'The Lime Grove Television Studios', *BBC Quarterly*, 5/3 (Autumn 1950).

Quéval, J., 'Cinema and Television', *Sight and Sound* (May 1950).

Rath, C. D., 'Live/life: Television as a Generator of Events in Everyday Life', in P. Drummond and R. Patterson (eds.), *Television and its Audience* (London: British Film Institute, 1988).

Rattigan, T., 'My First Television Play', *Radio Times*, 27 July 1951.

RAVAGE, J. W., *Television: The Director's Viewpoint* (Boulder: Westview Press, 1978).

RIDGMAN, J. (ed.), *Boxed Sets: Television Representations of Theatre* (Luton: Arts Council of England/John Libbey Media/University of Luton, 1998).

ROSEN, P., 'History of Image, Image of History', *Wide Angle*, 9/4 (1987).

ROSS, D., 'The Documentary in Television', *BBC Quarterly*, 5/1 (Spring 1950).

ROSS, G., *Television Jubilee* (London: W. H. Allen, 1961).

ROTHA, P. (ed.), *Television in the Making* (London and New York: Focal Press, 1956).

ROYAL, J. F. (ed.), *Television Production Problems* (New York: McGraw-Hill Book Co., 1948).

SALES, R., 'An Introduction to Broadcasting History', in D. Punter (ed.), *Introduction to Contemporary Cultural Studies* (London: Longman, 1986).

SALT, B., *Film Style and Technology: History and Analysis* (London: Starword, 1983).

SAMPSON, H. O., 'Television Lighting Technique', *Proceedings of the Institute of Electrical Engineers*, 99/3a/17 (April–May 1952).

SCANNELL, P., 'Public Service Broadcasting: The History of a Concept', in A. Goodwin and G. Whannel (eds.), *Understanding Television* (London: Routledge, 1990).

—— *Radio, Television and Modern Life* (Oxford: Blackwell, 1996).

—— and CARDIFF, D., *A Social History of Broadcasting*, 1. *1922–1939* (Oxford: Blackwell, 1991).

SCHIML, R., *Studio Drama: processes and procedures* (Boston and London: Focal Press, 1992).

SCROGGIE, M. G., *Television* (London and Glasgow: Blackie & Son, 1948).

SELF, D., *Television Drama: An Introduction* (London: Macmillan, 1984).

SENDALL, B., *Independent Television in Britain*, i. *Origin and Foundation, 1946–62* (London: Macmillan, 1982).

SETON, M., 'Television Drama', *Theatre Arts Monthly* (December 1938).

SHAFFER, L., 'Reflections on the Face in Film', *Film Quarterly*, 31/2 (Winter 1977–8).

SHAUGHNESSY, A., *Both Ends of the Candle* (London: Robin Clark, 1979).

SHIERS, G. (ed.), *Technical Development of Television* (New York: Arno Press, 1977).

SHUBIK, I., *Play For Today: The Evolution of Television Drama* (London: Davis-Poynter, 1975).

SLIDE, A., *The Television Industry: a historical dictionary* (New York and London: Greenwood, 1991).

SPIGEL, L., and MANN, D. (eds.), *Private Screenings: Television and the Female Consumer* (Minneapolis: University of Minneapolis Press, 1992).

STOKES, S., 'Radio Drama As I Hear It', *BBC Quarterly*, 5/3 (Autumn 1950).

STONIER, G. W., 'The Intimate Screen', *Sight and Sound*, 27/6 (Autumn 1958).

STURCKEN, F., *Live Television: The Golden Age of 1946–1958 in New York* (Jefferson, NC: McFarland, 1990).

SUTTON, S., *The Largest Theatre in the World: Thirty Years of Television Drama* (London: BBC, 1982).

SWIFT, J., 'Who Would be a Producer!', *Radio Times*, 14 January 1947.

—— 'The Interpretation of Drama', *Radio Times*, 14 March 1947.

—— *Adventure in Vision: The First Twenty-Five Years of Television* (London: John Lehman, 1950).

SWINSON, A., *Writing for Television* (London: Charles Black, 1955).

—— *Television* (Exeter: Wheaton, 1964).

TAYLOR, C. P., *Making a Television Play* (Newcastle-upon-Tyne: Oriel Press, 1970).

TAYLOR, D., 'Television: A Time to Speak', *New Statesman*, October 1981.

—— *Days of Vision* (London: Methuen, 1990).

TAYLOR, J. R. (ed.), *Anatomy of a Television Play* (London: Weidenfeld & Nicolson, 1962).

—— *Anger and After: A Guide to the New British Drama* (London: Methuen, 1962).

TERRACE, V., *The Complete Encyclopaedia of Television Programs, 1947–1979* (South Brunswick: Barnes, 1980).

THORPE, F. (ed.), *International Directory of Film and Television Documentation Centres* (Chicago and London: St. James, 1988).

TICHI, C., *Electronic Hearth: Creating an American Television Culture* (New York, Oxford: Oxford University Press, 1991).

TÖNQVIST, E., *Transposing Drama: Studies in Representation* (London: Macmillan, 1991).

TREWIN, J. C., *The Theatre Since 1900* (London: Andrew Dakers Ltd., 1951).

TRUFFAUT, F., *Hitchcock* (London: Secker and Warburg, 1968).

TULLOCH, J., *Television Drama: Agency, Audience, Myth* (London: Routledge, 1990).

TYNAN, K., 'Television and the Stage', *Drama*, 26 (1952).

URRICHIO, W., 'Introduction to the History of German Television, 1935–1944', *Historical Journal of Film, Radio and Television*, 10/2 (1990).

VAHIMAGI, T. (ed.), *British Television: An Illustrated Guide* (Oxford: Oxford University Press, 1994).

VEJRAZKA, V., 'The Stage Actor on Television', *World Theatre*, 9/4 (Winter 1960).

VERNA, T., *Live Television* (Boston and London: Focal Press, 1987).

WAGENFUHR, K., 'Developmental Possibilities of Television, 1939', *Historical Journal of Film, Radio and Television*, 10/3 (1990).

WALLIS, C., 'What Would Miss Austen Have Done?', *Radio Times*, 25 January 1952.

WATKINS, G. (ed.), *Tonight*, BFI Dossier, no. 15 (London: British Film Institute, 1982).

WEARING, J. P., *The London Stage 1930–1939*, 2 vols. (Metuchen, NJ, and London: Scarecrow Press, 1990).

WILK, M., *The Golden Age of Television: notes from the survivors* (New York, 1977).

WILLIAMS, R., *Television: Technology and Cultural Form* (London: Fontana, 1974).

WILLIS, T., *Woman in a Dressing Gown and other television plays* (London: Barrie & Rockliff, 1959).

WILSON, H. H., *Pressure Group* (London: Weidenfeld and Nicolson, 1961).

WINSTON, B., *Misunderstanding Media* (London: Routledge & Kegan Paul, 1986).

WITTS, A., *Television Cyclopaedia* (London: Chapman & Hall, 1937).

WOOD, R., *Hitchcock's Films Revisited* (New York: Columbia University Press, 1989).

YATES, R. F., *ABC of Television or seeing by radio* (London: Chapman & Hall, 1929).

ZETTL, H., *Television Production Handbook* (London: Pitman & Sons, 1961).

—— 'The Rare Case of Television Aesthetics', *Journal of the University Film Association*, 30/2 (Spring 1978).

ZUCKER, C., 'British Film, Stage and Television Performance: Training, Praxis, and Culture' in *CineAction*, 49 (July 1997).

Index

All titles refer to television versions. Major references are in **bold** type.

Adams, Mary 37
Adventure Story (1946) 98
Afternoon of a Nymph (1961) 144–5
Amyes, Julian 158
Anastasia (1953) 13, 139
'Armchair Theatre' 1, 3, 144
Armed Robbery (1947) 99
Arnheim, Rudolph 123
Ascent of F6, The (1937/8) **63–75**
Atkins, Ian 144
Auden, W. H. 63, 64

Baby, The (1954) 114
Baird, John Logie 19, 32–4, 41
Baker-Smith, Malcolm 78, 99
Balcon, Michael 160
Barnes, George 96 n. 64, 97
Barnouw, Eric 8
Barr, Charles 3–4, 97
Barr, Robert 99
Barry, Michael 9, 36, 37, 81, 95, 98,
    120, 123, 130, 132, 134–5, 144,
    156–9
Bartlett, Basil 109, 111, 128
Bazin, André 158
Beau Brummell (1954) 139
Bennett, Alan 133 n. 75
Bennett, Holland 113
Beveridge Committee 21
Birkenshaw, Douglas 40, 42, 46
Black, Peter 82
Bogarde, Dirk 107
Bordwell, David 16
Boucicault, Dion 17
Bower, Dallas 26, 37, 45, 103
Briggs, Asa 8–9, 20, 21
Broken Horseshoe, The (1952) 112
Broken Jug, The (1953) 114
Bunyip, The (1947) 101
Burch, Noel 16
Buscombe, Ed 8–9
Bussell, Jan 78, 98, 132–3, 135

Campbell, D. R. 42
Captain Banner (1954) 132 n. 73,
    134
Carroll, Noël 122 n. 45, 160
Cartier, Rudolph 1, 113–14, 130–9,
    148–9, 152–3, 155, 156, 159
Caughie, John 4, 12, 15, 21, 36, 116
Cavalcanti, Alberto 30
Clive of India (1938) 12, **49–56**, 59,
    64, 65, 119
Cock, Gerald 32, 40, 137
Collins, Norman 21, 78, 81, 87–90,
    94, 96 n. 64, 98–100
Constant Nymph, The (1938) 36,
    57–9, 65
Creature, The (1955) 138, 139 n. 92
Crozier, Eric 36, 38
Cushing, Peter 113 n. 21, 139, 143,
    146–52

Davis, Desmond 78, 158
Dear Murderer (1949) 99–100
Dorté, Philip 79, 81
Durbridge, Francis 112

Elsaesser, Thomas 16
EMI–Marconi 19, 32–4, 41
End of the Beginning, The (1938) 36
Epitaph for a Spy (1953) 139
Epstein, Jean 122

Fabian of Scotland Yard (1954) 112
Fame of Grace Darling, The (1939) 42
Fawcett, Eric 78, 101

Gardner, Carl 2–3, 7, 17, 51
Gielgud, Val 77, 81, 88, 90–6, 130,
    156
Goldie, Grace Wyndham 26, 31–2,
    63, 75, 76, 118, 160
Gorham, Maurice 21, 47, 78, 79,
    81–2, 88, 90, 113

Graves, Cecil 20
Greene, Hugh Carleton 12
Grierson, John 30

Hale, Lionel 125
Haley, William 21, 27, 78, 79, 81–2
Hankey Committee 20, 21, 78
Harrison, Stephen 37, 78, 103–4,
     106
Hickethier, Knut 43
Hindle Wakes (1947) 102
Hitchcock, Alfred 104, 126

I Am the Law (1954) 112
Importance of Being Earnest, The
     (1938) 36, 71
Inch Man, The (1951) 112
intimacy 7–8, 28–32, 98, 117–20,
     127, 159
Isherwood, Christopher 63, 64

Jeans, Ursula 120
Johnston, Denis 37, 58, 75, 78–9,
     82–3, 157
Journey's End (1937) 25, 36
Juno and the Paycock (1938) **59–63**,
     65

Kennedy, Margaret 57
Kennedy Martin, Troy 1, 6
Kneale, Nigel 12, 109, 111, 112, 130,
     133–7, 139, 153, 156

Lejeune, C. A. 112
Leman, Joy 133
Libel (1938) 36
Lindgren, Ernest 123
Lipscomb, W. P. 49–53
Livesey, Roger 120
Look Back in Anger 157
Lury, Karen 118

MacDermot, Robert 82–3, 85–8, 97,
     157
McGivern, Cecil 21, 82–8, 91–4, 97,
     99–100, 114, 124
Mackie, Philip 12, 111
McLoone, Martin 116
Madden, Cecil 27–8, 32, 33, 37,
     38–40, 50–1, 78, 85
Manvell, Roger 125–6, 135

Martin's Nest (1954) 114
Marty (1953) 151
Mendelson, Edward 63
Midsummer Fire (1955) 114
Minney, R. J. 49, 50
Mitchell, Yvonne 139
More, Kenneth 98–9
Morell, André 139
Morley, Royston 12, 37, 64, 66,
     70–1, 78, 89, 102, 111, 158
Mother of Men (1946) 101
Mourning Becomes Electra (1947)
     102–3
Mungo's Mansion (1948) 99
Munro, D. H. 45, 46
Murder Rap, The (1946) 99
Musser, Charles 47

Nelson, Robin 5
Newbiggin-Watts, Imlay 84
Newman, Sydney 1, 2–3, 7, 17, 79,
     130–1, 137, 144, 157–8
Nicolls, Basil 81
Nineteen Eighty-Four (1954) 10,
     100, 131, 132, 138, **139–55**, 158
Noah Gives Thanks (1955) 114
Norden, Denis 15
Norman, Bruce 41

Odets, Clifford 38
O'Donovan, Fred 37, 48, 59–63, 65,
     78, 101, 102, 126, 135
O'Ferrall, George More 1, 25, 36, 37,
     48, 49–58, 76, 78, 89, 121–2,
     135, 158
Once in a Lifetime (1937) 36
Orwell, George 139, 154–5
Osborne, John 157

Party Manners (1950) 96 n. 64
Perkins, V. F. 123
Petrified Forest, The (1951) 12
Pleasance, Donald 146, 148
Potter, Dennis 1, 159
Pride and Prejudice (1952) 112
Purbeck, Peter 34
Purser, Philip 131, 157

Quatermass Experiment, The (1953)
     10, 100, 112, 113, 115, 132, 134,
     138

Quatermass II (1955) 115, 138
Quatermass and the Pit (1959) 136

Rakoff, Alvin 158
Rebecca (1954) 132 n. 73, 134
Reith, John 2, 18–19
Renoir, Jean 158–9
Rivals, The (1938) 36
Rookery Nook (1953) 139
Rope (1947/50) 36, 99, **103–8**, 126, 145
Rossellini, Roberto 158
Rotha, Paul 123

St Simeon Stylites (1938) **58–9**
Salt, Barry 16
Scannell, Paddy 7
Scarlet Pimpernel, The (1939) 12
Scarlet Pimpernel, The (1950) 102
Sea Fever (1946) 98
Selsdon Committee 19, 41
Seton, Marie 46
Silence of the Sea, The (1946) 98
Spicer, Joanna 96–7, 113
Steiger, Rod 151
Streeton, William 39
Streets of New York, The (1939) 17
Swift, John 44, 61, 102

Telecrimes 99
telerecording 10–13, 23–4, 79–80, 113–15
Television Comes to London (1936) 23

Thank You, Mr Pepys 50–1
'Theatre Parade' 34–5, 37–8, 41, 43, 57, 58, 64, 157
They Flew Through Sand (1946) 98
Thomas, Stephen 37
Thompson, Kristin 16
Thorndike, Sybil 118
Three Hostages, The (1952) 112
Traveller Returns, The (1946) 99
TV Demonstration Film (1937) 23, 33
23rd Mission, The (1953) 114
Two Mrs Carrolls, The (1947) 99

Vance, Dennis 158

Waiting for Lefty 38
Ward, Bill 52
Warden, The (1951) 112
Web, The (1946) 99
'Wednesday Play, The' 1, 3
When We Are Married (1938) 34–5
Williams, Raymond 26
Williams, W. E. 119–20, 125, 128–9, 135
Willis, Ted 7
Winston, Brian 23
Wuthering Heights (1953) 132
Wyngarde, Peter 107
Wyver, John 2–3, 7, 17, 51

Zanuck, Darryl 50